The Gospel Medley

Every Word of Jesus in One Story

Jeffry Smith

The Gospel Medley

First Edition

Cover illustration and jacket design: Sean Flanagan and Tori Smith
Edited by: Lisa Thompson
Formatting by: Rik - Wild Seas Formatting

Published by: Jule Inc.
Peoria, Illinois
PO Box 10705
Peoria, Illinois 61612
jeffryjsmith@jeffryjsmith.com
jeffryjsmith.com

Library of Congress Control Number: 2021925085
ISBN: 978-0-9978234-7-9

Published in the United States of America

Copyright Page Contents

Source of Sources

Often when I quote from these books, I cite the original source.

Twenty-Six Translations of the Bible, Volume 3

1. *The Epistles of Paul* by W. I. Conybeare
2. *The New Testament in Basic English*
3. *The New Testament in the Language of Today* by William F. Beck
4. *The Revised Stand Version of the Bible*
5. *The New Testament, A New Translation* by James Moffatt
6. *Weymouth's New Testament in Modern Speech*
7. *The Holy Bible From Ancient Eastern Manuscripts* by George M. Lamsa
8. *The New Testament in Modern English* by Helen Montgomery
9. *The Emphasized New Testament* by Joseph Rotherham
10. *The New American Standard Bible, New Testament*
11. *The New Testament in Modern English* by J.B. Phillips
12. *The New Testament: A Translation in the Language of the People* by Charles Williams
13. *The Twentieth Century New Testament*
14. *The New English Bible*
15. *The Four Gospels* by E. V. Rieu
16. *The Acts of the Apostles* by C. H. Rieu
17. *The New Testament in the Translation of Monsignor Ronald Knox*
18. *Living Gospels* by Kenneth Taylor

19. The New Testament: An American Translation by Edgar Goodspeed

20. The New Testament of Our Lord and Savior Jesus Christ by John Broadus

21. The Amplified New Testament

22. The Holy Bible, The Berkeley Version in Modern English by Gerrit Verkuyl

23. The New Testament, A New Translation by Olaf Norlie

24. The New International Version

25. The King James Version

The Zondervan Parallel New Testament in Greek and English

1. The Nestle's Greek New Testament by Eberhard Nestle

2. The King James Version

3. The New International Version

The Merged Gospels: The Ultimate Word-by-Word Gospel Harmony

1. Textus Receptus

2. Greek critical texts

Grateful acknowledgement is given to Bible Gateway dot com for the use of their website, which made accessing the numerous Bible versions I used easy and user friendly. These are the translations I used or consulted in this book.

21st Century King James Version (KJ21)

American Standard Version (ASV)

Amplified Bible (AMP)

Amplified Bible, Classic Edition (AMPC)

BRG Bible (BRG)

Christian Standard Bible (CSB)

Common English Bible (CEB)

Complete Jewish Bible (CJB)

Contemporary English Version (CEV)

Darby Translation (DARBY)

Disciples' Literal New Testament (DLNT)

Douay-Rheims 1899 American Edition (DRA)

Easy-to-Read Version (ERV)

Evangelical Heritage Version (EHV)

English Standard Version (ESV)

English Standard Version Anglicised (ESVUK)

Expanded Bible (EXB)

1599 Geneva Bible (GNV)

GOD'S WORD Translation (GW)

Good News Translation (GNT)

Holman Christian Standard Bible (HCSB)

International Standard Version (ISV)

J.B. Phillips New Testament (PHILLIPS)

King James Version (KJV)

Authorized (King James) Version (AKJV)

Lexham English Bible (LEB)

Living Bible (TLB)

The Message (MSG)

Modern English Version (MEV)

Mounce Reverse-Interlinear New Testament (MOUNCE)

Names of God Bible (NOG)

New American Bible (Revised Edition) (NABRE)

New American Standard Bible (NASB)

New Century Version (NCV)

New English Translation (NET Bible)

New International Reader's Version (NIRV)

New International Version (NIV)

New International Version – UK (NIVUK)

New King James Version (NKJV)

New Life Version (NLV)

New Living Translation (NLV)

New Matthew Bible (NMB)

New Revised Stand Version (NRSV)

New Revised Stand Version, Anglicised Catholic Edition (NRSVACE)

New Revised Stand Version Catholic Edition (NRSVCE)

New Testament for Everyone (NTE)

Orthodox Jewish Bible (OJB)

The Passion Translation (TPT)

Revised Geneva Translation (RGT)

Revised Stand Version (RSV)

Revised Stand Version Catholic Edition (RSVCE)

Tree of Life Version (TLV)

The Voice (VOICE)

World English Bible (WEB)

Worldwide English (New Testament) (WE)

Wycliffe Bible (WYC)

Young's Literal Translation (YLT)

Contents

Preface: The Story of this Book

In 1981, after I finished Bible studies on faith, Proverbs, and the prophetic books of the Bible, I was at a loss as to what to study next. At my conversion in my mid-teens, the Worldwide Church of God had impressed upon me the importance of daily Bible study—the need for study was equal to or greater than daily food. I needed a huge topic to challenge me and occupy me for years as the prophetic books had.

I had attended services for nine years since my conversion and had grown accustomed to going through one- to two-hour sermons covering thirty to a hundred Scriptures. Speakers often read the same passage in each of the Gospels, and I had to flip from Matthew, to Mark, to Luke, to John to understand all the nuances of each evangelist. I had gone through Robertson's *Harmony of the Gospels* and Frederick Coulter's *A Harmony of the Gospels in Modern English: The Life of Jesus Christ* and found the parallel column format helpful, but still lacking. "Why couldn't the four Gospels be interwoven as a single narrative?" I wondered. Such a Bible help did not seem to be available, so I sought to write one as my daily Bible study.

I began handwriting each verse from my copy of *Nelson's Holy Bible: The New King James Version*. I had a bookmark in each of the four Gospels and read each one, verse by verse. I quickly realized this task was quite a bit more challenging than I first expected. I intended to organize the Gospels in chronological order, but occasionally the order of events slightly differed. The differences in wording between the narratives were very subtle as well, with one Gospel adding just one or two words to another's account. I could not miss a single word, and I had to keep the entire narrative in mind to resolve the chronological conflicts as well. This was just the sort of puzzle I loved to solve.

With much prayer and persistence (not necessarily in that order), I finished my handwritten version in 1988. We had just purchased our first personal computer. I then edited my hand-written version, typing it into the computer.

I finished this edit in 1992 and printed out my first version. Our computer failed, and we switched the hard drives to a new computer. I then transferred the files to a new word processor and edited it again, focusing on areas where I was uncertain or unclear on the order and placement of the narrative. I also purchased Zondervan's *26 Translations of the Bible*, and I used that to clarify and correct some passages when the New King James translation was unclear. I also bought a copy of Zondervan's *Parallel New Testament In Greek and English* to cross-check wording in some of the translations.

All along, I had been footnoting my changes to the New King James and noting Old Testament references. I used *Strong's Exhaustive Concordance* to decide which translation to use when I was unsure. I printed out this second edit and read it, noting typographical errors and order and placement errors. I corrected them and then submitted a sample of the book to be published in 1997. It was rejected.

I was not surprised, but I was discouraged. I studied other topics, predestination, transubstantiation, and the book of Psalms, but I always intended to return to *The Gospel Medley* and try and publish it again.

At a church book sale, I bought *The Life of Christ in Stereo* by Johnston M. Cheney. To my great pleasure, this book had achieved what I sought: a full harmonization of all the details of the four Gospels. I avidly studied the book, comparing it in detail with my version.

I learned a great deal. I was pleased when our works matched closely and startled at the differences. As a result, I changed several areas of *The Gospel Medley*.

I transferred my manuscript to Microsoft Word and edited it, adding index references and correcting errors. I have added this preface because I have studied self-publishing, and prefaces are a great way for an author to introduce himself. I added an appendix, explaining some of the decisions I made in the arrangement of the four Gospels.

Then in 2011, I purchased a copy of Dr. Gary Crossland's *Merged Gospels*. Here was a scholarly work that achieved what I desired, translated from the original Greek into a single narrative. I compared it verse by verse, word by word, with mine. Again, I was surprised at the similarities and differences. Since we differed in our philosophies of how to harmonize the Gospels, the differences were not surprising. I believed that each Gospel was written in chronological order and equal in authority for harmonizing the time sequence. Dr. Crossland instead used Luke as the principle harmonizing component.

Most recently, in 2018, in my sixth revision, I switched my translation from the New King James version, copyrighted by Thomas Nelson, to the World English Bible, which is in the public domain. This change allows me to self-publish my work.

My fervent desire and prayer has been to release *The Gospel Medley* free from any error, just as the four Gospels are. I beseech you, the reader, to notify me of any factual error you find.

Naturally, differences of opinion on the harmonization of the Gospels exist just as there are differences between this book and Mr. Cheney's and Dr. Crossland's. The Gospels contain enough ambiguity that the exact timing and arrangement of events is subjective. Indeed, the very view of the four Gospels as historical records is subjective; some scholars believe they were written primarily as theological treatises rather than historical documents.

I look forward to hearing from you, the reader. May God bless you in the life of His Son Jesus Christ

Jeffry J. Smith

August 2019

Introduction

The Goal of This Book

I wrote this book to help people study the Bible. Each of the four Gospels contains unique information with their own unique ordering of events. A harmony of the Gospels is very helpful in synchronizing and comparing the four accounts in four columns. However, a single narrative that includes all information from the four Gospels would help a reader greatly and in a different way. Such a work would be simpler, shorter, and easier to read than a harmony. It would contain all the differences between the Gospels with none of the redundancies.

I wrote this book to supply that need. Since the narrative thread alternates from one Gospel to another instead of laying out four books simultaneously, the result is more like a medley of four songs rather than a four-part harmony—hence the name of this work, *The Gospel Medley*.

Principles of Composition

1. Links to the Gospels

Since the four Gospels are tightly woven together in this work, the reader needs to be able to link back to the original passage or passages from each one. The reader needs to be able to unweave the fabric to discern the individual threads. I have listed the Scripture(s) of origin as headings for each paragraph, sentence, phrase, or word. The reader will be able to see the verse numbers and determine which Gospel the passage is from. Occasionally, the verse numbers are the same. In these cases, the reader will need to check the Bible for clarification.

2. Choice of Translation

Originally, I chose the New King James version for this work. In my latest revision, I switched to the public domain World English Bible (WEB). The Authorized or King James version of the Bible is the most well-known and widely used translation. The WEB translation retains the fidelity of the King James to the original Greek and Hebrew while modernizing the English.

3. Reconciling Differences

The Gospels will often differ in their accounts of the same event. Several biblical principles apply:

1) The Additive Principle: Since all of God's word is truth (John 17:17; I Timothy 3:16), every detail from every Gospel is true. The primary method of reconciliation is to take the details from each Gospel and add them together. This principle is stated as a general rule in Isaiah 27:9–10:

> "To whom will he teach knowledge? And whom will he make to understand the message? Those just weaned from milk? Those just drawn from the breasts? For precept must be upon precept, precept upon precept, line upon line, line upon line, here a little, there a little."

This verse indicates God has scattered His truth on any one subject throughout the Bible. The responsible Bible student will search out all truth on a subject and assemble it. When several different points from different Gospels are put together, sentences often become lists.

Gospel harmonies traditionally gather similar subject matter together. This medley does that only if the subject matter and the time ordering are similar. Luke 11 contains material similar to Matthew 23, but the timing differs by several months, so the material is not combined.

2) The Two Witnesses Principle: Occasionally, the additive principle falls short. When two or more Gospels differ as to the time order of two events, there can be only one order. In this case, Jesus's instruction in Matthew18:16 applies: "By the mouth of two or three witnesses every word may be established," quoted from Deuteronomy 19:15. If two of the Gospels indicate one order and a third indicates another order, the order of the majority is followed. For example, the three temptations Satan gave to Christ are in one order in Matthew and Mark and in another in Luke Luke's order is not used.

If these biblical principles do not reconcile differences, the following rules are applied:

A) The Repetition Rule: If two accounts in two Gospels differ in a seemingly irreconcilable manner, the flow of the medley is worded so that these two accounts are separate events. For example, consider the Sermon on the Mount. Matthew and Mark's accounts do not fit with the time flow in Luke in the Sermon on the Plain. Accordingly, this medley shows the Sermon on the Mount and the Sermon on the Plain as two separate but similar sermons.

B) The Context Rule: Sometimes two or more accounts have very subtle differences in nuances of phrasing. Although all the details may be included in the sentence, only one version of phrasing is possible. The selection is chosen based upon the context of what is happening and the known audiences of the authors. Matthew wrote primarily to a Jewish audience. Mark wrote mostly to a Gentile audience. Luke wrote to a general audience. John wrote a summary of all that had not been said by the other writers with the aim of preserving truth that was being lost by false teachers. With this background knowledge, when the context indicated a specialty of one of the writers, that writer's style was used.

C) The Simultaneous Rule: When the Gospels differ about the time order of certain events, the events may be occurring simultaneously. Thus, a supposed order may be strictly the result of the need to tell the story in a linear manner. Christ's entry into Jerusalem illustrates this principle.

4. Old Testament References

The Old Testament is often quoted in the Gospels. For those interested in reading these references, I footnote all quotes from the Old Testament. Since Jesus's hearers were familiar with the Old Testament, they would think about these quotes. I encourage the readers of *The Gospel Medley* to read the footnotes as they read each page for the same effect and to gain understanding of the passages.

In addition, much of the New Testament fulfills Old Testament prophecy. When the fulfillment occurs, the prophecy is also footnoted.

5. Explanations

Occasionally, the WEB translation falls short of fidelity to the Greek text. In these cases, the literal Greek translation is cited as well as other translations that are faithful to the Greek text. These are added as end notes by letter. Since these are my opinions, I've placed them in the Appendix.

Sometimes the events of the Gospels are merged in a manner contrary to expectation, that is, contrary to other harmonies. These sections are added as end notes by letter along with my explanation for the order.

I've added more detailed explanations in the appendices and end notes.

Bibliography

Appendix A: Chart of Jesus

Appendix B: The Timing and Structure of Jesus

Appendix C: Currency

Appendix D: Measurements

Appendix E: Time Table

Appendix F: Translation Decisions

Appendix G: Gospel Sequence Decisions

Appendix H - Draft History.

Scripture Index

Subject Index

I've put distance and weight conversions in [brackets] in line with the text to help the reader understand the passage.

6. Added [Bracketed] Words

I added minor connective words, such as "and," "but," and "for," along with pronouns and their antecedents to smooth the narrative flow from one Gospel to another. These are enclosed in [brackets].

7. The Chronological Assumption

Each Gospel is assumed to be in chronological order unless contradicted by two or more other Gospels. *The Gospel Medley* seeks to preserve the order of each Gospel as much as possible.

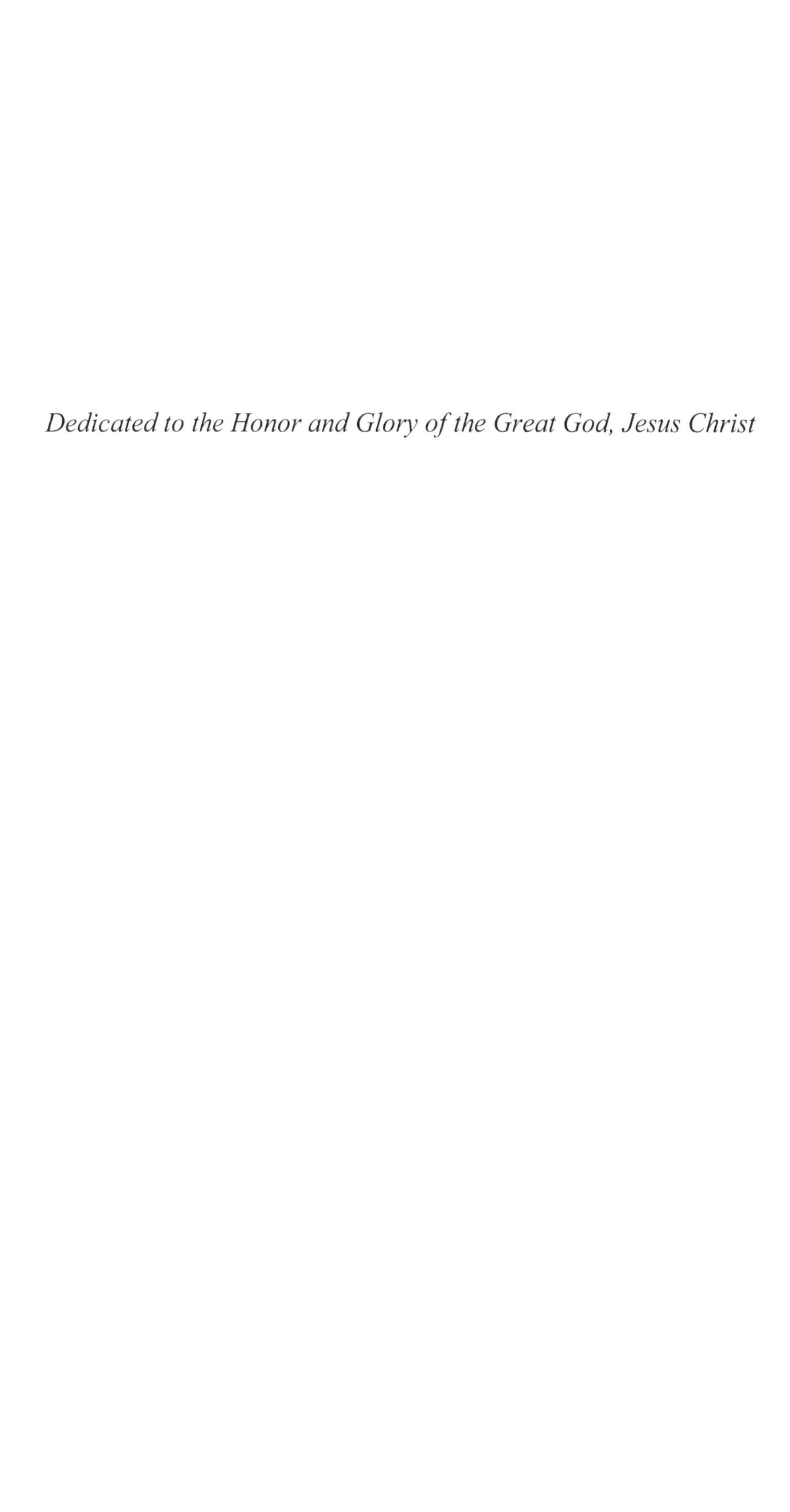

Dedicated to the Honor and Glory of the Great God, Jesus Christ

Pre-Existence and the Early Years of Jesus Christ

Mark 1:1

1 The beginning of the good news of Jesus Christ, the Son of God.

The Pre-Existence of Jesus Christ

John 1:1–5, 10–13

1 In the beginning was the Word, and the Word was with God, and the Word was God.[1] 2 The same was in the beginning with God. 3 All things were made through Him. Without Him was not anything made that has been made. 4 In Him was life, and the life was the light of men. 5 The light shines in the darkness, and the darkness hasn't overcome it[2].

Luke's Narrative Preface

Luke 1:1–4

1 Since many have undertaken to set in order a narrative concerning those matters which have been fulfilled among us, 2 even as those who from the beginning were, eyewitnesses and servants of the word delivered them to 3 it seemed good to me also, having traced the course of all things accurately from the first, to write to you in order, most excellent Theophilus; 4 that you might know the certainty concerning the things in which you were instructed.

John the Baptist's Conception

Luke 1:5–25

5 There was in the days of Herod, the king of Judea, a certain priest

---

[1] **Genesis 1:1** In the beginning, God created the heavens and the earth.

[2] The word translated "overcome" (*katelaben*) can also be translated "comprehended." It refers to getting a grip on an enemy to defeat him (WEB).

named Zacharias, of the priestly division of Abijah. He had a wife of the daughters of Aaron, and her name was Elizabeth. 6 They were both righteous before God, walking blamelessly in all the commandments and ordinances of the Lord. 7 But they had no child, because Elizabeth was barren, and they both were well advanced in years. 8 Now while he executed the priest's office before God in the order of his division, 9 according to the custom of the priest's office, his lot was to enter into the temple of the Lord and burn incense. 10 The whole multitude of the people were praying outside at the hour of incense.

11 An angel of the Lord appeared to him, standing on the right side of the altar of incense. 12 Zacharias was troubled when he saw him, and fear fell upon him.

13 But the angel said to him, "Don't be afraid, Zacharias, because your request has been heard, and your wife, Elizabeth, will bear you a son, and you shall call his name John. 14 You will have joy and gladness; and many will rejoice at his birth. 15 For he will be great in the sight of the Lord, and he will drink no wine nor strong drink. He will be filled with the Holy Spirit, even from his mother's womb. 16 He will turn many of the children of Israel to the Lord, their God. 17 He will go before Him in the spirit and power of Elijah,

> 'to turn the hearts of the fathers to the children,' and the disobedient to the wisdom of the just; to prepare a people prepared for the Lord[3]."

18 Zacharias said to the angel, "How can I be sure of this? For I am an old man, and my wife is well advanced in years."

19 The angel answered him, "I am Gabriel, who stands in the presence of God. I was sent to speak to you, and to bring you this good news. 20 Behold, you will be silent and not able to speak, until the day that these things will happen, because you didn't believe my words, which will be fulfilled in their proper time."

21 The people were waiting for Zacharias, and they marveled that he

---

[3] **Malachi 4:5** "Behold, I will send you Elijah the prophet before the great and terrible day of Yahweh comes. 6 He will turn the hearts of the fathers to the children, and the hearts of the children to their fathers, lest I come and strike the earth with a curse."

delayed in the temple. 22 When he came out, he could not speak to
them, and they perceived that he had seen a vision in the temple. He
continued making signs to them, and remained mute. 23 When the
days of his service were fulfilled, he departed to his house.

24 After these days Elizabeth, his wife, conceived, and she hid herself
five months, saying, 25 "Thus has the Lord done to me in the days in
which he looked at me, to take away my reproach among men."

The Genealogies of Jesus Christ

Matthew 1:1–17; Luke 3:38–32, 27, 31–23; Luke 4:31[4]

1 The book of the genealogy of Jesus Christ, the son of David, the son of Abraham.

38 Adam, the son of God,

Seth, the son of Adam,

Enos, the son of Seth,

Cainan, 38 the son of Enos,

Mahalaleel, the son of Cainan,

Jared, the son of Mahalaleel,

Enoch, the son of Jared,

Methuselah, the son of Enoch,

Lamech, 37 the son of Methuselah,

Noah, the son of Lamech,

Shem, the son of Noah,

Arphaxad, the son of Shem,

Cainan, the son of Arphaxad,

Shelah, 36 the son of Cainan,

35 Eber, the son of Shelah,

---

[4] Since Luke genealogy runs backward to Adam and Matthew's runs forward from Abraham's I harmonized them by citing Luke's verses backward. I group each generation together once Matthew and Luke begin to differ at Solomon.

Peleg, the son of Eber,

Reu, the son of Peleg,

Serug, the son of Reu,

34 Nahor, 35 the son of Serug,

34 Terah, the son of Nahor,

1 Abraham, the son of Terah.

2 Abraham became the father of Isaac.

Isaac became the father of Jacob.

Jacob became the father of Judah and his brothers.

3 Judah became the father of Perez and Zerah by Tamar.

Perez became the father of Hezron.

Hezron became the father of Ram.

4 Ram became the father of Amminadab.

Amminadab became the father of Nahshon.

Nahshon became the father of Salmon.

5 Salmon became the father of Boaz by Rahab.

Boaz became the father of Obed by Ruth.

Obed became the father of Jesse.

6 Jesse became the father of King David.

David became the father of Solomon by her who had been Uriah's wife.

31 Nathan, the son of David,[5]
7 Solomon became the father of Rehoboam.

31 Mattatha, the son of Nathan,
7 Rehoboam became the father of Abijah.

31 Menan, the son of Mattatha,

---

[5] **1 Chronicles 3:5** and these were born to him [David] in Jerusalem: Shimea, Shobab, Nathan, and Solomon, four, of Bathshua the daughter of Ammiel;

7 Abijah became the father of Asa.

31 Melea, the son of Menan,
8 Asa became the father of Jehoshaphat.

30 Eliakim, 31 the son of Melea,
8 Jehoshaphat became the father of Joram.

30 Jonan, the son of Eliakim,
8 Joram became the father of Uzziah.

30 Joseph, the son of Jonan,
9 Uzziah became the father of Jotham.

30 Judah, the son of Joseph,
9 Jotham became the father of Ahaz.

30 Simeon, the son of Judah,
9 Ahaz became the father of Hezekiah.

29 Levi, 30 the son of Simeon,
10 Hezekiah became the father of Manasseh.

29 Matthat, the son of Levi,
10 Manasseh became the father of Amon.

29 Jorim, the son of Matthat,
10 Amon became the father of Josiah.

29 Eliezer, the son of Jorim,
11 Josiah became the father of Jechoniah and his brothers, at the time of the exile to Babylon.

29 Jose, the son of Eliezer,
12 After the exile to Babylon, Jechoniah became the father of Shealtiel.

28 Er, 29 the son of Jose,
12 Shealtiel became the father of Zerubbabel.

28 Elmodam, the son of Er,
13 Zerubbabel became the father of Abiud.

28 Cosam, the son of Elmodam,
13 Abiud became the father of Eliakim

28 Addi, the son of Cosam,

13 Eliakim became the father of Azor.

28 Melchi, the son of Addi,
14 Azor became the father of Zadok.

27 Neri, 28 the son of Melchi,
14 Zadok became the father of Achim.

27 Shealtiel, the son of Neri,
14 Achim became the father of Eliud.

27 Zerubbabel, the son of Shealtiel,
15 Eliud became the father of Eleazar.

27 Rhesa, the son of Zerubbabel,
15 Eleazar became the father of Matthan.

27 Joanan, the son of Rhesa,
15 Matthan became the father of Jacob.

26 Judah, 27 the son of Joanan,
16 Jacob became the father of Joseph, the husband of Mary, from whom was born Jesus, who is called Christ.

17 So all the generations from Abraham to David are fourteen generations; from David to the exile to Babylon fourteen generations; and from the carrying away to Babylon to the Christ, fourteen generations.

26 Joseph, the son of Judah,

26 Semein, the son of Joseph,

26 Mattathias, the son of Semein,

26 Maath, the son of Mattathias,

25 Naggai 26 the son of Maath,

25 Esli, the son of Naggai,

25 Nahum, the son of Esli,

25 Amos, the son of Nahum,

25 Mattathias, the son of Amos,

24 Joseph, 25 the son of Mattathias,

24 Jannai, the son of Joseph,

24 Melchi, the son of Jannai,

24 Levi, the son of Melchi,

24 Matthat, the son of Levi,

23 Heli, 24 the son of Matthat,

23 Joseph, the son of Heli,

23 Jesus himself, being the son (as was supposed) of Joseph,[6] the Christ.

The Conception of Jesus

Luke 1:26–56; John 1:14

26 Now in the sixth month, the angel Gabriel was sent from God to a
city of Galilee, named Nazareth, 27 to a virgin pledged to be married
to a man whose name was Joseph, of David's house. The virgin's
name was Mary. 28 Having come in, the angel said to her, "Rejoice,
you highly favored one! The Lord is with you. Blessed are you among
women!"

29 But when she saw him, she was greatly troubled at the saying, and
considered what kind of salutation this might be. 30 The angel said to
her, "Don't be afraid, Mary, for you have found favor with God. 31
Behold, you will conceive in your womb, and give birth to a son, and
will call his name 'Jesus.' 32 He will be great, and will be called the
Son of the Most High. The Lord God will give Him the throne of His
father, David, 33 and He will reign over the house of Jacob forever.
There will be no end to His Kingdom[7]."

34 Mary said to the angel, "How can this be, seeing I am a virgin?"

---

[6] Note that in Luke's genealogy that Joseph is a son of Heli whereas in Matthew's, Jacob begot Joseph. "Son of" can also be used to represent "son-in-law." Thus Luke's genealogy represents Mary's genealogy through Heli while Matthew is Joseph's genealogy.

[7] **2 Samuel 7:12** When your days are fulfilled, and you sleep with your fathers, I will set up your offspring after you, who will proceed out of your body, and I will establish his kingdom. 13 He will build a house for my name, and I will establish the throne of his kingdom forever. 14 I will be his father, and he will be my son.

35 The angel answered her, "The Holy Spirit will come on you, and the power of the Most High will overshadow you. Therefore also the holy one who is born from you will be called the Son of God. 36
Behold, Elizabeth, your relative, also has conceived a son in her old age; and this is the sixth month with her who was called barren. 37
For nothing spoken by God is impossible."

38 Mary said, "Behold, the servant of the Lord; let it be done to me according to your word."

14 The Word became flesh . . .

38 The angel departed from her. 39 Mary arose in those days and went into the hill country with haste, into a city of Judah, 40 and entered into the house of Zacharias and greeted Elizabeth.

41 When Elizabeth heard Mary's greeting, the baby leaped in her womb, and Elizabeth was filled with the Holy Spirit. 42 She called out with a loud voice, and said, "Blessed are you among women, and blessed is the fruit of your womb! 43 Why am I so favored, that the mother of my Lord should come to me? 44 For behold, when the voice of your greeting came into my ears, the baby leaped in my womb for joy! 45 Blessed is she who believed, for there will be a fulfillment of the things which have been spoken to her from the Lord!"

46 And Mary said, "My soul doth magnify the Lord, 47 And my spirit hath rejoiced in God my Savior. 48 For He hath regarded the low estate of His handmaiden: for, behold, from henceforth all generations shall call me blessed. 49 For He that is mighty hath done to me great things; and holy is His name. 50 And His mercy is on them that fear Him from generation to generation. 51 He hath shewed strength with his arm; He hath scattered the proud in the imagination of their hearts.
52 He hath put down the mighty from their seats, and exalted them of low degree. 53 He hath filled the hungry with good things; and the rich He hath sent empty away. 54 He hath helped His servant Israel, in remembrance of His mercy; 55 As He spake to our fathers, to Abraham, and to his seed for ever."

56 Mary stayed with her about three months, and then returned to her house.

During Mary's Pregnancy

Matthew 1:18–25

18 Now the birth of Jesus Christ was like this; for after his mother, Mary, was engaged to Joseph, before they came together, she was found pregnant by the Holy Spirit. 19 Joseph, her husband, being a righteous man, and not willing to make her a public example, intended to put her away secretly.

20 But when he thought about these things, behold, an angel of the Lord appeared to him in a dream, saying, "Joseph, son of David, don't be afraid to take to yourself Mary, your wife, for that which is conceived in her is of the Holy Spirit. 21 She shall give birth to a son. You shall call his name Jesus, for it is He who shall save His people from their sins."

22 Now all this has happened, that it might be fulfilled which was spoken by the Lord through the prophet, saying,

> 23 "Behold, the virgin shall be with child, and shall give birth to a son. They shall call his name Immanuel[8] which is, being interpreted, 'God with us.'"

24 Joseph arose from his sleep, and did as the angel of the Lord commanded him, and took his wife to himself; 25 and didn't know her sexually until she had given birth to her firstborn son. He named him Jesus.

The Birth of John the Baptist

Luke 1:57–80

57 Now the time that Elizabeth should give birth was fulfilled, and she gave birth to a son. 58 Her neighbors and her relatives heard that the Lord had magnified His mercy towards her, and they rejoiced with her. 59 On the eighth day, they came to circumcise the child; and they would have called him Zacharias, after the name of the father.

60 His mother answered, "Not so; but he will be called John."

---

[8] **Isaiah 7:14** Therefore the Lord himself will give you a sign. Behold, the virgin will conceive, and bear a son, and shall call his name Immanuel.

61 They said to her, “There is no one among your relatives who is called by this name.” 62 They made signs to his father, what he would have him called.

63 He asked for a writing tablet, and wrote, “His name is John.” They all marveled.

64 His mouth was opened immediately, and his tongue freed, and he spoke, blessing God. 65 Fear came on all who lived around them, and all these sayings were talked about throughout all the hill country of Judea. 66 All who heard them laid them up in their heart, saying, “What then will this child be?”

The hand of the Lord was with him. 67 His father, Zacharias, was filled with the Holy Spirit, and prophesied, saying,

68 “Blessed be the Lord, the God of Israel, for He has visited and redeemed His people; 69 and has raised up a horn of salvation for us in the house of His servant David 70 (as He spoke by the mouth of His holy prophets who have been from of old), 71 salvation from our enemies, and from the hand of all who hate us; 72 to show mercy towards our fathers, to remember His holy covenant, 73 the oath which He spoke to Abraham, our father, 74 to grant to us that we, being delivered out of the hand of our enemies, should serve Him without fear, 75 In holiness and righteousness before Him all the days of our life.”

76 And you, child, will be called a prophet of the Most High, for you will go before the face of the Lord to prepare His ways, 77 to give knowledge of salvation to His people by the remission of their sins, 78 because of the tender mercy of our God, whereby the dawn from on high will visit us, 79 to shine on those who sit in darkness and the shadow of death; to guide our feet into the way of peace.”

80 The child was growing, and becoming strong in spirit, and was in the desert until the day of his public appearance to Israel.

The Birth of Jesus

Luke 2:1–39; Matthew 1:25

1 Now in those days, a decree went out from Caesar Augustus that all the world should be enrolled. 2 This was the first enrollment made

when Quirinius was governor of Syria. 3 All went to enroll themselves, everyone to his own city. 4 Joseph also went up from Galilee, out of the city of Nazareth, into Judea, to David's city, which is called Bethlehem, because he was of the house and family of David; 5 to enroll himself with Mary, who was pledged to be married to him as wife, being pregnant.

6 While they were there, the day had come for her to give birth. 7 She gave birth to her firstborn son. She wrapped him in bands of cloth, and laid him in a feeding trough, because there was no room for them in the guest room.[9]

25 He [Joseph] named him Jesus.

8 There were shepherds in the same country staying in the field, and keeping watch by night over their flock. 9 Behold, an angel of the Lord stood by them, and the glory of the Lord shone around them, and they were terrified.

10 The angel said to them, "Don't be afraid, for behold, I bring you good news of great joy which will be to all the people. 11 For there is born to you today, in David's city, a Savior, who is Christ the Lord. 12 This is the sign to you: you will find a baby wrapped in strips of cloth, lying in a feeding trough."

13 Suddenly, there was with the angel a multitude of the heavenly army praising God, and saying, 14 "Glory to God in the highest, and on earth peace, among men of good will."

15 When the angels went away from them into the sky, the shepherds said to one another, "Let's go to Bethlehem, now, and see this thing that has happened, which the Lord has made known to us."

16 They came with haste, and found both Mary and Joseph, and the

---

[9] The word used for "inn" in the Authorized Version is *kataluma* in Greek. It appears in Luke 22:11 and Mark 14:14 as well as here in Luke 2:7. In the other two passages, the Authorized Version renders it as "guest room." *Strong's Exhaustive Concordance of the Bible, with Hebrew, Chaldee and Greek Dictionaries* gives the definition as "lodging place, guest chamber, inn." Since Joseph had relatives in Bethlehem, he and Mary likely stayed with them instead of in a rented room. For a rented room in an inn, Luke used the Greek word *pandocheion* in Luke 10:34. For these reasons, the phrase "guest room" is used (https://www.amazon.com/Strongs-Exhaustive-Concordance-Chaldee-Dictionaries/dp/B000AMQT0S/).

baby was lying in the feeding trough.

17 When they saw it, they publicized widely the saying which was spoken to them about this child. 18 All who heard it wondered at the things which were spoken to them by the shepherds. 19 But Mary kept all these sayings, pondering them in her heart. 20 The shepherds returned, glorifying and praising God for all the things that they had heard and seen, just as it was told them.

20 The shepherds returned, glorifying and praising God for all the things that they had heard and seen, just as it was told them.

21 When eight days were fulfilled for the circumcision of the child, His name was called Jesus, which was given by the angel before He was conceived in the womb.

22 When the days of their purification according to the law of Moses were fulfilled, they brought Him up to Jerusalem, to present Him to the Lord

23 (as it is written in the law of the Lord, "Every male who opens the womb shall be holy to the Lord"),[10] 24 and to offer a sacrifice according to that which is said in the law of the Lord, "A pair of turtledoves, or two young pigeons."[11]

25 Behold, there was a man in Jerusalem whose name was Simeon. This man was righteous and devout, looking for the consolation of Israel, and the Holy Spirit was on him. 26 It had been revealed to him

---

[10] **Exodus 13:2, 12, 15** "Sanctify to me all the firstborn, whatever opens the womb among the children of Israel, both of man and of animal. It is mine." 12 that you shall set apart to Yahweh all that opens the womb, and every firstborn which you have that comes from an animal. The males shall be Yahweh's. 15 When Pharaoh stubbornly refused to let us go, Yahweh killed all the firstborn in the land of Egypt, both the firstborn of man, and the firstborn of animal. Therefore I sacrifice to Yahweh all that opens the womb, being males; but all the firstborn of my sons I redeem.'

[11] **Leviticus 12:2-4, 8 12** Say to the Israelites, If a woman conceives and bears a male child, she shall be unclean seven days, unclean as during her monthly discomfort. **3** And on the eighth day the child shall be circumcised. **4** Then she shall remain [separated] thirty-three days to be purified [from her loss] of blood; she shall touch no hallowed thing nor come into the [court of the] sanctuary until the days of her purifying are over. **8** If she cannot afford a lamb, then she shall take two turtledoves, or two young pigeons; the one for a burnt offering, and the other for a sin offering: and the priest shall make atonement for her, and she shall be clean.'"

by the Holy Spirit that he should not see death before he had seen the Lord's Christ. 27 He came in the Spirit into the temple. When the parents brought in the child, Jesus, that they might do concerning Him according to the custom of the law, 28 then he received Him into his arms, and blessed God, and said,

"Now You are releasing Your servant, Master, according to Your word, in peace; 30 for my eyes have seen Your salvation, 31 which You have prepared before the face of all peoples; 32 a light for revelation to the nations, and the glory of Your people Israel."[12]

33 Joseph and his mother were marveling at the things which were spoken concerning Him, 34 and Simeon blessed them, and said to Mary, His mother, "Behold, this child is set for the falling and the rising of many in Israel, and for a sign which is spoken against. 35 Yes, a sword will pierce through your own soul, that the thoughts of many hearts may be revealed."

36 There was one Anna, a prophetess, the daughter of Phanuel, of the tribe of Asher (she was of a great age, having lived with a husband seven years from her virginity, 37 and she had been a widow for about eighty-four years), who didn't depart from the temple, worshiping with fastings and petitions night and day. 38 Coming up at that very hour, she gave thanks to the Lord, and spoke of Him to all those who were looking for redemption in Jerusalem. 39 When they [Joseph and Mary had accomplished all things that were according to the law of the Lord, they returned into Galilee, to their own city, Nazareth.[13]

---

[12] **Isaiah 42:6-7** "I, Yahweh, have called you in righteousness, and will hold your hand, and will keep you, and make you a covenant for the people, as a light for the nations; 7 to open the blind eyes, to bring the prisoners out of the dungeon, and those who sit in darkness out of the prison. **Jeremiah 2:11** Has a nation changed its gods, which really are no gods? But my people have changed their glory for that which does not profit. **Zechariah 2:5** "For I," says Yahweh, "will be to her a wall of fire around it, and I will be the glory in the middle of her."

[13] Joseph and Mary eventually returned to Nazareth but moved to a house in Bethlehem by the time the wise men visited. Since Herod died in March of 4 BC, this episode had to take place before then but after Jesus's birth. "All these things" included the circumcision (nine days) and the purification (thirty days) plus at least three days for travel and three days back. At least two months passed before they fled to Egypt. We know the wise men visited them while they resided in Bethlehem. After their flight to Egypt, they returned to Nazareth.

The Visit of the Wise Men

Matthew 2:1–12

1 Now when Jesus was born in Bethlehem of Judea in the days of King Herod, behold, wise men from the east came to Jerusalem, saying, 2 "Where is He who is born King of the Jews? For we saw His star in the east, and have come to worship Him." 3 When King Herod heard it, he was troubled, and all Jerusalem with him. 4 Gathering together all the chief priests and scribes of the people, he asked them where the Christ would be born. 5 They said to him, "In Bethlehem of Judea, for this is written through the prophet,

> 6 'You Bethlehem, land of Judah, are in no way least among the princes of Judah: for out of you shall come a governor, who shall shepherd My people, Israel.'"[14]

7 Then Herod secretly called the wise men, and learned from them exactly what time the star appeared. 8 He sent them to Bethlehem, and said, "Go and search diligently for the young child. When you have found Him, bring me word, so that I also may come and worship Him."

9 They, having heard the king, went their way; and behold, the star, which they saw in the east, went before them, until it came and stood over where the young child was. 10 When they saw the star, they rejoiced with exceedingly great joy. 11 They came into the house and saw the young child with Mary, His mother and they fell down and worshiped Him. Opening their treasures, they offered to Him gifts: gold, frankincense, and myrrh. 12 Being warned in a dream that they shouldn't return to Herod, they went back to their own country another way.

The Flight to Egypt

Matthew 2:13–23

13 Now when they had departed, behold, an angel of the Lord

---

[14] **Micah 5:2** But you, Bethlehem Ephrathah, being small among the clans of Judah, out of you one will come out to me that is to be ruler in Israel; whose goings out are from of old, from ancient times.

appeared to Joseph in a dream, saying, "Arise and take the young child and His mother, and flee into Egypt, and stay there until I tell you, for Herod will seek the young child to destroy Him."

14 He arose and took the young child and His mother by night, and
departed into Egypt, 15 and was there until the death of Herod; that it might be fulfilled which was spoken by the Lord through the prophet, saying, "Out of Egypt I called My Son."[15]

16 Then Herod, when he saw that he was mocked by the wise men, was exceedingly angry, and sent out, and killed all the male children who were in Bethlehem and in all the surrounding countryside, from two years old and under, according to the exact time which he had
learned from the wise men. 17 Then that which was spoken by
Jeremiah the prophet was fulfilled, saying,

> 18 "A voice was heard in Ramah, lamentation, weeping and great mourning, Rachel weeping for her children; she wouldn't be comforted, because they are no more."[16]

19 But when Herod was dead, behold, an angel of the Lord appeared
in a dream to Joseph in Egypt, saying, 20 "Arise and take the young
child and his mother, and go into the land of Israel, for those who sought the young child's life are dead."

21 He arose and took the young child and his mother, and came into
the land of Israel. 22 But when he heard that Archelaus was reigning over Judea in the place of his father, Herod, he was afraid to go there. Being warned in a dream, he withdrew into the region of Galilee, 23
and came and lived in a city called Nazareth; that it might be fulfilled which was spoken through the prophets: "He will be called a Nazarene."[17]

---

[15] **Hosea 11:1** "When Israel was a child, then I loved him, and called my son out of Egypt."

[16] **Jeremiah 31:15** Yahweh says: A voice is heard in Ramah, lamentation, and bitter weeping, Rachel weeping for her children; she refuses to be comforted for her children, because they are no more.

[17] Expanded Bible: a person from the town of Nazareth; perhaps a reference to **Isaiah 11:1** "A ·new branch [sprout; shoot; ᶜthe Messiah] will grow from the stump of Jesse [ᶜking David's father; the Messiah will restore David's royal line]; a branch will ·come [sprout; *or* bear fruit] from his roots." where the Hebrew word

The Boyhood of Jesus

Luke 2:40–52

40 The child was growing, and was becoming strong in spirit, being filled with wisdom, and the grace of God was upon Him. 41 His parents went every year to Jerusalem at the feast of the Passover.

42 When He was twelve years old, they went up to Jerusalem according to the custom of the feast, 43 and when they had fulfilled the days, as they were returning, the boy Jesus stayed behind in Jerusalem. Joseph and His mother didn’t know it, 44 but supposing Him to be in the company, they went a day’s journey, and they looked for Him among their relatives and acquaintances. 45 When they didn’t find Him, they returned to Jerusalem, looking for Him.

46 After three days they found Him in the temple, sitting in the middle of the teachers, both listening to them, and asking them questions. 47 All who heard Him were amazed at His understanding and His answers. 48 When they saw Him, they were astonished, and His mother said to Him, “Son, why have You treated us this way? Behold, Your father and I were anxiously looking for You.”

49 He said to them, “Why were you looking for me? Didn’t you know that I must be in My Father’s house?” 50 They didn’t understand the saying which He spoke to them.

51 And He went down with them, and came to Nazareth. He was subject to them, and His mother kept all these sayings in her heart. 52 And Jesus increased in wisdom and stature, and in favor with God and men.

---

translated “branch” sounds like “Nazarene”].”

Early Ministry of Jesus and John the Baptist

John the Baptist's Judean Ministry

Luke 3:1–18; John 1:6–18; Matthew 3:1–12; Mark 1:2–8

1 Now in the fifteenth year of the reign of Tiberius Caesar, Pontius Pilate being governor of Judea, and Herod being tetrarch of Galilee, and his brother Philip tetrarch of the region of Ituraea and Trachonitis, and Lysanias tetrarch of Abilene, 2 in the high priesthood of Annas and Caiaphas,

6 There came a man, sent from God, whose name was John. 2 The word of God came to John, the son of Zacharias, in the wilderness. 7 The same came as a witness, that he might testify about the light, that all might believe through Him. 8 He was not the light, but was sent that he might testify about the light. 9 The true light that enlightens everyone was coming into the world.[18]

10 He was in the world, and the world was made through Him, and the world didn't recognize Him. 11 He came to His own, and those who were His own didn't receive Him. 12 But as many as received Him, to them He gave the right to become God's children, to those who believe in His name: 13 who were born not of blood, nor of the will of the flesh, nor of the will of man, but of God. 14 The Word became flesh, and lived among us. We saw His glory, such glory as of the one and only Son of the Father, full of grace and truth.

15 John testified about Him. He cried out, saying, "This was He of whom I said, 'He who comes after me has surpassed me, for He was before me.'"

16 From His fullness we all received grace upon grace. 17 For the law was given through Moses. Grace and truth were realized through Jesus Christ. 18 No one has seen God at any time. The one and only Son,

[18] The phrase "coming into the world" might refer to either "true Light" or "every man" in the Greek. The context of John favors the translation from the WEB, which is used in the Gospel Medley.

who is in the bosom of the Father, He has declared Him.

1 In those days 2 as it is written in the book of the words of 12 the prophet,

> "Behold, I send my messenger before your face, who will prepare your way before you. 3 The voice of one crying in the wilderness, 'Make ready the way of the Lord! Make His paths straight!'"[19]

1 John the Baptizer, 4 the Baptist, 1 came preaching in the wilderness of Judea, 3 into all the region around the Jordan, preaching the baptism of repentance for remission of sins.

Saying, 2 "Repent, for the Kingdom of Heaven is at hand!" 3 For this is He who was spoken of by Isaiah the prophet, saying,

> 4 "The voice of one crying in the wilderness, 'Make ready the way of the Lord. Make his paths straight. 5 Every valley will be filled. Every mountain and hill will be brought low. The crooked will become straight, and the rough ways smooth. 6 All flesh will see God's salvation.'"[20]

Now John himself wore clothing made of camel's hair, with a leather belt around his waist. His food 6 he was eating 4 was locusts and wild honey.

5 Then people from Jerusalem, all of Judea, and all the region around the Jordan 5 all 5 went out to him. 6 They were baptized by him in the Jordan, confessing their sins.

7 But when he saw many of the Pharisees and Sadducees coming for his baptism, he said to them, [and] 7 therefore to the multitudes who went out to be baptized by him, 7 "You offspring of vipers, who warned you to flee from the wrath to come? 8 Therefore produce fruit worthy of repentance! 9 Don't 8 begin 9 [to] think 9 to say 9 to

---

[19] **Malachi 3:1** "Behold, I send My messenger, and He will prepare the way before Me; and the Lord, Whom you seek, will suddenly come to His temple; and the messenger of the covenant, Whom you desire, behold, He comes!" says Yahweh of Armies.

[20] **Isaiah 40:3–5** The voice of one who calls out, "Prepare the way of Yahweh in the wilderness! Make a level highway in the desert for our God. 4 Every valley shall be exalted, and every mountain and hill shall be made low. The uneven shall be made level, and the rough places a plain. 5 Yahweh's glory shall be revealed, and all flesh shall see it together; for the mouth of Yahweh has spoken it."

yourselves, 'We have Abraham for our father,' for I tell you that God is able to raise up children to 9 Abraham from these stones. 10 Even now the 9 ax also lies at 9 the root of the trees. Every tree therefore that doesn't produce good fruit is cut down, and thrown into the fire."

10 The multitudes asked him, "What then must we do?"

11 He answered them, "He who has two coats, let him give to him who has none. He who has food, let him do likewise."

12 Tax collectors also came to be baptized, and they said to him, "Teacher, what must we do?"

13 He said to them, "Collect no more than that which is appointed to you."

14 Soldiers also asked him, saying, "What about us? What must we do?"

He said to them, "Extort from no one by violence, neither accuse anyone wrongfully. Be content with your wages."

15 As the people were in expectation, and all men reasoned in their hearts concerning John, whether perhaps he was the Christ.

And 16 John answered them all, 7 preaching, and saying, 11 "I indeed baptize you in water for repentance, but He who comes after me is mightier than I, 7 and I am not fit to stoop down and untie the thong of His sandals,[21] [and] 11 whose shoes I am not worthy to carry. He will baptize you in the Holy Spirit and with fire. 12 His winnowing fork is in His hand, and He will thoroughly cleanse His threshing floor. He will gather His wheat into the barn, but the chaff He will burn up with unquenchable fire."

18 Then with many other exhortations he preached good news to the people.

The Baptism of Jesus

Mark 1:9–11, 21; Luke 3:21–23; Matthew 3:13–17

Now 9 in those days 21 when all the people were baptized, Jesus 9

[21] A rabbi's disciples were to do all a slave does except untie his sandal. John said he wasn't worthy to be the Messiah's slave (Spencer Tverberg).

came from Nazareth in Galilee 13 to the Jordan to John, to be baptized by him.

14 But John would have hindered Him, saying, "I need to be baptized by You, and You come to me?"

15 But Jesus, answering, said to him, "Allow it now, for this is the fitting way for us to fulfill all righteousness." Then he allowed Him.

9 Jesus . . . was 21 also 9 baptized by John in the Jordan. 16 Jesus, when He was baptized, went up directly from the water 21 and was praying. 16 And behold, the heavens were opened to Him. He saw the Spirit of God descending as a dove, and coming on Him 22 in a bodily form like a dove.

22 And 17 behold, a voice 11 came 17 out of the heavens 22 saying, 17 "This [One], 11 You are 17 My beloved[22] Son,[23] with Whom 22 in You I am well pleased."[24]

23 Jesus Himself, when He began to teach, was about thirty years old.

Jesus Christ's Temptation by Satan

Luke 4:1–13; Mark 1:12–13; Matthew 4:1–11

1 Jesus, full of the Holy Spirit, returned from the Jordan,

12 Immediately the Spirit impelled Him out into the wilderness. 1 Then Jesus was led up by the Spirit into the wilderness to be tempted by the devil. 13 And He was in the wilderness forty days being tempted by Satan 2 the devil; and He was with the wild beasts. 2 He ate nothing in those days. Afterward, when He had fasted forty days and forty nights, He was hungry.

3 The tempter, 3 the devil, 4 came and said to Him, "If You are the Son of God, command that these stones become bread."

---

[22] **Genesis 22:2** He said, "Now take your son, your only son, whom you love, even Isaac, and go into the land of Moriah. Offer him there as a burnt offering on one of the mountains which I will tell you of."

[23] **Psalm 2:7** I will tell of the decree. Yahweh said to Me, "You are My Son. Today I have become Your Father."

[24] **Isaiah 42:1** "Behold, my servant, whom I uphold; my chosen, in whom my soul delights—I have put my Spirit on him. He will bring justice to the nations."

4 But 4 Jesus answered him, saying, "It is written,

> 'Man 4 shall not live by bread alone, but by every word 4 that proceeds out of the mouth of God.'"[25]

5 Then the devil took Him into the holy city, 9 Jerusalem, 5 set Him on the pinnacle of the temple, 6 and said to Him, "If You are the Son of God, throw Yourself down 9 from here, 5 for it is written, 'He will put his angels in charge of you.' and, 'On their hands they will bear you up, so that you don't dash your foot against a stone.'"[26]

12 Jesus answering, 7 said to him, "Again, it is written,

> 'You 7 shall not test the Lord your God.'"[27]

8 Again, the devil 5 leading Him up 8 to an exceedingly high mountain, and showed Him all the kingdoms of the world, and their glory 5 in a moment of time. 6 The devil said 9 to Him, "I will give You all of these things, 6 all this authority, and their glory, for it has been delivered to me; and I give it to whomever I want. 7 If You therefore will 9 fall down and 7 worship before me, it will all be Yours."

10 Then 8 Jesus answered him, "Get behind me Satan! For it is written,

> 'You shall worship the Lord your God, and you shall serve Him only.'"[28]

13 When the devil had completed every temptation, he departed from Him until another time.11 And behold, angels came and served Him.

---

[25] **Deuteronomy 8:3** . . . that he might teach you that man does not live by bread only, but man lives by every word that proceeds out of Yahweh's mouth.

[26] **Psalm 91:11–12** For he will put his angels in charge of you, to guard you in all your ways. 12 They will bear you up in their hands, so that you won't dash your foot against a stone.

[27] **Deuteronomy 6:16** You shall not tempt Yahweh your God, as you tempted Him in Massah.

[28] **Deuteronomy 6:13** You shall fear Yahweh your God; and you shall serve Him, and shall swear by His name.

John's Ministry at Bethabara Beyond Jordan

John 1:19–34

19 This is John's testimony, when the Jews sent priests and Levites from Jerusalem to ask him, "Who are you?"

20 He declared, and didn't deny, but he declared, "I am not the Christ."

21 They asked him, "What then? Are you Elijah?"[29]

He said, "I am not."

"Are you the prophet?"[30]

He answered, "No."

22 They said therefore to him, "Who are you? Give us an answer to take back to those who sent us. What do you say about yourself?"

23 He said, "I am the voice of one crying in the wilderness, 'Make straight the way of the Lord,'[31] as Isaiah the prophet said."

24 The ones who had been sent were from the Pharisees. 25 They
asked him, "Why then do you baptize, if you are not the Christ, nor Elijah, nor the prophet?"

26 John answered them, "I baptize in water, but among you stands one
Whom you don't know. 27 He is the one Who comes after me, Who
is preferred before me, Whose sandal strap I'm not worthy to loosen."
28 These things were done in Bethany beyond the Jordan, where John was baptizing.

29 The next day, he saw Jesus coming to him, and said, "Behold, the
Lamb of God, Who takes away the sin of the world! 30 This is He of

---

[29] **Malachi 4:5–6** "Behold, I will send you Elijah the prophet before the great and terrible day of Yahweh comes. 6 He will turn the hearts of the fathers to the children, and the hearts of the children to their fathers, lest I come and strike the earth with a curse."

[30] **Deuteronomy 18:15, 18** "Yahweh your God will raise up to you a prophet from among you, of your brothers, like me. You shall listen to him. 18 I will raise them up a prophet from among their brothers, like you. I will put my words in his mouth, and he shall speak to them all that I shall command him."

[31] **Isaiah 40:3** The voice of him that crieth in the wilderness, Prepare ye the way of the LORD, make straight in the desert a highway for our God (KJV).

Whom I said, 'After me comes a man Who is preferred before me, for He was before me.' 31 I didn't know Him, but for this reason I came baptizing in water: that He would be revealed to Israel."

32 John testified, saying, "I have seen the Spirit descending like a dove out of heaven, and it remained on Him. 33 I didn't recognize Him, but He who sent me to baptize in water, He said to me, 'On Whomever you will see the Spirit descending, and remaining on Him, the same is He Who baptizes in the Holy Spirit.' 34 I have seen, and have testified that this is the Son of God."

Jesus's First Disciples

John 1:35–42

35 Again, the next day, John was standing with two of his disciples, 36 and he looked at Jesus as He walked, and said, "Behold, the Lamb of God!" 37 The two disciples heard him speak, and they followed Jesus. 38 Jesus turned, and saw them following, and said to them, "What are you looking for?"

They said to Him, "Rabbi" (which is to say, being interpreted, Teacher), "where are you staying?"

39 He said to them, "Come, and see."

They came and saw where He was staying, and they stayed with Him that day. It was about the tenth hour.[32]

40 One of the two who heard John, and followed him, was Andrew, Simon Peter's brother. 41 He first found his own brother, Simon, and said to him, "We have found the Messiah!" (which is, being interpreted, Christ).

42 He brought him to Jesus. Jesus looked at him, and said, "You are Simon the son of Jonah. You shall be called Cephas" (which is by interpretation, Peter).

---

[32] John uses the Roman time system, which was divided into twelve hours from midnight to noon. Thus, this is 10:00 a.m. in modern usage. The other Gospels use the Jewish method of time, dividing the day and night into twelve hours from 6:00 a.m. to 6:00 p.m.

Jesus Calls Philip and Nathanael

John 1:43–51

43 On the next day, He was determined to go out into Galilee, and He found Philip. Jesus said to him, "Follow Me." 44 Now Philip was from Bethsaida, of the city of Andrew and Peter.

45 Philip found Nathanael, and said to him, "We have found Him, of whom Moses in the law, and the prophets, wrote: Jesus of Nazareth, the son of Joseph."

46 Nathanael said to him, "Can any good thing come out of Nazareth?"

Philip said to him, "Come and see."

47 Jesus saw Nathanael coming to Him, and said about him, "Behold, an Israelite indeed, in whom is no deceit!"[33]

48 Nathanael said to Him, "How do You know me?"

Jesus answered him, "Before Philip called you, when you were under the fig tree, I saw you."

49 Nathanael answered Him, "Rabbi, You are the Son of God! You are King of Israel!"

50 Jesus answered him, "Because I told you, 'I saw you underneath the fig tree,' do you believe? You will see greater things than these!"

51 He said to him, "Most certainly, I tell you, hereafter you will see heaven opened, and the angels of God ascending and descending on the Son of Man."

Water Turned into Wine

John 2:1–12

1 The third day, there was a marriage in Cana of Galilee. Jesus' mother was there. 2 Jesus also was invited, with his disciples, to the marriage. 3 When the wine ran out, Jesus's mother said to Him, "They have no

---

[33] **Psalm 32:2** Blessed is the man to whom Yahweh doesn't impute iniquity, in whose spirit there is no deceit.

wine."

4 Jesus said to her, "Woman, what does that have to do with you and Me? My hour has not yet come."

5 His mother said to the servants, "Whatever He says to you, do it."

6 Now there were six water pots of stone set there after the Jews' way of purifying, containing two or three metretes [about twenty to thirty gallons] apiece. 7 Jesus said to them, "Fill the water pots with water." They filled them up to the brim.

8 He said to them, "Now draw some out, and take it to the ruler of the feast." So they took it.

9 When the ruler of the feast tasted the water now become wine,[34] and didn't know where it came from (but the servants who had drawn the water knew), the ruler of the feast called the bridegroom, 10 and said to him, "Everyone serves the good wine first, and when the guests have drunk freely, then that which is worse. You have kept the good wine until now!" 11 This beginning of His signs Jesus did in Cana of Galilee, and revealed His glory; and His disciples believed in Him.

12 After this, He went down to Capernaum, He, and His mother, His brothers, and His disciples; and they stayed there a few days.

The First Passover of Jesus's Ministry

John 2:13–25

13 The Passover of the Jews was at hand, and Jesus went up to Jerusalem. 14 He found in the temple those who sold oxen, sheep, and doves, and the changers of money sitting.

15 He made a whip of cords, and threw all out of the temple, both the sheep and the oxen; and He poured out the changers' money, and overthrew their tables. 16 To those who sold the doves, He said, "Take these things out of here! Don't make My Father's house a marketplace!"

[34] **Isaiah 55:1** "Come, everyone who thirsts, to the waters! Come, he who has no money, buy, and eat! Yes, come, buy wine and milk without money and without price."

17 His disciples remembered that it was written, "Zeal for your house will eat me up."[35]

18 The Jews therefore answered Him, "What sign do You show us, seeing that You do these things?"

19 Jesus answered them, "Destroy this temple, and in three days I will raise it up."

20 The Jews therefore said, "It took forty-six years to build this
temple! Will you raise it up in three days?" 21 But He spoke of the
temple of His body. 22 When therefore He was raised from the dead,
His disciples remembered that He said this, and they believed the Scripture, and the word which Jesus had said.

23 Now when He was in Jerusalem at the Passover, during the feast,
many believed in His name, observing His signs which He did. 24 But
Jesus didn't trust Himself to them, because He knew everyone, 25 and
because He didn't need for anyone to testify concerning man; for He Himself knew what was in man.

Jesus Teaches Nicodemus

John 3:1–21

1 Now there was a man of the Pharisees named Nicodemus, a ruler of
the Jews. 2 The same came to Him by night, and said to Him, "Rabbi, we know that You are a teacher come from God, for no one can do these signs that You do, unless God is with Him."

3 Jesus answered him, "Most certainly, I tell you, unless one is born anew,[36] he can't see God's Kingdom."

4 Nicodemus said to Him, "How can a man be born when he is old? Can he enter a second time into his mother's womb, and be born?"

5 Jesus answered, "Most certainly I tell you, unless one is born of

---

[35] **Psalm 69:9** For the zeal of your house consumes me. The reproaches of those who reproach you have fallen on me.

36 *The Zondervan Interlinear and the Emphasized New Testament: A New Translation* by J. B. Rotherham both translate this phrase as "from above." The Greek may mean either "from above" or "again". (https://www.studylight.org/interlinear-study-bible/greek/john/3.html)

water and spirit, he can't enter into God's Kingdom! 6 That which is
born of the flesh is flesh. That which is born of the Spirit is spirit. 7
Don't marvel that I said to you, 'You must be born anew.' 8 The wind
blows where it wants to, and you hear its sound, but don't know where
it comes from and where it is going. So is everyone who is born of the
Spirit."

9 Nicodemus answered Him, "How can these things be?"

10 Jesus answered him, "Are you the teacher of Israel, and don't
understand these things? 11 Most certainly I tell you, We speak that
which We know, and testify of that which We have seen, and you
don't receive Our witness. 12 If I told you earthly things and you don't
believe, how will you believe if I tell you heavenly things?

13 "No one has ascended into heaven, but He Who descended out of
heaven, the Son of Man, Who is in heaven. 14 As Moses lifted up the
serpent in the wilderness, even so must the Son of Man be lifted up,
15 that whoever believes in Him should not perish, but have eternal
life. 16 For God so loved the world, that He gave His one and only
Son, that whoever believes in Him should not perish, but have eternal
life.

17 "For God didn't send His Son into the world to judge the world,
but that the world should be saved through Him. 18 He who believes
in Him is not judged. He who doesn't believe has been judged already,
because he has not believed in the name of the one and only Son of
God. 19 This is the judgment, that the light has come into the world,
and men loved the darkness rather than the light; for their works were
evil. 20 For everyone who does evil hates the light, and doesn't come
to the light, lest his works would be exposed. 21 But he who does the
truth comes to the light, that his works may be revealed, that they have
been done in God."

Jesus and His Disciples Baptize in Judea

John 3:22–36

22 After these things, Jesus came with His disciples into the land of
Judea. He stayed there with them, and baptized. 23 John also was
baptizing in Enon near Salim, because there was much water there.
They came, and were baptized. 24 For John was not yet thrown into

prison.

25 There arose therefore a questioning on the part of John's disciples with some Jews about purification. 26 They came to John, and said to him, "Rabbi, He who was with you beyond the Jordan, to whom you have testified, behold, the same baptizes, and everyone is coming to Him."

27 John answered, "A man can receive nothing, unless it has been given him from heaven. 28 You yourselves testify that I said, 'I am not the Christ,' but, 'I have been sent before Him.' 29 He who has the bride is the bridegroom; but the friend of the bridegroom, who stands and hears him, rejoices because of the bridegroom's voice. This, my joy, therefore is made full. 30 He must increase, but I must decrease.

31 He who comes from above is above all. He who is from the earth belongs to the earth, and speaks of the earth. He who comes from heaven is above all. 32 What He has seen and heard, of that He testifies; and no one receives His witness. 33 He who has received His witness has set his seal to this, that God is true. 34 For He Whom God has sent speaks the words of God; for God gives the Spirit without measure. 35 The Father loves the Son, and has given all things into His hand. 36 One who believes in the Son has eternal life, but one who disobeys the Son won't see life, but the wrath of God remains on him.

Jesus Begins Galilean Ministry

Jesus Meets the Samaritan Woman

Luke 3:19–20; John 4:1–44; Mark 1:14; Matthew 4:12

19 But Herod the tetrarch being reproved by him [John] for Herodias, his brother Philip's wife, and for all the evil things which Herod had done, 20 added this also to them all, that he shut up John in prison.

1 Therefore when the Lord knew that the Pharisees had heard that Jesus was making and baptizing more disciples than John 2 (although Jesus himself didn't baptize, but His disciples), [and] after John 14 was taken into custody, [and] 12 when Jesus heard that John was delivered up, 3 He left Judea, and departed into Galilee.

4 He needed to pass through Samaria. 5 So He came to a city of Samaria, called Sychar, near the parcel of ground that Jacob gave to his son, Joseph. 6 Jacob's well was there. Jesus therefore, being tired from His journey, sat down by the well. It was about the sixth hour [noon].

7 A woman of Samaria came to draw water. Jesus said to her, "Give Me a drink." 8 For His disciples had gone away into the city to buy food.

9 The Samaritan woman therefore said to Him, "How is it that you, being a Jew, ask for a drink from me, a Samaritan woman?" (For Jews have no dealings with Samaritans.)

10 Jesus answered her, "If you knew the gift of God, and Who it is Who says to you, 'Give Me a drink,' you would have asked Him, and He would have given you living water."

11 The woman said to him, "Sir, you have nothing to draw with, and the well is deep. So where do You get that living water? 12 Are You greater than our father, Jacob, who gave us the well, and drank of it himself, as did his children, and his livestock?"

13 Jesus answered her, "Everyone who drinks of this water will thirst again, 14 but whoever drinks of the water that I will give him will

never thirst again; but the water that I will give him will become in him a well of water springing up to eternal life."

15 The woman said to Him, "Sir, give me this water, so that I don't get thirsty, neither come all the way here to draw."

16 Jesus said to her, "Go, call your husband, and come here."

17 The woman answered, "I have no husband."

Jesus said to her, "You said well, 'I have no husband,' 18 for you have
had five husbands; and he whom you now have is not your husband.
This you have said truly."

19 The woman said to Him, "Sir, I perceive that you are a prophet. 20
Our fathers worshiped in this mountain, and you Jews say that in
Jerusalem is the place where people ought to worship."

21 Jesus said to her, "Woman, believe Me, the hour comes, when
neither in this mountain, nor in Jerusalem, will you worship the
Father. 22 You worship that which you don't know. We worship that
which we know; for salvation is from the Jews. 23 But the hour comes,
and now is, when the true worshipers will worship the Father in spirit
and truth, for the Father seeks such to be His worshipers. 24 God is
spirit, and those who worship Him must worship in spirit and truth."

25 The woman said to him, "I know that Messiah comes, He who is called Christ. When He has come, He will declare to us all things."

26 Jesus said to her, "I am He, the One Who speaks to you."

27 At this, His disciples came. They marveled that He was speaking with a woman; yet no one said, "What are You looking for?" or, "Why do You speak with her?"

28 So the woman left her water pot, and went away into the city, and
said to the people, 29 "Come, see a Man who told me everything that
I did. Can this be the Christ?"

30 They went out of the city, and were coming to Him. 31 In the
meanwhile, the disciples urged Him, saying, "Rabbi, eat."

32 But He said to them, "I have food to eat that you don't know about."

33 The disciples therefore said to one another, "Has anyone brought

Him something to eat?"

34 Jesus said to them, "My food is to do the will of Him who sent Me, and to accomplish His work. 35 Don't you say, 'There are yet four months until the harvest?' Behold, I tell you, lift up your eyes, and look at the fields, that they are white for harvest already. 36 He who reaps receives wages, and gathers fruit to eternal life; that both he who sows and he who reaps may rejoice together. 37 For in this the saying is true, 'One sows, and another reaps.' 38 I sent you to reap that for which you haven't labored. Others have labored, and you have entered into their labor."

39 From that city many of the Samaritans believed in Him because of the word of the woman, who testified, "He told me everything that I did." 40 So when the Samaritans came to Him, they begged Him to stay with them. He stayed there two days. 41 Many more believed because of His word. 42 They said to the woman, "Now we believe, not because of your speaking; for we have heard for ourselves, and know that this is indeed the Christ, the Savior of the world."

43 After the two days He went out from there and went into Galilee. 44 For Jesus Himself testified that a prophet has no honor in his own country.

Jesus Enters Galilee

Luke 4:14–15; Mark 1:14–15; John 4:45

14 Jesus returned in the power of the Spirit into Galilee, 14 preaching the good news of God's Kingdom, 15 and saying, "The time is fulfilled, and God's Kingdom is at hand! Repent, and believe in the good news."

45 So when He came into Galilee, the Galileans received Him, having seen all the things that He did in Jerusalem at the feast, for they also went to the feast. 14 And news about Him spread through all the surrounding area. 15 He taught in their synagogues, being glorified by all.

Jesus Heals a Nobleman's Son

John 4:46–54

46 Jesus came therefore again to Cana of Galilee, where He made the water into wine. There was a certain nobleman whose son was sick at Capernaum. 47 When he heard that Jesus had come out of Judea into Galilee, he went to Him, and begged Him that he would come down and heal his son, for he was at the point of death.

48 Jesus therefore said to him, "Unless you see signs and wonders, you will in no way believe."

49 The nobleman said to him, "Sir, come down before my child dies."

50 Jesus said to him, "Go your way. Your son lives."

The man believed the word that Jesus spoke to him, and he went his way. 51 As he was now going down, his servants met him and reported, saying "Your child lives!" 52 So he inquired of them the hour when he began to get better.

They said therefore to him, "Yesterday at the seventh hour [1:00 p.m.], the fever left him." 53 So the father knew that it was at that hour in which Jesus said to him, "Your son lives." He believed, as did his whole house. 54 This is again the second sign that Jesus did, having come out of Judea into Galilee.

Jesus Is Rejected at Nazareth

Mark 6:1–6; Matthew 13:54–58; Luke 4:16–30

1 He went out from there. He came into his own country, and His disciples followed him. 54 Coming into His own country, 16 where He had been brought up, 2 when the Sabbath had come, He entered, as was His custom, 16 into the synagogue on the Sabbath day, and stood up to read.

7 The book of the prophet Isaiah was handed to Him. He opened the book, and found the place where it was written,

> 18 "The Spirit of the Lord is on Me, because He has anointed me to preach good news to the poor. He has sent me to heal the broken hearted, to proclaim release to the captives, recovering of sight to the blind, to deliver those who are crushed, 19 and to

proclaim the acceptable year of the Lord."[37]

20 He closed the book, gave it back to the attendant, and sat down. The eyes of all in the synagogue were fastened on Him. 21 He began to tell them, "Today, this Scripture has been fulfilled in your hearing."

21 He began to teach 54 them in their synagogue, so that 22 all testified about Him, and wondered at the gracious words which proceeded out of His mouth, 54 so that they 2 and many hearing Him were astonished, saying, "Where did this man get these things?" 54 and "Where did this man get this wisdom, and these mighty works? 2 What is the wisdom that is given to this man, that such mighty works come about by His hands? 55 Isn't this 22 Joseph's 55 the carpenter's son? 3 Isn't this the carpenter, the Son of Mary? 55 Isn't His mother called Mary, and His brothers, James, Joses, Simon, and Judas? 56 Aren't all of His sisters 3 here 56 with us? Where then did this Man get all of these things?" 57 They were offended by Him.

But Jesus said to them, 23 "Doubtless you will tell Me this parable, 'Physician, heal yourself! Whatever we have heard done at Capernaum, do also here in Your hometown.'" 24 He said, "Most certainly I tell you, no prophet is acceptable in His hometown." 24 Then He said, 57 "A prophet is not without honor, except in his own country, 4 and among His own relatives, 57 and in His own house."

25 "But truly I tell you, there were many widows in Israel in the days of Elijah, when the sky was shut up three years and six months, when a great famine came over all the land. 26 Elijah was sent to none of them, except to Zarephath,[38] in the land of Sidon, to a woman who was a widow. 27 There were many lepers in Israel in the time of Elisha the prophet, yet not one of them was cleansed, except Naaman, the Syrian."[39]

---

[37] **Isaiah 61:1–2** The Lord Yahweh's Spirit is on Me; because Yahweh has anointed Me to preach good news to the humble. He has sent Me to bind up the broken hearted, to proclaim liberty to the captives, and release to those who are bound; 2 to proclaim the year of Yahweh's favor, and the day of vengeance of our God; to comfort all who mourn;

[38] **1 Kings 17:9** "Arise, go to Zarephath, which belongs to Sidon, and stay there. Behold, I have commanded a widow there to sustain you."

[39] **2 Kings 5:1** Now Naaman, captain of the army of the king of Syria, was a great man with his master, and honorable, because by him Yahweh had given victory to

28 They were all filled with wrath in the synagogue, as they heard these things. 29 They rose up, threw Him out of the city, and led Him to the brow of the hill that their city was built on, that they might throw Him off the cliff. 30 But He, passing through the middle of them, went His way.

58 He didn't do many mighty works there because of their unbelief. 5 He could do no mighty work there, except that He laid His hands on a few sick people, and healed them. 6 He marveled because of their unbelief.

He went around the villages teaching.

Jesus Goes to Capernaum

Matthew 4:13–17; Luke 4:31–32; Mark 1:22

13 Leaving Nazareth, He 31 came down to 13 and lived in Capernaum, 31 a city of Galilee 13 which is by the sea, in the region of Zebulun and Naphtali, 14 that it might be fulfilled which was spoken through Isaiah the prophet, saying,

> 15 "The land of Zebulun and the land of Naphtali, toward the sea, beyond the Jordan, Galilee of the Gentiles, 16 the people who sat in darkness saw a great light, to those who sat in the region and shadow of death, to them light has dawned."[40]

17 From that time, Jesus began to preach, and to say "Repent! For the Kingdom of Heaven is at hand." [and] 31 was teaching them on the Sabbath day, 32 and they were astonished at His teaching, for His word was with authority 22 and not as the scribes.

Jesus Calls the Disciples to Follow Him

Luke 5:1–11; Matthew 4:18–22; Mark 1:16–20

Syria: he was also a mighty man of valor, but he was a leper.

[40] **Isaiah 9:1–2** But there shall be no more gloom for her who was in anguish. In the former time, he brought into contempt the land of Zebulun and the land of Naphtali; but in the latter time he has made it glorious, by the way of the sea, beyond the Jordan, Galilee of the nations. 2 The people who walked in darkness have seen a great light. Those who lived in the land of the shadow of death, on them the light has shined.

1 Now while the multitude pressed on Him and heard the word of God, 18 walking by the sea of Galilee, 1 [while] He was standing by the lake of Gennesaret, 2 He saw two boats standing by the lake, but the fishermen had gone out of them, and were washing their nets. 18 [Then] Jesus saw two brothers: Simon, who is called Peter, and Andrew, his brother, casting a net into the sea; for they were fishermen. 3 He entered into one of the boats, which was Simon's, and asked him to put out a little from the land. He sat down and taught the multitudes from the boat.

4 When He had finished speaking, He said to Simon, "Put out into the deep, and let down your nets for a catch."

5 Simon answered Him, "Master, we worked all night, and took nothing; but at Your word I will let down the net."

6 When they had done this, they caught a great multitude of fish, and their net was breaking. 7 They beckoned to their partners in the other boat, that they should come and help them. They came, and filled both boats, so that they began sink. 8 But Simon Peter, when he saw it, fell down at Jesus's knees, saying, "Depart from me, for I am a sinful man, Lord." 9 For he was amazed, and all who were with him, at the catch of fish which they had caught; 10 and so also were James and John, sons of Zebedee who were partners with Simon.

He said to them, "Come after Me, and I will make you into 19 fishers for men."

20 They immediately left their nets and followed Him.

19 Going on a little further from there, He saw 21 two other brothers, 19 James the son of Zebedee, and John, his brother, who were also in the boat mending the nets 21 with Zebedee their father. 20 Immediately He called them, and they 22 immediately left the boat [and] 20 left their father, Zebedee, in the boat with the hired servants, and went after Him 22 and followed Him.

Jesus Casts Out a Demon and Teaches on the Sabbath

Mark 1:21–28; Luke 4:33–37

21 They went to Capernaum, and when the Sabbath came, Jesus went into the synagogue and began to teach. 33 In the synagogue there was

a man possessed by a demon, an impure spirit. He cried out at the top of his voice, 34 "Go away! What do You want with us, Jesus of Nazareth? Have You come to destroy us? I know who You are—the Holy One of God!"

35 "Be quiet!" Jesus said sternly. "Come out of him!" Then the 26 impure 35 demon 26 spirit 35 threw the man down before them all, 26 shook the man violently and came out of him with a shriek, 35 and came out without injuring him.

36 All the people were amazed and said to each other, 27 "What is this? A new teaching—and with authority! 36 What words these are! With authority and power He gives orders to 27 even 36 impure spirits and they 27 obey him [and] 36 come out!"

28 News about him spread quickly 37 throughout the surrounding area 28 over the whole region of Galilee.

Jesus Heals Peter's Mother-in-law

Mark 1:29–31; Matthew 8:14–15; Luke 4:38–39

29 As soon as they left the synagogue, they went with 14 James and John to the home of Simon and Andrew. 30 Simon's mother-in-law was in bed with a 38 high 30 fever, and they immediately told Jesus about her. 38 and they asked Jesus to help her.

14 When Jesus came into Peter's house, he saw Peter's mother- in-law lying in bed with a fever.

39 So 31 He came, 39 He bent over her and rebuked the fever, 15 He touched her hand, 31 took her hand and helped her up, 15 and the fever left her, and she got up and began to wait on 39 them.

Jesus Heals Many After the Sabbath

Mark 1:32–34; Luke 4:40–41; Matthew 8:16–17

32 That evening 40 at sunset, [and] 32 after sunset 40 the people brought to Jesus all 32 all the sick 40 who had various kinds of sickness, 32 and 16 many who were 32 possessed by demons. 33 All the city was gathered together at the door. 40 Laying His hands on each one, He healed 34 many—6 all the sick, 34 who had various

diseases. He also drove out many demons, 16 the spirits with a word 41 Moreover, demons came out of many people, shouting, "You are the Son of God!" But he rebuked them and would not allow them to speak, because they knew He was the Messiah.

> 17 This was to fulfill what was spoken through the prophet Isaiah: "He took up our infirmities and bore our diseases"[41]

Jesus Rises Early to Pray Before Traveling to Other Cities[42]

Mark 1:35–39; Luke 4:42–44; Matthew 4:23–25;

35 Very early in the morning, while it was still dark, Jesus got up, left the house and went off to a solitary place, 35 where He prayed. 42 When it was day. 36 Simon and his companions went to look for Him, 37 and when they found Him, they exclaimed: "Everyone is looking for You!"

38 Jesus replied, "Let us go somewhere else—to the nearby villages—so I can preach there also. That is why I have come."

42 The people were looking for Him and when they came to where He was, they tried to keep Him from leaving them. 43 But He said, "I must proclaim the good news of the kingdom of God to the other towns also, because that is why I was sent."

39 So 23 Jesus 39 traveled 23 throughout Galilee. 44 And He was preaching [and] teaching in their synagogues 44 of 39 Galilee, 23 proclaiming the good news of the kingdom, and healing every disease and sickness among the people 39 and driving out demons.

24 News about Him spread all over Syria, and people brought to Him all who were ill with various diseases, those suffering severe pain, the demon-possessed, those having seizures, and the paralyzed; and He healed them. 25 Large crowds from Galilee, Decapolis, Jerusalem, Judea and from beyond the Jordan followed Him.

[41] **Isaiah 53:4** Surely He took up our pain and bore our suffering, yet we considered Him punished by God, stricken by Him, and afflicted.

[42] The time order is determined by Mark and Luke here. Matthew is non-sequential.

The Sermon on the Mount: The Beatitudes

Matthew 5:1–12

1 Seeing the multitudes, He went up onto the mountain. When He had sat down, His disciples came to Him. 2 He opened his mouth and taught them, saying,

3 "Blessed are the poor in spirit, for theirs is the Kingdom of Heaven.[43]

4 "Blessed are those who mourn, for they shall be comforted[44]

5 "Blessed are the gentle, for they shall inherit the earth[45]

6 "Blessed are those who hunger and thirst after righteousness, for they shall be filled.

7 "Blessed are the merciful, for they shall obtain mercy.

8 "Blessed are the pure in heart, for they shall see God.

9 "Blessed are the peacemakers, for they shall be called children of God.

10 "Blessed are those who have been persecuted for righteousness's sake, for theirs is the Kingdom of Heaven.

11 "Blessed are you when people reproach you, persecute you, and say all kinds of evil against you falsely, for My sake. 12 Rejoice, and be exceedingly glad, for great is your reward in heaven. For that is how they persecuted the prophets who were before you.

---

[43] **Isaiah 57:15** For thus says the high and lofty One Who inhabits eternity, Whose name is Holy: "I dwell in the high and holy place, with him also who is of a contrite and humble spirit, to revive the spirit of the humble, and to revive the heart of the contrite." **Isaiah 66:2** For My hand has made all these things, and so all these things came to be," says Yahweh: "But to this man will I look, even to he who is poor and of a contrite spirit, and who trembles at my word."

[44] **Isaiah 61:2** To proclaim the year of Yahweh's favor, and the day of vengeance of our God; to comfort all who mourn. **Isaiah 66:10** "Rejoice with Jerusalem, and be glad for her, all you who love her. Rejoice for joy with her, all you who mourn over her." **Isaiah 66:13** "As one whom his mother comforts, so will I comfort you. You will be comforted in Jerusalem."

[45] **Psalm 37:11** But the humble shall inherit the land, and shall delight themselves in the abundance of peace.

Salt and Light

Matthew 5:13–16

13 "You are the salt of the earth, but if the salt has lost its flavor, with what will it be salted? It is then good for nothing, but to be cast out and trodden under the feet of men.

14 "You are the light of the world. A city located on a hill can't be hidden. 15 Neither do you light a lamp, and put it under a measuring basket, but on a stand; and it shines to all who are in the house. 16 Even so, let your light shine before men; that they may see your good works, and glorify your Father Who is in heaven.

The Fulfillment of the Law

Matthew 5:17–20

17 "Don't think that I came to destroy the law or the prophets. I didn't come to destroy, but to fulfill. 18 For most certainly, I tell you, until heaven and earth pass away, not even one smallest letter or one tiny pen stroke shall in any way pass away from the law, until all things are accomplished. 19 Whoever, therefore, shall break one of these least commandments, and teach others to do so, shall be called least in the Kingdom of Heaven; but whoever shall do and teach them shall be called great in the Kingdom of Heaven. 20 For I tell you that unless your righteousness exceeds that of the scribes and Pharisees, there is no way you will enter into the Kingdom of Heaven.

Murder

Matthew 5:21–26

21 "You have heard that it was said to the ancient ones, 'You shall not murder'[46] and 'Whoever murders will be in danger of the judgment.' 22 But I tell you, that everyone who is angry with his brother without a cause will be in danger of the judgment; and whoever says to his brother, 'Raca!' will be in danger of the council; and whoever says, 'You fool!' will be in danger of the fire of Gehenna.

---

[46] **Exodus 20:13** You shall not murder; **Deuteronomy 5:17** You shall not murder.

23 "If therefore you are offering your gift at the altar, and there remember that your brother has anything against you, 24 leave your gift there before the altar, and go your way. First be reconciled to your brother, and then come and offer your gift.

25 "Agree with your adversary quickly, while you are with him on the way; lest perhaps the prosecutor deliver you to the judge, and the judge deliver you to the officer, and you be cast into prison. 26 Most certainly I tell you, you shall by no means get out of there, until you have paid the last penny.

Jesus Teaches About Adultery

Matthew 5:27–32

27 "You have heard that it was said to the ancients 'You shall not commit adultery,'[47] 28 but I tell you that everyone who gazes at a woman to lust after her has committed adultery with her already in his heart. 29 If your right eye causes you to stumble, pluck it out and throw it away from you. For it is more profitable for you that one of your members should perish, than for your whole body to be cast into Gehenna. 30 If your right hand causes you to stumble, cut it off, and throw it away from you. For it is more profitable for you that one of your members should perish, than for your whole body to be cast into Gehenna.

31 "It was also said, 'whoever shall put away his wife, let him give her a writing of divorce.'[48] 32 but I tell you that whoever puts away his wife, except for the cause of sexual immorality, makes her an adulteress; and whoever marries her when she is put away commits adultery.

---

[47] **Exodus 20:14** You shall not commit adultery. **Deuteronomy 5:18** You shall not commit adultery.

[48] **Deuteronomy 24:1** When a man takes a wife and marries her, then it shall be, if she finds no favor in his eyes, because he has found some unseemly thing in her, that he shall write her a bill of divorce, and put it in her hand, and send her out of his house.

Jesus Teaches About Oaths

Matthew 5:33–37

33 “Again you have heard that it was said to the ancients, ‘You shall not make false vows,[49] but shall perform to the Lord your vows,’[50] 34 but I tell you, don’t swear at all: neither by heaven, for it is the throne of God; 35 nor by the earth, for it is the footstool of His feet; nor by Jerusalem, for it is the city of the great King. 36 Neither shall you swear by your head, for you can’t make one hair white or black. 37 But let your ‘Yes’ be ‘Yes’ and your ‘No’ be ‘No.’ Whatever is more than these is of the evil one.

Jesus Teaches About Loving Your Enemy

Matthew 5:38–48

38 “You have heard that it was said, ‘An eye for an eye, and a tooth for a tooth.’[51] But I tell you, don’t resist him who is evil; but whoever strikes you on your right cheek, turn to him the other also. 40 If anyone sues you to take away your coat, let him have your cloak also. 41 Whoever compels you to go one mile, go with him two. 42 Give to him who asks you, and don’t turn away him who desires to borrow from you.’”

Matthew 5:43–48

43 “You have heard that it was said, ‘You shall love your neighbor and hate your enemy.’[52] 44 But I tell you, love your enemies, bless

---

[49] **Leviticus 19:12** You shall not swear by my name falsely, and profane the name of your God. I am Yahweh.

[50] **Numbers 30:2** If a man makes a vow to the LORD, or swears an oath to bind himself by some agreement, he shall not break his word; he shall do according to all that proceeds out of his mouth. **Deuteronomy 23:23** You shall observe and do that which has gone out of your lips. Whatever you have vowed to Yahweh your God as a freewill offering, which you have promised with your mouth, you must do.

[51] **Exodus 21:24** Eye for eye, tooth for tooth, hand for hand, foot for foot **Leviticus 24:20** Fracture for fracture, eye for eye, tooth for tooth; as he has injured someone, so shall it be done to him. **Deuteronomy 19:21** Your eyes shall not pity: life for life, eye for eye, tooth for tooth, hand for hand, foot for foot.

[52] **Leviticus 19:18** ‘You shall not take vengeance, nor bear any grudge against the children of your people; but you shall love your neighbor as yourself. I am Yahweh.’

those who curse you, do good to those who hate you, and pray for those who mistreat you and persecute you, 45 that you may be children of your Father who is in heaven. For he makes his sun to rise on the evil and the good, and sends rain on the just and the unjust. 46 For if you love those who love you, what reward do you have? Don't even the tax collectors do the same? 47 If you only greet your friends, what more do you do than others? Don't even the tax collectors do the same? 48 Therefore you shall be perfect, just as your Father in heaven is perfect.

Jesus Teaches About Giving

Matthew 6:1–4

1 "Be careful that you don't do your charitable giving before men, to be seen by them, or else you have no reward from your Father who is in heaven. 2 Therefore when you do merciful deeds, don't sound a trumpet before yourself, as the hypocrites do in the synagogues and in the streets, that they may get glory from men. Most certainly I tell you, they have received their reward. 3 But when you do merciful deeds, don't let your left hand know what your right hand does, 4 so that your merciful deeds may be in secret, then your Father who sees in secret will reward you openly.

Jesus Teaches About Prayer

Matthew 6:5–15

5 "When you pray, you shall not be as the hypocrites, for they love to stand and pray in the synagogues and in the corners of the streets, that they may be seen by men. Most certainly, I tell you, they have received their reward. 6 But you, when you pray, enter into your inner room, and having shut your door, pray to your Father who is in secret, and your Father who sees in secret will reward you openly. 7 In praying, don't use vain repetitions, as the Gentiles do; for they think that they will be heard for their much speaking. 8 Therefore don't be like them, for your Father knows what things you need, before you ask Him.

9 "Pray like this: 'Our Father in heaven, may Your name be kept holy. 10 Let Your Kingdom come. Let Your will be done, as in heaven, so

on earth. 11 Give us today our daily bread. 12 Forgive us our debts, as we also forgive our debtors. 13 Bring us not into temptation, but deliver us from the evil one. For Yours is the Kingdom, the power, and the glory forever. Amen.'

14 "For if you forgive men their trespasses, your heavenly Father will also forgive you. 15 But if you don't forgive men their trespasses, neither will your Father forgive your trespasses.

Jesus Teaches About Fasting

Matthew 6:16–18

16 "Moreover when you fast, don't be like the hypocrites, with sad faces. For they disfigure their faces, that they may be seen by men to be fasting. Most certainly I tell you, they have received their reward. 17 But you, when you fast, anoint your head, and wash your face; 18 so that you are not seen by men to be fasting, but by your Father who is in secret, and your Father, who sees in secret, will reward you.

Jesus Teaches About Materialism

Matthew 6:19–34

19 "Don't lay up treasures for yourselves on the earth, where moth and rust consume, and where thieves break through and steal; 20 but lay up for yourselves treasures in heaven, where neither moth nor rust consume, and where thieves don't break through and steal; 21 for where your treasure is, there your heart will be also.

22 "The lamp of the body is the eye. If therefore your eye is sound, your whole body will be full of light. 23 But if your eye is evil, your whole body will be full of darkness. If therefore the light that is in you is darkness, how great is the darkness!

24 "No one can serve two masters, for either he will hate the one and love the other; or else he will be devoted to one and despise the other. You can't serve both God and Mammon.

25 "Therefore I tell you, don't be anxious for your life: what you will eat, or what you will drink; nor yet for your body, what you will wear. Isn't life more than food, and the body more than clothing? 26 See the birds of the sky, that they don't sow, neither do they reap, nor gather

into barns. Your heavenly Father feeds them. Aren't you of much more value than they?

27 "Which of you, by being anxious, can add one moment to his lifespan? 28 Why are you anxious about clothing? Consider the lilies of the field, how they grow. They don't toil, neither do they spin, 29 yet I tell you that even Solomon in all his glory was not dressed like one of these. 30 But if God so clothes the grass of the field, which today exists, and tomorrow is thrown into the oven, won't He much more clothe you, you of little faith?

31 "Therefore don't be anxious, saying, 'What will we eat?', 'What will we drink?' or, 'With what will we be clothed?' 32 For the Gentiles seek after all these things; for your heavenly Father knows that you need all these things.

33 "But seek first God's Kingdom, and His righteousness; and all these things will be given to you as well. 34 Therefore don't be anxious for tomorrow, for tomorrow will be anxious for itself. Each day's own evil is sufficient.

Jesus Teaches About Judging

Matthew 7:1–6

1 "Don't judge, so that you won't be judged. 2 For with whatever judgment you judge, you will be judged; and with whatever measure you measure, it will be measured to you. 3 Why do you see the speck that is in your brother's eye, but don't consider the beam that is in your own eye? 4 Or how will you tell your brother, 'Let me remove the speck from your eye,' and behold, the beam is in your own eye? 5 You hypocrite! First remove the beam out of your own eye, and then you can see clearly to remove the speck out of your brother's eye.

6 "Don't give that which is holy to the dogs, neither throw your pearls before the pigs, lest perhaps they trample them under their feet, and turn and tear you to pieces.

Jesus Teaches About Answered Prayer

Matthew 7:7–12

7 "Ask, and it will be given you. Seek, and you will find. Knock, and

it will be opened for you. 8 For everyone who asks receives. He who seeks finds. To him who knocks it will be opened.

9 "Or who is there among you, who, if his son asks him for bread, will give him a stone? 10 Or if he asks for a fish, who will give him a serpent? 11 If you then, being evil, know how to give good gifts to your children, how much more will your Father who is in heaven give good things to those who ask Him! 12 Therefore whatever you desire for men to do to you, you shall also do to them; for this is the law and the prophets.

The Narrow Gate

Matthew 7:13–14

13 "Enter in by the narrow gate; for wide is the gate and broad is the way that leads to destruction, and many are those who enter in by it. 14 Because narrow is the gate, and restricted is the way that leads to life! Few are those who find it.

False Prophets

Matthew 7:15–20

15 "Beware of false prophets, who come to you in sheep's clothing, but inwardly are ravening wolves. 16 By their fruits you will know them. Do you gather grapes from thorns, or figs from thistles? 17 Even so, every good tree produces good fruit; but the corrupt tree produces evil fruit. 18 A good tree can't produce evil fruit, neither can a corrupt tree produce good fruit. 19 Every tree that doesn't grow good fruit is cut down, and thrown into the fire. 20 Therefore by their fruits you will know them.

The Parable of the House on the Rock

Matthew 7:21–29

21 "Not everyone who says to Me, 'Lord, Lord,' will enter into the Kingdom of Heaven; but he who does the will of My Father who is in heaven. 22 Many will tell Me in that day, 'Lord, Lord, didn't we prophesy in Your name, in Your name cast out demons, and in Your name do many mighty works?' 23 Then I will tell them, 'I never knew

you. Depart from me, you who work iniquity.'

24 "Everyone therefore who hears these words of Mine, and does them, I will liken him to a wise man, who built his house on a rock. 25 The rain came down, the floods came, and the winds blew, and beat on that house; and it didn't fall, for it was founded on the rock.

26 "Everyone who hears these words of Mine, and doesn't do them will be like a foolish man, who built his house on the sand. 27 The rain came down, the floods came, and the winds blew, and beat on that house; and it fell—and great was its fall."

28 When Jesus had finished saying these things, the multitudes were astonished at His teaching, 29 for He taught them with authority, and not like the scribes.

Jesus Heals a Leper

Matthew 8:1–4; Luke 5:12–16; Mark 1:40–45

1 When He came down from the mountain, great multitudes followed Him. 12 While He was in one of the cities, behold, there 40 was a man full of leprosy. When he saw Jesus, 2 [the] leper came to Him and worshiped Him, [and] 40 kneeling down to Him, 12 he fell on his face, and begged Him, saying, "Lord, if you want to, You can make me clean."

3 Jesus 41 being moved with compassion, He stretched out His hand, 13 touched him, saying, 41 to him, "I want to. Be made clean." 42 When He had said this, immediately the leprosy departed from him, and he was made clean.

4 Jesus said to him, 43 He strictly warned him, and immediately sent him out, 14 He commanded him to tell no one 44 and said to him, "See you say nothing to anybody, but go show yourself to the priest, and offer for your cleansing the things 14 according to what 44 Moses commanded, for a testimony to them."

45 But he went out, and began to proclaim it much, and to spread about the matter. 15 But the report concerning Him spread much more, and great multitudes came together to hear, and to be healed by Him of their infirmities, 45 so that Jesus could no more openly enter into a city, but was outside in desert places: 16 But He withdrew himself into

the desert, and prayed. 45 And they came to Him from everywhere.

The Cost of Discipleship

Matthew 8:18–22

18 Now when Jesus saw great multitudes around Him, He gave the order to depart to the other side.

19 A scribe came, and said to Him, "Teacher, I will follow You wherever you go."

20 Jesus said to him, "The foxes have holes, and the birds of the sky have nests, but the Son of Man has nowhere to lay His head."

21 Another of His disciples said to Him, "Lord, allow me first to go and bury my father."

22 But Jesus said to him, "Follow me, and leave the dead to bury their own dead."

Jesus Heals a Paralytic

Matthew 9:1–8; Mark 2:1–12; Luke 5:17–26

1 He entered into a boat, and crossed over, 1 and He entered again 1 into His own city 1 Capernaum after some days, it was heard that He was in the house. 2 Immediately many were gathered together, so that there was no more room, not even around the door; and He spoke the word to them.

17 On one of those days, He was teaching; and there were Pharisees and teachers of the law sitting by, who had come out of every village of Galilee, Judea, and Jerusalem. The power of the Lord was with Him to heal them.

18 Behold, 3 four people, 18 men, brought a paralyzed man 3 carrying a paralytic, 2 lying 18 on a cot, [or] 2 bed 3 to Him 18 and they sought to bring him in to lay before Jesus.

4 When they could not 19 find a way to bring him in [and] 4 near to Him for the crowd, 19 they went up to the housetop, [and] 4 they removed the roof where He was. When they had broken it up, they let down the mat that the paralytic was lying on, 19 through the tiles with

his cot into the middle before Jesus.

Jesus, seeing their faith, said to the paralytic, "Son, cheer up! 20 Man, 2 your sins are forgiven you."

3 Behold, some of the scribes 21 and the Pharisees began to reason, saying, 3 to themselves, 6 sitting there, and reasoning in their hearts, 7 "Why does this Man speak blasphemies like that? 21 Who is this that speaks blasphemies? Who can forgive sins, but God alone? 3 This man blasphemes."

8 Immediately Jesus, perceiving in His spirit that they so reasoned within themselves, 22 answered them, [and] 8 said to them, "Why do you 4 think evil [and] 8 reason these things in your hearts? 5 For 9 which is easier, 23 to say 9 to the paralytic, 'Your sins are forgiven;' or to say, 'Arise, and take up your bed, and walk?' 10 But that you may know that the Son of Man has authority on earth to forgive sins"—6 (then He said to the paralytic), 11 "I tell you, arise, take up your mat, and go to your house."

25 Immediately he rose up before them, and took up that which he was laying on, 12 the mat, and went out in front of them all; 25 and departed to his house, glorifying God. 8 But when the multitudes saw it, they marveled and glorified God, who had given such authority to men. 26 Amazement took hold on all, and they glorified God. They were filled with fear, saying, 12 "We never saw anything like this!" [and] 26 "We have seen strange things today."

Jesus Calls Matthew

Luke 5:27–28; Matthew 9:9; Mark 2:13–14

27 After these things 9 Jesus 27 went out, 13 again by the 9 seaside. All the multitude came to Him, and He taught them. 14 As He passed by, 9 from there, 14 He saw 9 a man called Matthew 14 Levi, the son of Alphaeus, 27 a tax collector sitting at the tax office, and said to him, "Follow me!"

Matthew Gives a Feast in Jesus's Honor

Luke 5:29–32; Matthew 9:10–13; Mark 2:15–17

29 Levi made a great feast for Him in his house. There was a 10 great

crowd of tax collectors and others who were reclining with them. 10 As He sat in 15 Levi's[53] 10 house, behold, many tax collectors and sinners came and sat down with Jesus and His disciples, 15 for there were many, and they followed Him. 16 The scribes and the Pharisees, when they saw that He was eating with the sinners and tax collectors, 11 they 30 murmured against His disciples, saying, 11 "Why does your Teacher eat 16 and drink 11 with tax collectors and sinners?"

17 When Jesus heard it, 31 Jesus answered 17 [and] said to them, "Those who are healthy have no need for a physician, but those who are sick. 13 But you go and learn what this means: 'I desire mercy, and not sacrifice',[54] for I came not to call the righteous, but sinners to repentance.'"

A Question on Fasting

Mark 2:18–22; Matthew 9:14–17; Luke 5:33–39

18 John's disciples and the Pharisees were fasting, and they came and asked Him, 14 Then John's disciples came to Him, saying, 18 "Why do 14 we 18 John's disciples 33 often fast and pray, likewise also the disciples of the Pharisees, 18 but Your disciples don't fast, 33 Yours eat and drink?"

19 Jesus 34 said to them, "Can you make the friends of the bridegroom 15 mourn [and] 34 fast, while the bridegroom is with them? 19 As long as they have the bridegroom with them, they can't fast. 35 But the days will come when the bridegroom will be taken away from them. 15 and 35 then they will fast in those days."

The Parable of Cloth and Wineskins

36 He also told a parable to them. "No one 21 sews a piece of unshrunk cloth 36 from a new garment on an old garment, or else he will tear the new, [for] 21 the patch shrinks and the new 16 patch 21 tears away from the old 16 garment, 21 and a worse hole is made 36 and also the piece from the new will not match the old.

---

[53] From NKJV, GNT, CEB, Free Bible Version, and NT Psalms.

[54] **Hosea 6:6** For I desire mercy, and not sacrifice; and the knowledge of God more than burnt offerings.

37 "No one puts new wine into old wine skins, or else the new wine will burst the skins, and it will be spilled, and the skins will be destroyed. 38 But new wine must be put into fresh wine skins, and both are preserved. 39 No man having drunk old wine immediately desires new, for he says, 'The old is better.'"

Jairus Requests Healing for His Daughter

Matthew 9:18–19; Mark 5:22–24; Luke 8:41–42

18 While He told these things to them, 22 behold, one of the rulers of the synagogue, Jairus by name, came; and seeing Him, he fell at His feet, 18 and worshiped Him, 23 and begged Him much, 41 to come into his house, 42 for he had an only daughter, about twelve years of age, and she was dying, 23 saying, "My little daughter is at the point of death. Please come and lay your hands on her, that she may be made healthy, and live."

19 Jesus got up and followed him, as did His disciples. 42 But as he went, the multitudes pressed against Him 24 and a great multitude followed him, and they pressed upon Him on all sides.

Jesus Heals A Woman of a Hemorrhage

Mark 5:25–34; Luke 8:43–48; Matthew 9:19–22

25 A certain woman, who had an issue of blood for twelve years, 26 and had suffered many things by many physicians, and had spent all that she had, 43 all her living on physicians, and could not be healed by any, 26 and was no better, but rather grew worse. 27 Having heard the things concerning Jesus, came up behind him in the crowd, and touched 44 the fringe of 27 His clothes.[55] 28 For she said 21 within herself, 28 "If I just touch His clothes, I will be made well." 29 Immediately the flow of her blood was dried up, 44 and immediately

[55] **Leviticus 15:19–27** 19 "'If a woman has a discharge, and her discharge in her flesh is blood, she shall be in her impurity seven days. Whoever touches her shall be unclean until the evening. 25 "'If a woman has a discharge of her blood many days not in the time of her period, or if she has a discharge beyond the time of her period, all the days of the discharge of her uncleanness shall be as in the days of her period. She is unclean. **Malachi 4:2** But to you who fear My name The Sun of Righteousness shall arise with healing in His wings [same word as 'fringe'].

the flow of her blood stopped 29 and she felt in her body that she was healed of her affliction.

30 Immediately Jesus, perceiving in Himself that the power had gone out from Him, turned around in the crowd, and asked, 45 "Who touched me? 30 Who touched my clothes?"

45 When all denied it, Peter and those with Him 31 His disciples said to Him, 45 "Master, 31 You see the multitude pressing 45 and jostle You, 31 and You say, 'Who touched me?'"

46 But Jesus said, "Someone did touch Me, for I perceived that power has gone out of Me." 32 He looked around to see her who had done this thing. 22 But Jesus, [turned] around and [saw] her. 47 When the woman saw that she was not hidden, 33 fearing and trembling, knowing what had been done to her, came and fell down before Him, and told Him all the truth. 47 [She] declared to Him in the presence of all the people the reason why she had touched Him, and how she was healed immediately.

34 He said to her, 22 "Daughter, cheer up! 34 Daughter, your faith has made you well. Go in peace, and be cured of your disease." 22 And the woman was made well from that hour.

Jesus Resurrects Jairus's Daughter

Mark 5:35–43; Luke 8:49–56; Matthew 9:23–26

35 While He was still speaking, people came from the synagogue ruler's house saying, "Your daughter is dead. Why bother the Teacher any more? 49 Don't trouble the Teacher."

36 But Jesus, when He heard the message spoken, immediately 50 answered him, [and] 36 said to the ruler of the synagogue, "Don't be afraid, only believe 50 and she will be healed." 37 He allowed no one to follow Him, except Peter, James, and John the brother of James.

38 He came to the synagogue ruler's house, [and] 51 He didn't allow anyone to enter in, except Peter, John, James, the father of the child, and her mother. 52 All were weeping and mourning her. 23 When Jesus came into the ruler's house 38 and He saw an uproar, 23 and saw the flute players, and the crowd in noisy disorder, 39 weeping, and great wailing. 39 When He had entered in, He said to them, "Why

do you make an uproar and weep? 52 Don't weep. 24 Make room, because the girl, 39 the child is not dead, but is asleep."

40 They ridiculed Him, 53 knowing that she was dead. 40 But He, having put them all out, took the father of the child, her mother, and those who were with Him, and went in where the child was lying. 41 Taking the child by the hand, He said to her, "Talitha cumi!" which means, being interpreted, "Girl, I tell you, get up!"

55 Her spirit returned, and 42 immediately the girl rose up and walked, for she was twelve years old. 56 Her parents were amazed, 42 with great amazement. 43 He strictly ordered them that no one should know this, and commanded that something should be given to her to eat. 56 But He commanded them to tell no one what had been done. 26 The report of this went out into all that land.

The Second Passover of Jesus's Ministry

A Question on Sabbath Keeping

Luke 6:1–5; Matthew 12:1–8; Mark 2:23-28

1 Now on the second Sabbath after the first, [56] 1 Jesus went 1 on the Sabbath day through the grain fields. His disciples were hungry and began to pluck heads of grain and to eat, 1 and ate, rubbing them in their hands.[57]

2 But the Pharisees, when they saw it, said to Him, "Behold, Your disciples do what is not lawful to do on the Sabbath." 2 But some of the Pharisees said to them, "Why do you do that which is not lawful to do on the Sabbath day?"

3 Jesus, answering them, said, "Haven't you read what David did when 25 he had need, [and] 3 was hungry, he, and those who were with him; 26 when Abiathar was high priest, 4 how he entered into God's house, and took and ate the show bread, and gave also to those who were with him,[58] 4 which was not lawful for him to eat, neither

---

[56] This could also be rendered, "the second Sabbath of first rank," which would imply that this would be the second annual holy day, known as the Last Day of Unleavened Bread. This occurs seven days after the Passover. See **Leviticus 23:6–8** 6 And on the fifteenth day of the same month is the Feast of Unleavened Bread to the Lord; seven days you must eat unleavened bread. 7 On the first day you shall have a holy convocation; you shall do no customary work on it. 8 But you shall offer an offering made by fire to the Lord for seven days. The seventh day shall be a holy convocation; you shall do no customary work on it. See the Appendix B for further discussion of this verse.

[57] This is the official method of harvesting grain on the Sabbath. See Appendix B for details.

[58] **1 Samuel 21:3–6** "Now therefore, what have you on hand? Give me five loaves of bread in my hand, or whatever can be found." 4 And the priest answered David and said, "There is no common bread on hand; but there is holy bread, if the young men have at least kept themselves from women." 5 Then David answered the priest, and said to him, "Truly, women have been kept from us about three days since I came out. And the vessels of the young men are holy, and the bread is in effect common, even though it was consecrated in the vessel this day." 6 So the priest gave him holy bread; for there was no bread there but the showbread which had been

for those who were with him, but only for the priests 4 to eat?"[59]

5 "Or have you not read in the law, that on the Sabbath day, the priests in the temple profane the Sabbath, and are guiltless?[60] 6 But I tell you that one greater than the temple is here. 7 But if you had known what this means, 'I desire mercy, and not sacrifice'[61] you would not have condemned the guiltless." 27 He said to them, "The Sabbath was made for man, not man for the Sabbath. 28 Therefore the Son of Man is Lord even of the Sabbath."

Jesus Heals A Man with a Withered Hand on the Sabbath

Matthew 12:9–14; Mark 3:1–6; Luke 6:6–11

9 He departed there, and went 1 again 9 into their synagogue 6 on another Sabbath that He entered into the synagogue and taught. 10 And behold, 6 there was a man there, and his right hand was withered.

10 They asked Him, "Is it lawful to heal on the Sabbath day?" that they might accuse him. 7 The scribes and the Pharisees watched Him, to see whether He would heal 2 him 7 on the Sabbath, that they might find an accusation against Him.

8 But He knew their thoughts; and He said to the man who had the withered hand, "Rise up, and stand 3 up 8 in the middle." He arose and stood.

11 He said to them, "What man is there among you, who has one sheep, and if this one falls into a pit on the Sabbath day, won't he grab on to it, and lift it out? 12 Of how much more value then is a man than a sheep! Therefore it is lawful to do good on the Sabbath day."

---

taken from before the LORD, in order to put hot bread in its place on the day when it was taken away (NKJV).

[59] **Leviticus 24:9** And it shall be for Aaron and his sons, and they shall eat it in a holy place; for it is most holy to him from the offerings of the LORD made by fire, by a perpetual statute" (NKJV).

[60] **Numbers 28:9–10** And on the Sabbath day two lambs in their first year, without blemish, and two-tenths of an ephah of fine flour as a grain offering, mixed with oil, with its drink offering—10 this is the burnt offering for every Sabbath, besides the regular burnt offering with its drink offering.

[61] **Hosea 6:6** For I desire mercy and not sacrifice, And the knowledge of God more than burnt offerings.

9 Then Jesus said to them, “I will ask you something: Is it lawful on the Sabbath to do good, or to do harm? To save a life, or to kill?” 4 But they were silent.

5 When He had looked around at them 10 all 5 with anger, being grieved at the hardening of their hearts, 13 then 5 He said to the man, “Stretch out your hand.” He stretched it out, and his hand was restored as healthy as the other.

11 But they were filled with rage. 6 The Pharisees went out, and immediately conspired with the Herodians against Him, 11 and talked with one another about what they might do to Jesus, 6 how they might destroy Him.

Jesus Returns to Galilee to Preach and Heal

Matthew 12:15–21; Mark 3:7–12

15 Jesus, perceiving that, withdrew from there 7 to the sea with His disciples, and a great multitude followed Him from Galilee, from Judea, 8 from Jerusalem, from Idumaea, beyond the Jordan, and those from around Tyre and Sidon. A great multitude, hearing what great things He did, came to Him, 15 followed Him; and He healed them all. 9 He spoke to his disciples that a little boat should stay near Him because of the crowd, so that they wouldn’t press on Him. 10 For He had healed many, so that as many as had diseases pressed on Him that they might touch Him.

11 The unclean spirits, whenever they saw Him, fell down before Him, and cried, “You are the Son of God!” 12 He sternly warned them that they should not make Him known, 17 that it might be fulfilled which was spoken through Isaiah the prophet, saying,

> 18 “Behold, my servant Whom I have chosen; my beloved in Whom my soul is well pleased: I will put my Spirit on Him. He will proclaim justice to the nations. 19 He will not strive, nor shout; neither will anyone hear His voice in the streets. 20 He won’t break a bruised reed. He won’t quench a smoking flax, until He leads justice to victory. 21 In His name, the nations will

hope."[62]

Jesus Ordains the Apostles

Luke 6:12–16; Mark 3:12–19; Matthew 10:3

12 In these days, He went out to the mountain to pray, and He continued all night in prayer to God.

13 When it was day, He called His disciples, 12 those whom He wanted, and they went to Him. 13 and from them twelve, He chose [and] 14 appointed twelve, 13 whom He also named apostles: 14 that they might be with Him, and that He might send them out to preach, 15 and to have authority to heal sicknesses and to cast out demons: 16 Simon, to whom He 14 also 14 gave the name Peter; 14 Andrew, his brother; 17 James the son of Zebedee; John, the brother of James, and He called them Boanerges, which means, Sons of Thunder; 18 Andrew; Philip; Bartholomew; Matthew; 3 the tax collector; 18 Thomas, James the son of Alphaeus, 3 Lebbaeus, who was also called 18 Thaddaeus, [also known as] 16 Judas the son of James; 18 Simon 15 who was called the Zealot; 19 and Judas Iscariot, who also betrayed Him.

The Sermon on the Plain

Luke 6:17–49

17 He came down with them, and stood on a level place, with a crowd of his disciples, and a great number of the people from all Judea and Jerusalem, and the sea coast of Tyre and Sidon, who came to hear Him and to be healed of their diseases; 18 as well as those who were troubled by unclean spirits, and they were being healed. 19 All the multitude sought to touch Him, for power came out of Him and healed them all.

---

[62] **Isaiah 42:1–4** "Behold, my servant, Whom I uphold; my chosen, in Whom my soul delights—I have put my Spirit on Him. He will bring justice to the nations. 2 He will not shout, nor raise His voice, nor cause it to be heard in the street. 3 He won't break a bruised reed. He won't quench a dimly burning wick. He will faithfully bring justice. 4 He will not fail nor be discouraged, until He has set justice in the earth, and the islands will wait for His law."

The Beatitudes

20 He lifted up His eyes to His disciples, and said, "Blessed are you who are poor, God's Kingdom is yours.

21 "Blessed are you who hunger now, for you will be filled. Blessed are you who weep now, for you will laugh.

22 "Blessed are you when men shall hate you, and when they shall exclude and mock you, and throw out your name as evil, for the Son of Man's sake. 23 Rejoice in that day, and leap for joy, for behold, your reward is great in heaven, for their fathers did the same thing to the prophets.

24 "But woe to you who are rich! For you have received your consolation.

25 "Woe to you, you who are full now, for you will be hungry.

"Woe to you who laugh now, for you will mourn and weep.

26 "Woe to you when all men speak well of you, for their fathers did the same thing to the false prophets.

Love Your Enemies

27 "But I tell you who hear: love your enemies, do good to those who hate you, 28 bless those who curse you, and pray for those who mistreat you. 29 To him who strikes you on the cheek, offer also the other; and from him who takes away your cloak, don't withhold your coat also. 30 Give to everyone who asks you, and don't ask him who takes away your goods to give them back again.

31 "As you would like people to do to you, do exactly so to them.

32 "If you love those who love you, what credit is that to you? For even sinners love those who love them. 33 If you do good to those who do good to you, what credit is that to you? For even sinners do the same. 34 If you lend to those from whom you hope to receive, what credit is that to you? Even sinners lend to sinners, to receive back as much.

35 "But love your enemies, and do good, and lend, expecting nothing back; and your reward will be great, and you will be children of the

Most High; for He is kind toward the unthankful and evil.

Judging Others

36 "Therefore be merciful, even as your Father is also merciful.

37 "Don't judge and you won't be judged. Don't condemn, and you won't be condemned. Set free and you will be set free.

38 "Give and it will be given to you: good measure, pressed down, shaken together and running over, will be given to you. For with the same measure you measure it will be measured back to you."

The Parable of the Blind Guiding the Blind

39 He spoke a parable to them. "Can the blind guide the blind? Won't
they both fall into a pit? 40 A disciple is not above his teacher, but
everyone when he is fully trained will be like his teacher.

41 "Why do you see the speck of chaff that is in your brother's eye,
but don't consider the beam that is in your own eye? 42 Or how can
you tell your brother, 'Brother, let me remove the speck of chaff that is in your eye,' when you yourself don't see the beam that is in your own eye? You hypocrite! First remove the beam from your own eye, and then you can see clearly to remove the speck of chaff that is in your brother's eye.

The Parable of A Tree and Its Fruit

43 "For there is no good tree that produces rotten fruit; nor again a
rotten tree that produces good fruit. 44 For each tree is known by its
own fruit. For people don't gather figs from thorns, nor do they gather
grapes from a bramble bush. 45 The good man out of the good treasure
of his heart brings out that which is good, and the evil man out of the evil treasure of his heart brings out that which is evil, for out of the abundance of the heart, his mouth speaks.

The Parable of the House on the Rock

46 "Why do you call Me, 'Lord, Lord,' and don't do the things which
I say? 47 Everyone who comes to Me, and hears My words, and does

them, I will show you who he is like. 48 He is like a man building a house, who dug and went deep, and laid a foundation on the rock. When a flood arose, the stream broke against that house, and could not shake it, because it was founded on the rock. 49 But he who hears, and doesn't do, is like a man who built a house on the earth without a foundation, against which the stream broke, and immediately it fell, and the ruin of that house was great."

Jesus Heals the Centurion's Servant

Luke 7:1–10; Matthew 8:5–13

1 Now when He concluded all His sayings in the hearing of the people, He entered Capernaum. 2 A certain centurion's servant, who was dear to him, was sick and ready to die. 3 So when he heard about Jesus, he sent elders of the Jews to Him, pleading with Him to come and heal his servant. 4 And when they came to Jesus, they begged Him earnestly, saying that the one for whom He should do this was deserving, 5 "for he loves our nation, and has built us a synagogue."

7 And Jesus said to him, "I will come and heal him."

6 Then Jesus went with them. And when He was already not far from the house, the centurion sent friends to Him, saying to Him, "Lord, do not trouble Yourself; for I am not worthy that You should enter under my roof. 7 Therefore I did not even think myself worthy to come to You. But say the word, and my servant will be healed. 8 For I also am a man placed under authority, having soldiers under me. And I say to one, 'Go,' and he goes; and to another, 'Come,' and he comes; and to my servant, 'Do this,' and he does it."

9 When Jesus heard these things, He marveled at him, and turned and said to the multitude who followed him, "I tell you, 10 assuredly, I say to you, I have not found such great faith, not even in Israel! 11 And I say to you that many will come from east and west, and sit down with Abraham, Isaac, and Jacob in the Kingdom of Heaven. 12 But the sons of the kingdom will be cast out into outer darkness. There will be weeping and gnashing of teeth."

13 Then Jesus said to the centurion, "Go your way; and as you have believed, so let it be done for you." And his servant was healed that same hour. 10 And those who were sent, returning to the house, found

the servant well who had been sick.

Jesus Resurrects a Widow's Son

Luke 7:11–17

11 Soon afterwards, He went to a city called Nain. Many of His disciples, along with a great multitude, went with Him. 12 Now when He came near to the gate of the city, behold, one who was dead was carried out, the only son of his mother, and she was a widow. Many people of the city were with her. 13 When the Lord saw her, He had compassion on her, and said to her, "Don't cry." 14 He came near and touched the coffin, and the bearers stood still. He said, "Young man, I tell you, arise!" 15 He who was dead sat up, and began to speak. And He gave him to his mother.

16 Fear took hold of all, and they glorified God, saying, "A great prophet has arisen among us!" and, "God has visited his people!" 17 This report went out concerning Him in the whole of Judea, and in all the surrounding region.

John the Baptist Sends Messengers to Jesus

Luke 7:18–35; Matthew11:2–19

18 The disciples of John told him about all these things. 2 When John heard in the prison 2 the works of Christ. 19 John, calling to himself two of his disciples, sent 2 word by 19 them to Jesus, saying, "Are you the one Who is coming, or should we look for another?"

20 When the men had come to Him, they said, "John the Baptizer has sent us to you, saying, 'Are you He Who comes, or should we look for another?'"

21 In that hour He cured many of diseases and plagues and evil spirits; and to many who were blind He gave sight. 22 Jesus answered them, "Go and tell John the things which you have seen and heard: that the blind receive their sight, the lame walk, the lepers are cleansed, the deaf hear, the dead are raised up, and the poor have good news preached to them.[63] 23 Blessed is he who finds no occasion for

---

[63] **Isaiah 35:3–6** Strengthen the weak hands, and make firm the feeble knees. 4 Tell

stumbling in Me."

24 When John's messengers had departed, 7 Jesus spoke to the crowds about John: "What did you go out to the wilderness to see? A stalk blowing in the wind? 8 What did you go out to see? A man dressed up in refined clothes? 8 Look, those who wear refined clothes [and] 25 are gorgeously dressed, and live delicately, are in kings' 8 [or] royal palaces [and] 25 courts 9 What did you go out to see? A prophet? Yes, I tell you, and more than a prophet. 10 He is the one of whom it is written:

> 'Look, I'm sending my messenger before you, who will prepare your way before you'[64]

28 "For 11 I assure you that no one who has ever been born is [a] greater 28 prophet 11 than John the Baptist. Yet whoever is least in 28 God's 11 Kingdom of Heaven is greater than he. 12 From the days of John the Baptist until now the Kingdom of Heaven is violently attacked as violent people seize it. 13 All the prophets and the law prophesied until John came. 14 If you are willing to accept it, he is Elijah who is to come. 15 Let the person who has ears, hear.

29 When all the people and the tax collectors heard this, they declared God to be just, having been baptized with John's baptism. 30 But the Pharisees and the lawyers rejected the counsel of God, not being baptized by him themselves.

---

those who have a fearful heart, "Be strong. Don't be afraid. Behold, your God will come with vengeance, God's retribution. He will come and save you." 5 Then the eyes of the blind will be opened, and the ears of the deaf will be unstopped. 6 Then the lame man will leap like a deer, and the tongue of the mute will sing; for waters will break out in the wilderness, and streams in the desert. **Isaiah 61:1–2** The Lord Yahweh's Spirit is on Me; because Yahweh has anointed Me to preach good news to the humble. He has sent Me to bind up the broken hearted, to proclaim liberty to the captives, and release to those who are bound; 2 to proclaim the year of Yahweh's favor, and the day of vengeance of our God; to comfort all who mourn; **Isaiah 29:18–19** In that day, the deaf will hear the words of the book, and the eyes of the blind will see out of obscurity and out of darkness. 19 The humble also will increase their joy in Yahweh, and the poor among men will rejoice in the Holy One of Israel.

[64] **Malachi 3:1** Look, I am sending My messenger who will clear the path before Me; suddenly the LORD whom you are seeking will come to His temple. The messenger of the covenant in whom you take delight is coming, says the LORD of heavenly forces.

31 But the Lord said, "To what then will I liken the people of this generation? What are they like? 32 They are like children who sit in the marketplace, and call to one another, saying, 'We piped to you, and you didn't dance. We mourned, and you didn't weep.' 33 For John the Baptizer came neither eating bread nor drinking wine, and you say, 'He has a demon.' 34 The Son of Man has come eating and drinking, and you say, 'Behold, a gluttonous man, and a drunkard; a friend of tax collectors and sinners!' 35 Wisdom is justified by all her children."

Jesus Reproves Cities for Lack of Repentance

Matthew 11:20–30

20 Then he began to scold the cities where he had done his greatest miracles because they didn't change their hearts and lives. 21 "How terrible it will be for you, Chorazin! How terrible it will be for you, Bethsaida! For if the miracles done among you had been done in Tyre and Sidon, they would have changed their hearts and lives and put on funeral clothes and ashes a long time ago. 22 But I say to you that Tyre and Sidon will be better off on Judgment Day than you. 23 And you, Capernaum, will you be honored by being raised up to heaven? No, you will be thrown down to the place of the dead. After all, if the miracles that were done among you had been done in Sodom, it would still be here today. 24 But I say to you that it will be better for the land of Sodom on the Judgment Day than it will be for you."

Jesus Praises God for Calling the Simple

25 At that time, Jesus answered, "I thank You, Father, Lord of heaven and earth, that You hid these things from the wise and understanding, and revealed them to infants. 26 Yes, Father, for so it was well-pleasing in Your sight.

27 "All things have been delivered to Me by My Father. No one knows the Son, except the Father; neither does anyone know the Father, except the Son, and he to whom the Son desires to reveal him.

28 "Come to Me, all you who labor and are heavily burdened, and I will give you rest. 29 Take my yoke upon you, and learn from Me, for I am gentle and humble in heart; and you will find rest for your souls. 30 For My yoke is easy, and My burden is light."

Jesus Anointed by a Sinful Woman and Parable of Two Debtors

Luke 7:36–50

36 One of the Pharisees invited Him to eat with him. He entered into the Pharisee's house, and sat at the table.

37 Behold, a woman in the city who was a sinner, when she knew that
He was reclining in the Pharisee's house, she brought an alabaster jar
of ointment. 38 Standing behind at His feet weeping, she began to wet
His feet with her tears, and she wiped them with the hair of her head,
kissed His feet, and anointed them with the ointment.

39 Now when the Pharisee who had invited Him saw it, he said to himself, "This man, if He were a prophet, would have perceived who and what kind of woman this is who touches Him, that she is a sinner."

40 Jesus answered him, "Simon, I have something to tell you."

He said, "Teacher, say on."

41 "A certain lender had two debtors. The one owed five hundred
denarii, and the other fifty. 42 When they couldn't pay, he forgave
them both. Which of them therefore will love him most?"

43 Simon answered, "He, I suppose, to whom he forgave the most."

He said to him, "You have judged correctly."

44 Turning to the woman, He said to Simon, "Do you see this woman?
I entered into your house, and you gave me no water for My feet, but
she has wet My feet with her tears, and wiped them with the hair of
her head. 45 You gave Me no kiss, but she, since the time I came in,
has not ceased to kiss My feet. 46 You didn't anoint My head with oil,
but she has anointed My feet with ointment. 47 Therefore I tell you,
her sins, which are many, are forgiven, for she loved much. But to
whom little is forgiven, the same loves little."

48 He said to her, "Your sins are forgiven."

49 Those who sat at the table with Him began to say to themselves, "Who is this who even forgives sins?"

50 He said to the woman, "Your faith has saved you. Go in peace."

Jesus Travels with the Apostles

Luke 8:1–3; Matthew 9:35–38; Mark 3:19–21

1 Soon afterward, Jesus traveled through the cities and villages, preaching and proclaiming the good news of God's kingdom. The Twelve were with Him, 2 along with some women who had been healed of evil spirits and sicknesses. Among them were Mary Magdalene (from whom seven demons had been thrown out), 3 Joanna (the wife of Herod's servant Chuza), Susanna, and many others who provided for them out of their resources.

35 Jesus traveled among all the cities and villages, teaching in their synagogues, announcing the good news of the kingdom, and healing every disease and every sickness.

36 Now when Jesus saw the crowds, He had compassion for them because they were troubled and helpless, like sheep without a shepherd. 37 Then He said to his disciples, "The size of the harvest is bigger than you can imagine, but there are few workers. 38 Therefore, plead with the Lord of the harvest to send out workers for His harvest."

19 He came into a house. 20 The multitude came together again, so that they could not so much as eat bread. 21 When His family heard it, they went out to seize Him: for they said, "He is insane."

Jesus Heals a Blind Mute and the Pharisees' Blasphemy

Matthew 12:22–37; Mark 3:22–30

22 Then one possessed by a demon, blind and mute, was brought to Him and He healed him, so that the blind and mute man both spoke and saw. 23 All the multitudes were amazed, and said, "Can this be the son of David?"

22 The legal experts [and] 24 Pharisees 22 came down from Jerusalem. 24 When [they] heard, 22 over and over 24 they said, 22 [and] charged, "He's possessed by Beelzebul," [and] 24 "This man throws out demons only by the authority of Beelzebul, 22 by the prince, 24 the ruler of the demons."

25 Because Jesus knew what they were thinking, [and] 23 when Jesus

called them together He spoke to them in a parable [and] 25 replied: 23 “How can Satan throw Satan out? 24 A kingdom involved in civil war will collapse. 25 Every kingdom involved in civil war becomes a wasteland. 25 And a house torn apart by divisions will collapse. 25 Every city or house torn apart by divisions will collapse. 26 If Satan rebels against himself and is divided, then he can’t endure. He’s done for. 26 If Satan throws out Satan, he is at war with himself. How then can his kingdom endure?

27 “And if I throw out demons by the authority of Beelzebul, then by whose authority do your followers throw them out? Therefore, they will be your judges. 28 But if I throw out demons by the power of God’s Spirit, then God’s kingdom has already overtaken you. 29 Can people go into a house that belongs to a strong man and steal his possessions, unless they first tie up the strong man? 27 No one gets into the house of a strong person and steals anything without first tying up the strong person. Only then can the house be burglarized. 29 Then they can rob his house. 30 Whoever isn’t with Me is against Me, and whoever doesn’t gather with Me scatters.”

28 “I assure you that 31 every sin and insult to God [and] 28 human beings will be forgiven for everything, for all sins and insults of every kind. 31 But insulting the Holy Spirit won’t be forgiven. 32 And whoever speaks a word against the Son of Man will be forgiven, but whoever speaks against the Holy Spirit, it will not be forgiven him, neither in this age, nor in that which is to come. 29 But whoever may blaspheme against the Holy Spirit never has forgiveness, but is subject to eternal condemnation.” 30 —because they said, “He has an unclean spirit.”

33 “Either make the tree good, and its fruit good, or make the tree corrupt, and its fruit corrupt; for the tree is known by its fruit. 34 You offspring of vipers, how can you, being evil, speak good things? For out of the abundance of the heart, the mouth speaks. 35 The good man out of his good treasure brings out good things, and the evil man out of his evil treasure of the heart brings out evil things. 36 I tell you that every idle word that men speak, they will give account of it in the Day of Judgment. 37 For by your words you will be justified, and by your words you will be condemned.”

The Scribes and Pharisees Ask for a Sign

Matthew 12:38–45

38 Then certain of the scribes and Pharisees answered, "Teacher, we want to see a sign from You."

39 But He answered them, "An evil and adulterous generation seeks after a sign, but no sign will be given it but the sign of Jonah the prophet. 40 For as Jonah was three days and three nights in the belly of the whale, so will the Son of Man be three days and three nights in the heart of the earth.

41 The men of Nineveh will stand up in the judgment with this generation, and will condemn it, for they repented at the preaching of Jonah; and behold, someone greater than Jonah is here. 42 The queen of the south will rise up in the judgment with this generation, and will condemn it, for she came from the ends of the earth to hear the wisdom of Solomon; and behold, someone greater than Solomon is here.

Unclean Spirits

43 When an unclean spirit has gone out of a man, he passes through waterless places, seeking rest, and doesn't find it. 44 Then he says, 'I will return into my house from which I came out,' and when he has come back, he finds it empty, swept, and put in order. 45 Then he goes, and takes with himself seven other spirits more evil than he is, and they enter in and dwell there. The last state of that man becomes worse than the first. Even so will it be also to this evil generation."

Jesus's Physical and Spiritual Family

Matthew 12:46–50; Mark 3:31–35; Luke 8:19–21

46 While He was yet speaking to the multitudes, 31 His mother and His brothers came, 19 to Him, and they could not come near Him for the crowd. 46 Behold, His mother and His brothers stood outside 31 and standing outside, they sent to Him, calling Him.

32 A multitude was sitting around Him, and 20 some people told Him, 32 "Behold, Your mother, Your brothers, and Your sisters 20 stand 32 outside looking for You, 47 seeking, 20 desiring to see You, 47 to

speak to You."

48 But He answered him who spoke to Him, "Who is My mother? Who are My brothers?" 34 Looking around at those who sat around Him, 49 He stretched out His hand towards His disciples, and said, "Behold, My mother and My brothers! 50 For whoever does the will of My Father who is in heaven, he is My brother, and 35 My 50 sister, and mother. 21 My mother and My brothers are these who hear the word of God, and do it."

The Parable of the Sower

Matthew 13:1–9; Mark 4:1–9; Luke 8:4–8

1 On that day Jesus went out of the house, and sat by the seaside. 1 Again He began to teach by the seaside. A great multitude 4 came together, 1 to Him, and people from every 4 city were coming to Him, 1 so that He entered into a boat in the sea, and sat down. All the multitude were on the land by the sea, 2 standing on the beach.

3 He spoke to them [and] 2 He taught them many things in parables, and told them in His teaching, 4 by a parable, 3 "Listen! Behold, the farmer went out to sow, 5 his seed 4 and as he sowed, some seed fell by the road, 5 and it was trampled underfoot, 5 and the birds came and devoured it. 5 Others fell on the rocky ground, where it had little soil, and immediately it sprang up, because it had no depth of soil. 6 And as soon as it grew, 6 when the sun had risen, it was scorched; and because it had no root, it withered away, 6 because it had no moisture.

7 "Others fell among the thorns, and the thorns grew up, 7 with it, 7 and choked it, and it yielded no fruit. 8 Others fell into the good ground, and yielded fruit, growing up and increasing. 8 Some produced thirty times, some sixty times, and some one hundred times as much 8 fruit. (8 some one hundred times as much, some sixty, and some thirty.)" 8 As He said these things, He called out, "He who has ears to hear, let him hear!"

The Purpose of Parables

Mark 4:10–20; Matthew 13:10–23; Luke 8:8–15

10 When He was alone, those who were around Him with the twelve

10 disciples 10 asked Him about the parables.

8 Then His disciples asked Him, 10 "Why do You speak to them in parables? 8 What does this parable mean?"

11 He answered them, "To you it is given to know the mysteries of the Kingdom 11 [of] God 11 of Heaven, but 10 the rest, 11 but to those who are outside, 11 it is not given to them [and] 11 all things are done in parables, 12 For whoever has, to him will be given, and he will have abundance, but whoever doesn't have, from him will be taken away even that which he has. 13 Therefore I speak to them in parables, because 'seeing they don't see, and hearing, they don't hear, neither do they understand, 12 lest perhaps they should turn again, and their sins should be forgiven them.' 14 In them the prophecy of Isaiah is fulfilled, which says,

'By hearing you will hear, and will in no way understand; Seeing you will see, and will in no way perceive: 15 for this people's heart has grown callous, their ears are dull of hearing, they have closed their eyes; or else perhaps they might perceive with their eyes, hear with their ears, understand with their heart, and would turn again; and I would heal them.'[65]

16 "But blessed are your eyes, for they see; and your ears, for they hear. 17 For most certainly I tell you that many prophets and righteous men desired to see the things which you see, and didn't see them; and to hear the things which you hear, and didn't hear them.

Then His disciples asked Him, "What does this parable mean?"

He said to them, "Don't you understand this parable? How will you understand all of the parables? 18 Hear, then, the parable of the farmer. 11 Now the parable is this: 14 The farmer sows the word. 11 The seed is the word of God. 19 When anyone hears the word of the Kingdom, and doesn't understand it, the evil one, 12 the devil 15 immediately Satan comes, 19 and snatches away 15 the word 19 which has been sown in his heart, 12 that they may not believe and be

---

[65] **Isaiah 6:9–10** He said, "Go, and tell this people, 'You hear indeed, but don't understand; and you see indeed, but don't perceive.' 10 Make the heart of this people fat. Make their ears heavy, and shut their eyes; lest they see with their eyes, and hear with their ears, and understand with their heart, and turn again, and be healed."

saved. 15 The ones by the road are 12 those 15 where the word is sown 19 by the roadside.

16 "These in the same way are 20 what was sown on the rocky places, this is he who hears the word, and immediately with joy receives it; 21 yet he has no root in himself, 13 who believe for a while, 17 but are short-lived. 21 When oppression or persecution arises because of the word, immediately he stumbles, 13 then falls away in time of temptation.

18 "Others are 22 what was sown among the thorns, this is he 18 those 22 who hear the word, 14 and as they go on their way 22 the cares of this age and the deceitfulness of riches 14 and pleasures of life, 19 and the lusts of other things entering in 22 choke the word, and he becomes unfruitful. 14 They bring no fruit to maturity.

20 "Those which were sown on the good ground are those 23 who hear the word, and understand it, 20 accept it, 15 in an honest and good heart, having heard the word, hold it tightly, 23 who most certainly bears fruit, 15 with patience. 23 And produces, some one hundred times as much, some sixty, and some thirty. (20 some thirty times, some sixty times, and some one hundred times.)"

The Parable of the Lamp and the Bushel Basket

Mark 4:21–25; Luke 8:16–18

21 He said to them, "Is the lamp brought to be put under a basket or under a bed? Isn't it put on a stand? 16 No one, when he has lit a lamp, covers it with a container, or puts it under a bed; but puts it on a stand, that those who enter in may see the light. 17 For nothing is hidden, that will not be revealed; nor anything 22 covered up, 17 that will not be known 22 but that it should come to light. 23 If any man has ears to hear, let him hear."

24 He said to them, 18 "Be careful therefore, 24 take heed what you hear. With whatever measure you measure, it will be measured to you, and more will be given to you who hear. 25 For whoever has, to him will more be given, and he who doesn't have, even that which 18 he thinks he has 25 will be taken away from him."

The Parable of the Tares

Matthew 13:24–30

24 He set another parable before them, saying, “The Kingdom of
Heaven is like a man who sowed good seed in his field, 25 but while
people slept, his enemy came and sowed darnel weeds[66] also among
the wheat, and went away. 26 But when the blade sprang up and
produced fruit, then the darnel weeds appeared also. 27 The servants
of the householder came and said to him, ‘Sir, didn’t you sow good
seed in your field? Where did these darnel weeds come from?’

28 “He said to them, ‘An enemy has done this.’

“The servants asked him, ‘Do you want us to go and gather them up?’

29 “But he said, ‘No, lest perhaps while you gather up the darnel
weeds, you root up the wheat with them. 30 Let both grow together
until the harvest, and in the harvest time I will tell the reapers, “First,
gather up the darnel weeds, and bind them in bundles to burn them;
but gather the wheat into my barn.”’”[67]

The Parable of the Growing Seed

Mark 4:26–29

26 He said, “God’s kingdom is as if a man should cast seed on the
earth, 27 and should sleep and rise night and day, and the seed should
spring up and grow, he doesn’t know how. 28 For the earth bears fruit:
first the blade, then the ear, then the full grain in the ear. 29 But when
the fruit is ripe, immediately he puts in the sickle, because the harvest
has come.”

---

[66] Darnel is a weed grass (probably bearded darnel or *lolium temulentum*) that looks very much like wheat until it is mature when the difference becomes very apparent.

[67] **Joel 3:13** “Put in the sickle, for the harvest is ripe. Come, go down; For the winepress is full, The vats overflow—For their wickedness is great.” **Revelation 14:14–16** Then I looked, and behold, a white cloud, and on the cloud sat One like the Son of Man, having on His head a golden crown, and in His hand a sharp sickle. 15 And another angel came out of the temple, crying with a loud voice to Him who sat on the cloud, “Thrust in Your sickle and reap, for the time has come for You to reap, for the harvest of the earth is ripe.” 16 So He who sat on the cloud thrust in His sickle on the earth, and the earth was reaped.

The Parable of the Mustard Seed

Matthew 13:31–32; Mark 4:30–32

31 He set another parable before them, saying, 30 "How will we liken
God's kingdom? Or with what parable will we illustrate it? 31 The
Kingdom of Heaven is like a grain of mustard seed, which a man took,
and sowed in his field; 32 which indeed is smaller than all seeds [and]
31 though it is less than all the seeds that are on the earth yet when it
is sown, grows up, 32 [and] when it is grown, 32 becomes greater than
all the herbs, 32 [and] becomes a tree, 32 and puts out great branches,
32 so that the birds of the air come and lodge in its branches 32 under
its shadow."[68]

The Kingdom of God Compared to Leaven

Matthew 13:33–35; Mark 4:32–34

33 He spoke another parable to them. "The Kingdom of Heaven is like
yeast, which a woman took, and hid in three measures of meal,[69] until
it was all leavened."

With many such parables He spoke the word to them, as they were
able to hear it. 36 Then Jesus sent the multitudes away, and went into
the house.

34 Jesus spoke all these things in parables to the multitudes; and
without a parable, He didn't speak to them, 35 that it might fulfilled

[68] **Daniel 4:10–12** Thus were the visions of my head on my bed: I saw, and behold, a tree in the middle of the earth; and its height was great. 11 The tree grew, and was strong, and its height reached to the sky, and its sight to the end of all the earth. 12 The leaves of it were beautiful, and its fruit much, and in it was food for all: the animals of the field had shadow under it, and the birds of the sky lived in its branches, and all flesh was fed from it. **Ezekiel 17:22–23** Thus says the Lord Yahweh: I will also take of the lofty top of the cedar, and will set it; I will crop off from the topmost of its young twigs a tender one, and I will plant it on a high and lofty mountain: 23 in the mountain of the height of Israel will I plant it; and it shall produce boughs, and bear fruit, and be a goodly cedar: and under it shall dwell all birds of every wing; in the shade of its branches shall they dwell.

[69] **Genesis 18:6** Abraham hurried into the tent to Sarah, and said, "Quickly prepare three seahs of fine meal, knead it, and make cakes." (se'ah = 1/3 ephah, = 12.148 litres = 10.696 qts.) - Brown-Driver-Briggs

which was spoken through the prophet, saying,

> "I will open my mouth in parables; I will utter things hidden from the foundation of the world."[70]

34 But privately to His own disciples He explained everything.

The Parable of the Tares Explained

Matthew 13:36–43

36 His disciples came to Him, saying, "Explain to us the parable of the darnel weeds of the field."

37 He answered them, "He who sows the good seed is the Son of Man, 38 the field is the world; and the good seed, these are the children of the Kingdom; and the darnel weeds are the children of the evil one. 39 The enemy who sowed them is the devil. The harvest is the end of the age, and the reapers are angels. 40 As therefore the darnel weeds are gathered up and burned with fire; so will it be at the end of this age. 41 The Son of Man will send out His angels, and they will gather out of His Kingdom all things that cause stumbling, and those who do iniquity, 42 and will cast them into the furnace of fire. There will be weeping and the gnashing of teeth.[71] 43 Then the righteous will shine like the sun in the Kingdom of their Father. He who has ears to hear, let him hear.

The Kingdom of God Is Like Hidden Treasure

Matthew 13:44

44 "Again, the Kingdom of Heaven is like a treasure hidden in the field, which a man found, and hid. In his joy, he goes and sells all that he has, and buys that field.

---

[70] **Psalm 78:2** I will open my mouth in a parable. I will utter dark sayings of old.

[71] **Revelation 14:17–18** Another angel came out of the temple which is in heaven. He also had a sharp sickle. 18 Another angel came out from the altar, he who has power over fire, and he called with a great voice to him who had the sharp sickle, saying, "Send your sharp sickle, and gather the clusters of the vine of the earth, for the earth's grapes are fully ripe!"

The Kingdom of God Is Like the Pearl of Great Price

Matthew 13:45–46

45 "Again, the Kingdom of Heaven is like a man who is a merchant seeking fine pearls, 46 who having found one pearl of great price, he went and sold all that he had, and bought it.

The Kingdom Is Like a Dragnet

Matthew 13:47–53; Luke 8:22; Mark 4:35

47 "Again, the Kingdom of Heaven is like a dragnet, that was cast into the sea, and gathered some fish of every kind, 48 which, when it was filled, they drew up on the beach. They sat down, and gathered the good into containers, but the bad they threw away. 49 So will it be in the end of the world. The angels will come and separate the wicked from among the righteous, 50 and will cast them into the furnace of fire. There will be the weeping and the gnashing of teeth."

51 Jesus said to them, "Have you understood all these things?"

They answered him, "Yes, Lord."

52 He said to them, "Therefore every scribe who has been made a disciple in the Kingdom of Heaven is like a man who is a householder, who brings out of his treasure new and old things."

53 When Jesus had finished these parables, he departed from there.

22 Now on one of those days, 35 on that day, when evening had come, 22 He entered into a boat, Himself and His disciples, and He said to them, "Let's go over to the other side of the lake." So they launched out.

Jesus Calms a Storm

Mark 4:36–41; Luke 8:23–25; Matthew 8:23–27

36 Leaving the multitude, they took Him with them, even 23 as He was, in the boat. Other small boats were also with Him. 23 When He got into a boat, His disciples followed Him. 23 But as they sailed, He fell asleep. 37 A big 23 violent 23 wind storm came down on the lake, 37 and the waves beat into the boat, 23 so much that the boat was

covered with the waves, 23 and they were 37 already filled, 23 taking on dangerous amounts of water. 38 He Himself was in the stern, asleep on the cushion, and 24 they came to Him, and awoke Him, saying, 25 "Save us, Lord! 24 Master, Master, we are dying!" 38 and told Him, "Teacher, don't you care that we are dying?"

24 He awoke, and 26 He said to them, "Why are you fearful, O you of little faith?" Then He got up, 24 rebuked the wind and the raging of the water, 39 and said to the sea, "Peace! Be still!" The wind ceased, and 24 they [the waves] ceased, and 39 there was a great calm. 25 He said to them, 40 "Why are you so afraid? How is it that you have no faith? 25 Where is your faith?"

25 Being 41 greatly 25 afraid 27 the men 25 marveled, saying to one another, "Who is this, then, that He commands even the winds and the water, and they obey Him?"

Jesus Casts Out a Legion of Demons

Mark 5:1–20; Matthew 8:28–34; Luke 8:26–39

1 They came to the other side of the sea, into the country of the Gadarenes. 28 Gergesenes, 26 which is opposite Galilee.

2 When 27 Jesus 2 had come out of the boat, [and] 27 stepped ashore, 2 immediately 27 certain 28 two people 27 who had 28 possessed by 2 an unclean spirit 27 demons for a long time 28 met Him there, coming out of the tombs, exceedingly fierce, so that nobody could pass that way.

[They] wore no clothes, and didn't live in a house, but 3 lived in the tombs. 29 For the unclean spirit had often seized the man. He was kept under guard, and bound with chains and fetters. 3 Nobody could bind him any more, not even with chains, 4 because he had been often bound with fetters and chains, and the chains had been torn apart by him, and the fetters broken in pieces. Nobody had the strength to tame him. 29 He was driven by the demon into the desert. 5 Always, night and day, in the tombs and in the mountains, he was crying out, and cutting himself with stones. 6 When he saw Jesus from afar, he ran, 28 cried out, and fell down before Him, 6 and bowed down to Him.

7 And 29 behold, they cried out, 7 with a loud voice said, 29 saying,

"What do we have 7 to do with You, Jesus, You Son of the Most High God? 29 Have You come here to torment us before the time? 7 I beg You, don't torment me!"

29 For Jesus was commanding the unclean spirit to come out of the man 8 [and] said to him, "Come out of the man, you unclean spirit!" 9 He asked him, "What is your name?"

9 He said to Him, "My name is Legion, for we are many." 10 He begged Him much that He would not send them away out of the country, 31 into the abyss. 11 Now on the mountainside there was a great herd of pigs feeding 30 far away from them. 12 All the demons begged Him, saying, 31 "If you cast us out, permit us to go away into the herd of pigs, 12 that we may enter into them."

13 At once Jesus gave them permission. 32 He said to them, "Go!"

13 The unclean spirits came out 33 of the man, 13 and entered into the pigs. 32 Behold, the whole 13 herd of about two thousand, rushed down the steep bank [or] 32 cliff into the sea, [of Galilee or], 33 lake [Gennesaret], 13 and they were drowned in the sea.

14 Now 34 when those who fed them saw what had happened, they fled, 33 and went away into the city, and told everything, including what happened to those who were possessed with demons, 14 in the city and in the country. 34 Behold, all the city came out to meet Jesus. [and] 14 to see what it was that had happened.

15 They came to Jesus, and saw him who had been possessed by demons sitting, clothed, 35 sitting at Jesus's feet, clothed 15 and in his right mind, even him who had the legion; and they were afraid. 36 Those who saw it told them how he who had been possessed by demons was healed 16 and about the pigs. 34 When they saw him, 37 all the people of the surrounding country of the Gadarenes asked, 17 [then] began to beg Him to depart from their region [and] 37 from them, for they were very much afraid. He entered into the boat, and returned.

18 As He was entering into the boat, he who had been possessed by demons, 38 from whom the demons had gone out 18 begged Him that he might be with Him.

19 He didn't allow him, but 38 Jesus sent him away, saying, 19 to

him, "Go, 38 return 19 to your house, to your friends, 19 and tell them what great things the Lord has done for you, and how He had mercy on you."

37 He went his way, 20 and departed, 39 proclaiming throughout the whole city what great things Jesus had done for him 20 and began to proclaim in Decapolis how Jesus had done great things for him, and everyone marveled.

Jesus Returns to the Crowds Across the Lake

Mark 5:21; Luke 8:40

21 When Jesus had crossed back over in the boat to the other side, a great multitude was gathered to Him; [and] 40 the multitude welcomed Him, for they were all waiting for Him. 21 And He was by the sea.

Jesus Heals Two Blind Men

Matthew 9:27–31

27 As Jesus passed by from there, two blind men followed Him, calling out and saying, "Have mercy on us, son of David!"

28 When He had come into the house, the blind men came to Him. Jesus said to them, "Do you believe that I am able to do this?"

They told Him, "Yes, Lord."

29 Then He touched their eyes, saying, "According to your faith be it done to you." 30 Their eyes were opened. Jesus strictly commanded them, saying, "See that no one knows about this." 31 But they went out and spread abroad His fame in all that land.

Jesus Heals a Mute Man

Matthew 9:32–34; Luke 11:14–28

32 As they went out, behold, a mute man who was demon possessed was brought to Him. 14 He was casting out a demon, and it was mute. 33 When the demon was cast out, the mute man spoke. The multitudes marveled, saying, "Nothing like this has ever been seen in Israel!"

34 But 15 some of 34 the Pharisees said, 15 "He casts out demons by Beelzebul, the prince of the demons." 16 Others, testing Him, sought from Him a sign from heaven.

17 But He, knowing their thoughts, said to them, "Every kingdom divided against itself is brought to desolation. A house divided against itself falls. 18 If Satan also is divided against himself, how will his kingdom stand? For you say that I cast out demons by Beelzebul. 19 But if I cast out demons by Beelzebul, by whom do your children cast them out? Therefore will they be your judges. 20 But if I by God's finger[72] cast out demons, then God's kingdom has come to you.

21 "When the strong man, fully armed, guards his own dwelling, his goods are safe. 22 But when someone stronger attacks him and overcomes him, he takes from him his whole armor in which he trusted, and divides his plunder. 23 "He that is not with me is against me. He who doesn't gather with me scatters.

24 "The unclean spirit, when he has gone out of the man, passes through dry places, seeking rest, and finding none, he says, 'I will turn back to my house from which I came out.' 25 When he returns, he finds it swept and put in order. 26 Then he goes, and takes seven other spirits more evil than himself, and they enter in and dwell there. The last state of that man becomes worse than the first."

27 It came to pass, as He said these things, a certain woman out of the multitude lifted up her voice, and said to Him, "Blessed is the womb that bore You, and the breasts which nursed You!"

28 But He said, "On the contrary, blessed are those who hear the word of God, and keep it."

Jesus Celebrates the Fall Holy Days in Jerusalem

John 5:1–47

1 After these things, there was a feast of the Jews, and Jesus went up to Jerusalem. 2 Now in Jerusalem by the sheep gate, there is a pool, which is called in Hebrew, "Bethesda," having five porches. 3 In these lay a great multitude of those who were sick, blind, lame, or paralyzed,

---

[72] **Exodus 8:19** Then the magicians said to Pharaoh, "This is God's finger:" and Pharaoh's heart was hardened, and he didn't listen to them; as Yahweh had spoken.

waiting for the moving of the water; 4 for an angel went down at certain times into the pool, and stirred up the water. Whoever stepped in first after the stirring of the water was healed of whatever disease he had.

Jesus Heals a Paralytic at the Pool of Bethseda

5 A certain man was there, who had been sick for thirty-eight years. 6
When Jesus saw him lying there, and knew that he had been sick for a long time, he asked him, "Do you want to be made well?"

7 The sick man answered him, "Sir, I have no one to put me into the pool when the water is stirred up, but while I'm coming, another steps down before me."

8 Jesus said to him, "Arise, take up your mat, and walk."

9 Immediately, the man was made well, and took up his mat and walked.

10 Now it was the Sabbath on that day. 10 So the Jews said to him who was cured, "It is the Sabbath. It is not lawful for you to carry the mat."

11 He answered them, "He who made me well, the same said to me, 'Take up your mat, and walk.'"

12 Then they asked him, "Who is the man who said to you, 'Take up your mat, and walk'?"

13 But he who was healed didn't know Who it was, for Jesus had withdrawn, a crowd being in the place.

14 Afterward Jesus found him in the temple, and said to him, "Behold, you are made well. Sin no more, so that nothing worse happens to you."

15 The man went away, and told the Jews that it was Jesus who had made him well.

Jews Plot Jesus's Death During the Feast

16 For this cause the Jews persecuted Jesus, and sought to kill Him, because He did these things on the Sabbath.

17 But Jesus answered them, “My Father is still working, so I am working, too.”

18 For this cause therefore the Jews sought all the more to kill Him, because He not only broke the Sabbath, but also called God His own Father, making Himself equal with God.

19 Jesus therefore answered them, “Most certainly, I tell you, the Son can do nothing of Himself, but what He sees the Father doing. For whatever things He does, these the Son also does likewise. 20 For the Father has affection for the Son, and shows Him all things that He Himself does. He will show Him greater works than these, that you may marvel. 21 For as the Father raises the dead and gives them life, even so the Son also gives life to whom He desires. 22 For the Father judges no one, but He has given all judgment to the Son, 23 that all may honor the Son, even as they honor the Father. He who doesn’t honor the Son doesn’t honor the Father who sent Him.

Life and Judgment Through the Son

24 “Most certainly I tell you, he who hears My word, and believes Him who sent Me, has eternal life, and doesn’t come into judgment, but has passed out of death into life. 25 Most certainly, I tell you, the hour comes, and now is, when the dead will hear the Son of God’s voice; and those who hear will live. 26 For as the Father has life in Himself, even so He gave to the Son also to have life in Himself. 27 He also gave Him authority to execute judgment, because He is a son of man. 28 Don’t marvel at this, for the hour comes, in which all that are in the tombs will hear His voice, 29 and will come out; those who have done good, to the resurrection of life; and those who have done evil, to the resurrection of judgment. 30 I can of Myself do nothing. As I hear, I judge, and My judgment is righteous; because I don’t seek My own will, but the will of My Father Who sent Me.

Testimonies About Jesus

31 “If I testify about Myself, My witness is not valid. 32 It is another who testifies about Me. I know that the testimony which He testifies about Me is true. 33 You have sent to John, and he has testified to the truth. 34 But the testimony which I receive is not from man. However,

I say these things that you may be saved. 35 He was the burning and shining lamp, and you were willing to rejoice for a while in his light.

36 "But the testimony which I have is greater than that of John, for the works which the Father gave Me to accomplish, the very works that I do, testify about Me, that the Father has sent Me. 37 The Father Himself, Who sent Me, has testified about Me. You have neither heard His voice at any time, nor seen His form. 38 You don't have His word living in you; because you don't believe Him whom He sent.

39 "You search the Scriptures, because you think that in them you have eternal life; and these are they which testify about Me. 40 Yet you will not come to Me, that you may have life. 41 I don't receive glory from men. 42 But I know you, that you don't have God's love in yourselves. 43 I have come in My Father's Name, and you don't receive Me. If another comes in his own name, you will receive him. 44 How can you believe, who receive glory from one another, and you don't seek the glory that comes from the only God?

45 "Don't think that I will accuse you to the Father. There is one who accuses you, even Moses, on whom you have set your hope. 46 For if you believed Moses, you would believe Me; for he wrote about Me. 47 But if you don't believe his writings, how will you believe My words?"

Jesus Sends Out the Twelve Apostles

Matthew 10:1–15; Luke 9:1–16; Mark 6:7–13

1 He called to Himself His twelve disciples, 1 together, 1 and gave them, 1 power and authority over all demons, 1 [and] unclean spirits, to cast them out, and to heal every disease and every sickness. 2 He sent them out 7 out two by two 2 to preach God's kingdom and to heal the sick.

2 Now the names of the twelve apostles are these. The first, Simon, who is called Peter; Andrew, his brother; James the son of Zebedee; John, his brother; 3 Philip; Bartholomew; Thomas; Matthew the tax collector; James the son of Alphaeus; Lebbaeus, who was also called Thaddaeus; 4 Simon the Canaanite; and Judas Iscariot, who also betrayed him.

5 Jesus sent these twelve out, and commanded them, saying, “Don’t go among the Gentiles, and don’t enter into any city of the Samaritans. 6 Rather, go to the lost sheep of the house of Israel.

7 “As you go, preach, saying, ‘The Kingdom of Heaven is at hand!’ 8 Heal the sick, cleanse the lepers, and cast out demons. Freely you received, so freely give.

8 He commanded them that they should take nothing for their journey, except a staff only: 3 He said to them, “Take nothing for your journey—neither staffs, nor money; 9 Don’t take any gold, silver, or brass in your money belts, 3 nor wallet, nor bread. 10 Take no bag for your journey, neither two coats 3 apiece, 10 nor shoes, nor staff: 9 But wear sandals, and [do] not put on two tunics, 10 for the laborer is worthy of his food.

11 “Into whatever city or village you enter, find out who in it is worthy; 10 Wherever you enter into a house 4 whatever house you enter, 11 stay there until you go on 4 and 10 depart from there.12 As you enter into the household, greet it. 13 If the household is worthy, let your peace come on it, but if it isn’t worthy, let your peace return to you.

14 “Whoever doesn’t receive you, nor hear your words, as you go out of that house or that city, shake off 5 even the14 dust from 11 under 14 your feet 11 for a testimony against them. 15 Most certainly I tell you, it will be more tolerable for the land of Sodom and Gomorrah in the day of judgment than for that city.

Persecutions Are Coming

Matthew 10:16–42; 11:1; Mark 6:12–13; Luke 9:6

16 “Behold, I send you out as sheep among wolves. Therefore be wise as serpents, and harmless as doves. 17 But beware of men: for they will deliver you up to councils, and in their synagogues they will scourge you. 18 Yes, and you will be brought before governors and kings for my sake, for a testimony to them and to the nations. 19 But when they deliver you up, don’t be anxious how or what you will say, for it will be given you in that hour what you will say. 20 For it is not you who speak, but the Spirit of your Father who speaks in you.

21 "Brother will deliver up brother to death, and the father his child. Children will rise up against parents, and cause them to be put to death. 22 You will be hated by all men for my name's sake, but he who endures to the end will be saved. 23 But when they persecute you in this city, flee into the next, for most certainly I tell you, you will not have gone through the cities of Israel, until the Son of Man has come.

24 "A disciple is not above his teacher, nor a servant above his lord. 25 It is enough for the disciple that he be like his teacher, and the servant like his lord. If they have called the master of the house Beelzebul, how much more those of his household! 26 Therefore don't be afraid of them, for there is nothing covered that will not be revealed; and hidden that will not be known.

27 "What I tell you in the darkness, speak in the light; and what you hear whispered in the ear, proclaim on the housetops. 28 Don't be afraid of those who kill the body, but are not able to kill the soul. Rather, fear him who is able to destroy both soul and body in Gehenna."

29 "Aren't two sparrows sold for an assarion coin? Not one of them falls on the ground apart from your Father's will, 30 but the very hairs of your head are all numbered. 31 Therefore don't be afraid. You are of more value than many sparrows.

32 "Everyone therefore who confesses me before men, him I will also confess before My Father Who is in heaven. 33 But whoever denies me before men, him I will also deny before My Father Who is in heaven.

34 "Don't think that I came to send peace on the earth. I didn't come to send peace, but a sword. 35 For I came to

> 'set a man at odds against his father, and a daughter against her mother, and a daughter-in-law against her mother-in-law 36 A man's foes will be those of his own household.'[73]

36 "He who loves father or mother more than Me is not worthy of Me;

[73] **Micah 7:6** For the son dishonors the father, the daughter rises up against her mother, the daughter-in-law against her mother-in-law; a man's enemies are the men of his own house.

and he who loves son or daughter more than Me isn't worthy of Me. 38 He who doesn't take his cross and follow after Me, isn't worthy of Me. 39 He who seeks his life will lose it; and he who loses his life for My sake will find it.

40 "He who receives you receives Me, and he who receives Me receives Him who sent Me. 41 He who receives a prophet in the name of a prophet will receive a prophet's reward. He who receives a righteous man in the name of a righteous man will receive a righteous man's reward. 42 Whoever gives one of these little ones just a cup of cold water to drink in the name of a disciple, most certainly I tell you he will in no way lose his reward."

1 When Jesus had finished directing His twelve disciples, He departed from there to teach and preach in their cities.

12 They went out [and] 6 departed, and went throughout the villages, preaching the good news, 12 and preached that people should repent. 13 They cast out many demons, and anointed many with oil who were sick, and healed them 6 everywhere.

Herod Hears of Jesus's Works

Luke 9:7–9; Matthew 14:1–12; Mark 6:14–29

7 Now 1 at that time, 14 King Herod 1 the tetrarch heard the report concerning Jesus, 7 all that was done by Him; 14 for His Name had become known, 7 and he was very perplexed, because it was said by some that John had risen from the dead, 8 and by some that Elijah had appeared, and by others that one of the old prophets had risen again. 9 Herod said, "John I beheaded, but who is this, about Whom I hear such things?" 14 and he said, 2 to his servants, 14 "John the Baptizer has risen from the dead, and therefore these powers are at work in him."

15 But others said, "He is Elijah."

Others said, "He is a prophet, or like one of the prophets."

16 But Herod, when he heard this, said, "This is John, whom I beheaded. He has risen from the dead."

9 He sought to see him. For Herod himself had sent out and arrested

John, and bound him in prison for the sake of Herodias, his brother Philip's wife, for he had married her. 18 For John said to Herod, "It is not lawful for you to have your brother's wife."[74] 19 Herodias set herself against him, and desired to kill him, but she couldn't, 20 for Herod feared John, knowing that he was a righteous and holy man, and kept him safe. 5 When he [Herod] would have put him to death, [too], he feared the multitude, because they counted him as a prophet. 20 When he heard him, he did many things, and he heard him gladly.

21 Then a convenient day came, that Herod 6 celebrated 21 on his birthday [and] made a supper for his nobles, the high officers, and the chief men of Galilee. 22 When the daughter of Herodias herself came in and danced, 6 among them and 22 she pleased Herod and those sitting with him. 7 Whereupon 22 the king said to the young lady, "Ask me whatever you want, and I will give it to you." 23 He swore to her, 7 with an oath 23 "Whatever you shall ask of me, I will give you, up to half of my kingdom."

24 She went out, and said to her mother, "What shall I ask?"

She said, "The head of John the Baptizer."

25 She came in immediately with haste to the king, and asked, 8 being prompted by her mother, 25 "I want you to give me right now the head of John the Baptizer on a platter."

26 The king was exceedingly sorry, but for the sake of his oaths, and of his dinner guests, 9 at the table with him, he didn't wish to refuse her. 27 Immediately the king sent out a soldier of his guard, and commanded to bring John's head [and] 9 it to be given. 26 He went 9 and beheaded John in the prison 28 and brought his head on a platter, and gave it to the young lady; and the young lady gave it to her mother.

28 When his disciples heard this, they came and took up his corpse 12 and buried it 29 in a tomb, 12 and they went and told Jesus. 1 After these things, 13 when Jesus heard this, He withdrew from there in a boat, to a deserted place apart [with His disciples.]

---

[74] **Leviticus 18:16** "'You shall not uncover the nakedness of your brother's wife. It is your brother's nakedness." **Leviticus 20:21** "'If a man takes his brother's wife, it is an impurity. He has uncovered his brother's nakedness. They shall be childless."

The Apostles Return from their Mission

Luke 9:10–11; Mark 6:30–32

10 When they had returned, 30 the apostles gathered themselves together to Jesus, and they told Him all things, whatever they had done, and whatever they had taught

10 He took them, and withdrew apart [and] 31 He said to them, "You come apart into a deserted place, and rest awhile." For there were many coming and going and they had no leisure so much as to eat.

John 6:1

1 Jesus [and] 32 they went away in the boat 1 to the other side of the sea of Galilee, which is also called the Sea of Tiberias. 32 to a deserted place 10 of a city called Bethsaida 32 by themselves.

The Third Passover of Jesus's Ministry

The Feeding of the Five Thousand

Matthew 14:13–21; Mark 6:33–44; John 6:2–14; Luke 9:12–17

13 When the multitudes heard it, they followed Him on foot from the cities. 33 They saw them going, and many recognized Him and ran there on foot from all the cities.

They arrived before them and came together to Him. 2 A great multitude followed Him, because they saw His signs which He did on those who were sick. 3 Jesus went up into the mountain, and He sat there with his disciples. Now the Passover, the feast of the Jews, was at hand.[75]

34 Jesus came out, saw a great multitude, and He had compassion on them, because they were like sheep without a shepherd, 11 He welcomed them, 34 and He began to teach them many things 11 and spoke to them of God's kingdom, and He cured 14 their sick, 11 those who needed healing.

35 When it was late in the day, 1 when evening had come, [and] 12 the day began to wear away 35 His 12 twelve 35 disciples came to Him, and said, "This place is deserted, and it is late in the day. 36 Send 15 the multitudes 36 away, that they may go into the surrounding country and villages, 12 and farms, and lodge, and get food, 36 and buy themselves bread, for they have nothing to eat, 12 for we are here in a deserted place."

5 Jesus therefore lifting up His eyes, and seeing that a great multitude was coming to Him, 16 but Jesus said to them, 37 [and] answered them, 16 "They don't need to go away. You give them something to eat." 5 Jesus said to Philip, "Where are we to buy bread, that these may eat?" 6 This He said to test him, for He Himself knew what He would do.

---

[75] **Leviticus 23:5** In the first month, on the fourteenth day of the month in the evening, is Yahweh's Passover.

37 They asked Him, "Shall we go and buy two hundred denarii worth of bread, and give them something to eat?"

7 Philip answered Him, "Two hundred denarii worth of bread is not sufficient for them, that everyone of them may receive a little."

38 He said to them, "How many loaves do you have? Go see."

When they knew, they said, "Five, and two fish."

8 One of His disciples, Andrew, Simon Peter's brother, said to Him, 9 "There is a boy here who has five barley loaves and two fish, but what are these among so many? 13 Unless we should go and buy food for all these people." 14 For they were about five thousand men.

18 He said, "Bring them here to me." 14 He said to His disciples, "Make them sit down in groups of about fifty each." 15 They did so, and made them all sit down, 39 in groups on the green grass. 10 Now there was much grass in that place. 40 They sat down in ranks, by hundreds and by fifties. 10 So the men sat down, in number about five thousand.

19 And He took the five loaves and the two fish, and looking up to heaven, He blessed, broke 41 the loaves, 19 and gave the loaves to the disciples 41 to set before them, 16 the multitude. 41 And He divided the two fish among them all, 11 He distributed to the disciples, 11 and the disciples 19 gave to the multitudes, 11 to those who were sitting down; likewise also of the fish as much as they desired.

20 They all ate, and were filled. 12 When they were filled, He said to His disciples, "Gather up the broken pieces which are left over, that nothing be lost."

13 So they gathered them up, and filled twelve baskets with broken pieces from the five barley loaves, 20 twelve baskets full, 13 which were left over by those who had eaten 43 and also of the fish 20 of that which remained left over. 21 Those who ate were about five thousand men, besides women and children.

14 When therefore the people saw the sign which Jesus did, they said, "This is truly the prophet who comes into the world."

Jesus Prays Alone on a Mountain

John 6:15–18; Mark 6:45–46; Matthew 14:22–23

15 Jesus therefore, perceiving that they were about to come and take Him by force, to make Him king, 45 immediately He made His disciples get into the boat, and to go ahead to the other side, to Bethsaida, while He Himself sent the multitude away. 46 After He had taken leave of them, 22 [and] had sent the multitudes away, 15 22 He 15 withdrew again to the mountain by Himself 46 to pray. 23 When evening had come, He was there alone 47 on the land.

6 When evening came, His disciples went down to the sea, 17 and they entered into the boat, and were going over the sea to Capernaum. It was now dark, and Jesus had not come to them. 18 The sea was tossed by a great wind blowing.

Jesus Walks on Water

Mark 6:47–52; Matthew 14:24–33; John 6:19–21

47 When evening had come, the boat was in the middle of the sea, and He was alone on the land. 24 But the boat was now in the middle of the sea, distressed by the waves, for the wind was contrary. 48 Seeing them distressed in rowing, for the wind was contrary to them, 19 when therefore they had rowed about twenty-five or thirty stadia [five to six kilometers or three to four miles], 48 [and it was] about the fourth watch of the night [3:00 a.m.] 19 Jesus 48 came to them, walking on the sea,[76] 19 and drawing near to the boat; 48 and He would have passed by them, 49 but they, when they saw Him walking on the sea, supposed that it was a ghost, and cried out; 26 saying, "It's a ghost!" 50 for they all saw Him, and were troubled. 26 And they cried out for fear.

27 But immediately Jesus spoke to them, saying "Cheer up! I AM! Don't be afraid."

28 Peter answered Him and said, "Lord, if it is You, command me to come to You on the waters."

---

[76] **Job 9:8** He alone stretches out the heavens, and treads on the waves of the sea.

29 He said, "Come!"

Peter stepped down from the boat, and walked on the waters to come to Jesus. 30 But when he saw that the wind was strong, he was afraid, and beginning to sink, he cried out, saying, "Lord, save me!"

31 Immediately Jesus stretched out His hand, took hold of him, and said to him, "You of little faith, why did you doubt?"

21 They were willing therefore to receive Him into the boat. 51 He got into the boat with them; and 32 when they got up into the boat, the wind ceased. 33 Those who were in the boat came and worshiped Him, saying, "You are truly the Son of God!"

51 And they were very amazed among themselves, and marveled; 52 for they hadn't understood about the loaves, but their hearts were hardened. 21 Immediately the boat was at the land where they were going.

Jesus Preaches About the Bread from Heaven

John 6:22–40

22 On the next day, the multitude that stood on the other side of the sea saw that there was no other boat there, except the one in which His disciples had embarked, and that Jesus hadn't entered with His disciples into the boat, but His disciples had gone away alone. 23 However boats from Tiberias came near to the place where they ate the bread after the Lord had given thanks. 24 When the multitude therefore saw that Jesus wasn't there, nor His disciples, they themselves got into the boats, and came to Capernaum, seeking Jesus.

25 When they found Him on the other side of the sea, they asked Him, "Rabbi, when did You come here?"

26 Jesus answered them, "Most certainly I tell you, you seek Me, not because you saw signs, but because you ate of the loaves, and were filled. 27 Don't work for the food which perishes, but for the food which remains to eternal life, which the Son of Man will give to you. For God the Father has sealed Him."

28 They said therefore to Him, "What must we do, that we may work the works of God?"

29 Jesus answered them, "This is the work of God, that you believe in
Him Whom He has sent."

30 They said therefore to Him, "What then do You do for a sign, that
we may see, and believe You? What work do You do? 31 Our fathers
ate the manna in the wilderness. As it is written, 'He gave them bread
out of heaven to eat.'"[77]

32 Jesus therefore said to them, "Most certainly, I tell you, it wasn't
Moses who gave you the bread out of heaven, but My Father gives
you the true bread out of heaven. 33 For the bread of God is that which
comes down out of heaven, and gives life to the world."

34 They said therefore to Him, "Lord, always give us this bread."

35 Jesus said to them, "I am the bread of life. He who comes to Me
will not be hungry, and he who believes in Me will never be thirsty.
36 But I told you that you have seen Me, and yet you don't believe.
37 All those whom the Father gives me will come to Me. He who
comes to Me I will in no way throw out. 38 For I have come down
from heaven, not to do My own will, but the will of Him who sent Me.
39 This is the will of My Father who sent Me, that of all He has given
to Me I should lose nothing, but should raise him up at the last day.
40 This is the will of the One who sent Me, that everyone who sees
the Son, and believes in Him, should have eternal life; and I will raise
him up at the last day."

Jesus Rejected by His Own

John 6:41–59

41 The Jews therefore murmured concerning Him, because He said,
"I am the bread which came down out of heaven."

42 They said, "Isn't this Jesus, the son of Joseph, whose father and

---

[77] **Exodus 16:4** Then Yahweh said to Moses, "Behold, I will rain bread from the sky for you, and the people shall go out and gather a day's portion every day, that I may test them, whether they will walk in my law, or not." **Nehemiah 9:15** And gave them bread from the sky for their hunger, and brought water out of the rock for them for their thirst, and commanded them that they should go in to possess the land which you had sworn to give them. **Psalm 78:24–25** He rained down manna on them to eat, and gave them food from the sky. 25 Man ate the bread of angels. He sent them food to the full.

mother we know? How then does He say, 'I have come down out of heaven?'"

43 Therefore Jesus answered them, "Don't murmur among yourselves. 44 No one can come to Me unless the Father who sent Me draws him, and I will raise him up in the last day. 45 It is written in the prophets, 'They will all be taught by God.'[78] Therefore everyone who hears from the Father, and has learned, comes to Me. 46 Not that anyone has seen the Father, except He Who is from God. He has seen the Father.

47 "Most certainly, I tell you, he who believes in Me has eternal life. 48 I am the bread of life. 49 Your fathers ate the manna in the wilderness, and they died. 50 This is the bread which comes down out of heaven, that anyone may eat of it and not die. 51 I am the living bread which came down out of heaven. If anyone eats of this bread, he will live forever. Yes, the bread which I will give for the life of the world is My flesh."

52 The Jews therefore contended with one another, saying, "How can this man give us His flesh to eat?"

53 Jesus therefore said to them, "Most certainly I tell you, unless you eat the flesh of the Son of Man and drink His blood, you don't have life in yourselves. 54 He who eats My flesh and drinks My blood has eternal life, and I will raise Him up at the last day. 55 For My flesh is food indeed, and My blood is drink indeed. 56 He who eats My flesh and drinks My blood lives in Me, and I in him. 57 As the living Father sent me, and I live because of the Father; so he who feeds on Me, he will also live because of Me. 58 This is the bread which came down out of heaven—not as our fathers ate the manna, and died. He who eats this bread will live forever."

59 He said these things in the synagogue, as He taught in Capernaum.

Many of Jesus's Disciples Turn Away

John 6:60–71

60 Therefore many of His disciples, when they heard this, said, "This

[78] **Isaiah 54:13** All your children will be taught by Yahweh; and your children's peace will be great.

is a hard saying! Who can listen to it?"

61 But Jesus knowing in Himself that His disciples murmured at this, said to them, "Does this cause you to stumble? 62 Then what if you would see the Son of Man ascending to where He was before? 63 It is the Spirit Who gives life. The flesh profits nothing. The words that I speak to you are spirit, and are life. 64 But there are some of you who don't believe."

For Jesus knew from the beginning who they were who didn't believe, and who it was who would betray Him.

66 At this, many of his disciples went back, and walked no more with Him. 67 Jesus said therefore to the twelve, "You don't also want to go away, do you?"

68 Simon Peter answered Him, "Lord, to whom would we go? You have the words of eternal life. 69 We have come to believe and know that You are the Christ, the Son of the living God."

70 Jesus answered them, "Didn't I choose you, the twelve, and one of you is a devil?" 71 Now he spoke of Judas, the son of Simon Iscariot, for it was he who would betray him, being one of the twelve.

Jesus Goes Through Galilee, Avoiding the Jews

John 7:1

1 After these things, Jesus was walking in Galilee, for He wouldn't walk in Judea, because the Jews sought to kill Him.

Jesus Heals People From Gennesaret

Mark 6:53–56; Matthew 14:34–36

53 When they had crossed over, they came to land at Gennesaret, and moored to the shore. 54 When they had come out of the boat, immediately the people recognized Him. 35 When the people of that place recognized Him, they sent into all that surrounding region, 55 and ran around that whole region, and began to bring those who were sick, on their mats, to where they heard He was. 56 Wherever He entered, into villages, or into cities, or into the country, they laid the sick in the marketplaces, and begged Him that they might touch just

the fringe of His garment; and as many as touched Him 36 as many as touched it were made whole.

The Pharisees Complain About Washing of Hands

Mark 7:1–5; Matthew 15:1–2

1 Then the Pharisees and some of the scribes gathered 1 together to 1 Jesus, 1 having come from Jerusalem. 2 Now when they saw some of His disciples eating bread with defiled, that is unwashed, hands, they found fault. 3 (For the Pharisees and all the Jews, don't eat unless they wash their hands and forearms, holding to the tradition of the elders. 4 They don't eat when they come from the marketplace unless they bathe themselves, and there are many other things, which they have received to hold to: washings of cups, pitchers, bronze vessels, and couches.)

5 The Pharisees and the scribes asked Him, "Why don't Your disciples walk according to the tradition of the elders, 2 [but] disobey the tradition of the elders? For they don't wash their hands when they eat bread 5 but eat their bread with unwashed hands?"

Jesus Reproves Pharisees for Their Hypocrisy

Mark 7:6–13; Matthew 15:3–9

3 He answered them, "Why do you also disobey the commandment of God because of your tradition? 4 For God commanded, [through] 10 for Moses said, 4 'Honor your father and your mother,'[79] and, 'He who speaks evil of father or mother, let him be put to death.'[80] 5 But you say, 'Whoever may tell his father or his mother, "Whatever help you might otherwise have gotten from me 11 is Corban, that is to say, 5 a gift devoted to God," 6 he shall not honor his father or mother,' 12 then you no longer allow him to do anything for his father or his

---

[79] **Exodus 20:12** "Honor your father and your mother, that your days may be long in the land which Yahweh your God gives you." **Deuteronomy 5:16** "Honor your father and your mother, as Yahweh your God commanded you; that your days may be long, and that it may go well with you, in the land which Yahweh your God gives you."

[80] **Exodus 21:17** "Anyone who curses his father or his mother shall surely be put to death."

mother, 13 making void the word of God [and] 6 the commandment of God 13 by your tradition, which you have handed down. You do many things like this."

7 "You hypocrites! Well did Isaiah prophesy 6 of you, saying,

> 8 'These people draw near to Me with their mouth, and 8 honor Me with their lips; but their heart is far from Me. 9 And in vain do they worship Me, teaching as doctrine rules made by men.'"[81]

8 "For you set aside the commandment of God, and hold tightly to the tradition of men—the washing of pitchers and cups, and you do many other such things." 9 He said to them, "Full well do you reject the commandment of God, that you may keep your tradition."

Unwashed Hands Do not Defile One Spiritually

Mark 7:14–37; Matthew 15:10–20

14 He called all the multitude to Himself, and said to them, "Hear me, all of you, and understand. 15 There is nothing from outside of the man, that going into him 11 which enters into the mouth doesn't 15 defile him; but the things which proceed out of the man 11 which proceeds out of the mouth, 15 are those that defile the man. 16 If anyone has ears to hear, let him hear!"

17 When He had entered into a house away from the multitude, 12 then the disciples came, and said to Him, "Do you know that the Pharisees were offended, when they heard this saying?"

13 But He answered, "Every plant which My heavenly Father didn't plant will be uprooted. 14 Leave them alone. They are blind guides of the blind. If the blind guide the blind, both will fall into a pit."

15 Peter [and] 17 His disciples 15 answered Him, [and] 17 asked Him about the parable, 15 "Explain the parable to us."

18 He said to them, "Are you also 16 still 18 without understanding? Don't you perceive [and] 17 understand 18 that whatever goes into the man from outside can't defile him, 19 because it doesn't go into his

[81] **Isaiah 29:13** The Lord said, "Because this people draws near with their mouth and with their lips to honor me, but they have removed their heart far from me, and their fear of me is a commandment of men which has been taught."

heart, but 17 goes into the mouth passes into the belly, 17 and then out of the body 19 then into the latrine, thus purifying all foods?

20 He said, 18 "But the things which proceed out of the mouth [of] 20 the man 18 come out of the heart, and they defile the man. 21 For from within, out of the hearts of men, proceed evil thoughts, adulteries, sexual sins, murders, thefts, 19 false testimony, 22 covetings, wickedness, deceit, lustful desires, an evil eye, 19 blasphemies, 22 pride, and foolishness. 23 All these evil things come from within, and defile the man, 20 but to eat with unwashed hands doesn't defile the man."

Jesus Goes to Tyre and Sidon

Mark 7:24–30; Matthew 15:21–28

24 From there, 21 Jesus 24 arose and 21 went out from there, and withdrew into the region of 24 the borders of 21 Tyre and Sidon. 24 He entered into a house, and didn't want anyone to know it, but He couldn't escape notice. 25 For 22 behold, 22 a Canaanite woman came out from those borders, 25 whose little daughter had an unclean spirit, having heard of Him, came and fell down at His feet 22 and cried, saying, "Have mercy on me, Lord, You Son of David! My daughter is severely possessed by a demon!" 26 Now the woman was a Greek, a Syrophoenician by race. She begged Him that He would cast the demon out of her daughter.

23 But He answered her not a word.

24 His disciples came and begged Him, saying, "Send her away; for she cries after us."

25 But He answered, "I wasn't sent to anyone but the lost sheep of the house of Israel."

26 But she came and worshiped Him, saying, "Lord, help me."

27 But Jesus said to her, "Let the children be filled first, for it is not appropriate to take the children's bread and throw it to the dogs."[82]

28 But she answered Him, "Yes, Lord. Yet even the dogs under the table eat the children's crumbs 27 which fall from their masters'

[82] The Jews commonly called the Gentiles "dogs."

table."

28 Then Jesus answered her, [and] 29 said to her, 28 "Woman, great is your faith! Be it done to you even as you desire. 29 For this saying, go your way. The demon has gone out of your daughter." 28 And her daughter was healed from that hour.

30 She went away to her house, and found the child having been laid on the bed, with the demon gone out.

Jesus Heals a Deaf Mute

Mark 7:31–37; Matthew 15:29–30

31 Again He departed from the borders of Tyre and Sidon, through the middle of the region of Decapolis, 29 and came near to the sea of Galilee; 30 and He went up into the mountain, and sat there. 32 They brought to Him one who was deaf and had an impediment in his speech. They begged Him to lay His hand on him.

33 He took him aside from the multitude, privately, and put His fingers into his ears, and He spat, and touched his tongue. 34 Looking up to heaven, He sighed, and said to him, "Ephphatha!" that is, "Be opened!"

35 Immediately his ears were opened, and the impediment of his tongue was released, and he spoke clearly. 36 He commanded them that they should tell no one, but the more He commanded them, so much the more widely they proclaimed it.

37 They were astonished beyond measure, saying, "He has done all things well. He makes even the deaf hear, and the mute speak!"

Jesus Heals Many in Galilee

Matthew 15:30–31

30 Great multitudes came to Him, having with them the lame, blind, mute, maimed, and many others, and they put them down at His feet. He healed them, 31 so that the multitude wondered when they saw the mute speaking, injured whole, lame walking, and blind seeing—and they glorified the God of Israel.

The Feeding of the Four Thousand

Mark 8:1–10; Matthew 15:32–39

1 In those days, when there was a very great multitude, and they had nothing to eat, 1 Jesus called [and] 32 summoned 1 His disciples to Himself, and said to them, 2 "I have compassion on the multitude, because they have stayed with Me now [and] 32 continue 2 three days, and have nothing to eat. 32 I don't want to send them away fasting. 3 If I send them away fasting to their home, they will faint on the way, for some of them have come a long way."

4 His disciples answered Him, "From 33 where should we get so many loaves in a deserted place as to satisfy so great a multitude?"

34 Jesus said to them, 5 He asked them, "How many loaves do you have?"

And they said, "Seven, 34 and a few small fish."

6 He commanded the multitude to sit down on the ground, and He took the seven loaves. Having given thanks, He broke them, and gave them to His disciples to serve, and they served the multitude. 7 They had a few small fish. Having blessed them, He said to serve these also.

8 They 37 all 8 ate, and were filled. They took up seven baskets of broken pieces that were left over. 9 Those who had eaten were about four thousand 38 men, besides women and children.

39 Then He sent away the multitudes [and] 10 immediately He entered into the boat with His disciples, and came into the region of Dalmanutha 38 and came into the borders of Magdala.

The Pharisees and Sadducees Seek a Sign

Matthew 16:1–4; Mark 8:11–13

1 The Pharisees and Sadducees came 11 out and began to question Him, seeking from Him a sign from heaven, and testing Him.

12 He sighed deeply in His spirit, and 2 He answered them, 12 "Why does this generation seek a sign? 2 When it is evening, you say, 'It will be fair weather, for the sky is red.' 3 In the morning, 'It will be foul weather today, for the sky is red and threatening.' Hypocrites!

You know how to discern the appearance of the sky, but you can't discern the signs of the times! 4 An evil and adulterous generation seeks after a sign, and 12 most certainly I tell you, 4 there will be no sign given to it, except the sign of the prophet Jonah."[83] He left them, and departed, 13 and again entering into the boat, departed to the other side.

The Leaven of the Pharisees

Matthew 16:5–12; Mark 8:14–21

5 The disciples came to the other side and had forgotten to take bread 14 and they didn't have more than one loaf in the boat with them. 15 He warned them, saying, "Take heed: beware of the yeast of the Pharisees 6 and Sadducees, 15 and the yeast of Herod."

16 They reasoned with one another, saying, "It's because we have no bread."

8 Jesus, 17 perceiving it, said to them, 8 "Why do you reason among yourselves, you of little faith, 'because you have brought no bread?' 17 Don't you perceive yet, neither understand? Is your heart still hardened? 18 Having eyes, don't you see? Having ears, don't you hear?[84] Don't you remember? 19 When I broke the five loaves among the five thousand, how many baskets full of broken pieces did you take up?"

They told him, "Twelve."

20 "When the seven loaves fed the four thousand, how many baskets full of broken pieces did you take up?"

They told him, "Seven."

21 He asked them, "Don't you understand, yet?" 11 How is it that you don't perceive that I didn't speak to you concerning bread? But beware of the yeast of the Pharisees and Sadducees."

12 Then they understood that He didn't tell them to beware of the

---

[83] **Jonah 1:17** Yahweh prepared a great fish to swallow up Jonah, and Jonah was in the belly of the fish three days and three nights.

[84] **Jeremiah 5:21** 'Hear now this, foolish people, and without understanding; who have eyes, and don't see; who have ears, and don't hear.'

yeast of bread, but of the teaching of the Pharisees and Sadducees.

Jesus Heals a Blind Man at Bethsaida

Mark 8:22–26

22 He came to Bethsaida. They brought a blind man to Him, and begged Him to touch him. 23 He took hold of the blind man by the hand, and brought him out of the village. When He had spit on his eyes, and laid His hands on him, He asked him if he saw anything.

24 He looked up, and said, "I see men; for I see them like trees walking."

25 Then again He laid his hands on his eyes. He looked intently, and was restored, and saw everyone clearly. 26 He sent him away to his house, saying, "Don't enter into the village, nor tell anyone in the village."

Peter's Declaration of Jesus as Christ at Caesarea Philippi

Matthew 16:13–20; Mark 8:27–30; Luke 9:18–21

13 Now when Jesus came into the parts of Caesarea Philippi, 27 Jesus went out, with His disciples, into the villages of Caesarea Philippi. On the way, 18 as He was praying alone, the disciples were with Him, and 13 He asked His disciples, saying, "Who do men 18 the multitudes 13 say that I, the Son of Man, am?"

14 They said, "Some say John the Baptizer, 19 but 14 some, 19 others say, 14 Elijah, and others, 19 that 14 Jeremiah, or one of the prophets, 19 that one of the old prophets is risen again."

15 He said to them, "But who do you say that I am?"

16 Simon Peter answered, "You are the Christ, the Son of the living God."

17 Jesus answered him, "Blessed are you, Simon Bar Jonah, for flesh and blood has not revealed this to you, but my Father who is in heaven. 18 I also tell you that you are Peter, and on this rock I will build my assembly, and the gates of Hades will not prevail against it. 19 I will give to you the keys of the Kingdom of Heaven, and whatever you bind on earth will have been bound in heaven; and whatever you

release on earth will have been released in heaven." 20 Then He 21 warned them, and 20 commanded the disciples that they should tell no one 30 about Him 20 that He was Jesus the Christ.

Jesus Predicts His Death and Resurrection

Matthew16:21–23; Mark 8:31–33; Luke 9:22

21 From that time, Jesus began to show his disciples [and] 31 teach them that the Son of Man must 21 go to Jerusalem and suffer many things from the elders, chief priests, and scribes, 31 and be rejected by the elders, the chief priests, and the scribes, and be killed, and after three days rise again, 21 and the third day be raised up.[85]

32 He spoke to them openly 22 saying, "The Son of Man must suffer many things, and be rejected by the elders, chief priests, and scribes, and be killed, and the third day be raised up."

22 Peter took Him aside, and began to rebuke Him, saying, "Far be it from You, Lord! This will never be done to You."

33 But He, turning around, and seeing His disciples, rebuked Peter, and said, 23 "Get behind Me, Satan! You are a stumbling block to Me, for you are not setting your mind on the things of God, but on the things of men."

The Total Commitment Required of a Christian

Mark 8:34–38; 9:1; Matthew 16:24–28; Luke 9:23–27

34 He called the multitude to himself with his disciples, and said to them, 24 "If anyone desires to come after Me, let him deny himself, and take up his cross, 23 daily, 24 and follow Me. 25 For whoever desires to save his life will lose it, and whoever will lose his life for My sake 35 and the sake of the good news 25 will find it [and] 24 save it. 26 For what will it profit a man, if he gains the whole world, and

---

[85] This seems more repetitious than necessary, but the three Gospels differ in subtle but important points. Jesus said that the time He would be in the tomb was the sign He was the Messiah. These three accounts indicate that this time was first, after three days, and second, on the third day. Both of these could be true only if He was in the tomb for exactly seventy-two hours and if He was resurrected at the very end of the third day after His burial.

forfeits his life? 25 and loses or forfeits his own self? 26 Or what will a man give in exchange for his life? 38 For whoever will be ashamed of Me and of My words in this adulterous and sinful generation, the Son of Man also will be ashamed of Him, when He comes in His Father's glory, with the holy angels."

27 "For the Son of Man will come in 26 in His glory, and 27 the glory of His Father with His 26 holy angels 27 and then He will render to everyone according to his deeds.[86] 28 Most certainly I tell you, there are some standing here who will in no way taste of death, until they see the Son of Man coming in His Kingdom [and] 1 until they see God's kingdom come with power."

The Transfiguration

Matthew 17:1–9; Luke 9:28–36; Mark 9:2–10

1 After six days, Jesus took with him Peter, James, and John his brother, and brought them up into a high mountain by themselves. 28 About eight days after these sayings[87] [they] went up onto the mountain to pray. As He was praying, the appearance of His face was altered, and 2 He was transfigured before them 2 and He was changed into another form in front of them. 2 His face shone like the sun, and His garments became as white as the light. 29 His clothing became white and dazzling, 3 glistening, exceedingly white, like snow, such as no launderer on earth can whiten them. 30 Behold, two men were talking with Him, 4 Elijah and Moses appeared to them, and they were talking with Jesus. 3 Moses and Elijah 31 appeared in glory, and spoke of His departure, which He was about to accomplish at Jerusalem.

32 Now Peter and those who were with Him were heavy with sleep, but when they were fully awake, they saw His glory, and the two men who stood with Him. 33 As they were parting from Him, 4 Peter

---

[86] **Psalm 62:12** Also to you, Lord, belongs loving kindness, for you reward every man according to his work. **Proverbs 24:12** If you say, "Behold, we didn't know this;" doesn't he who weighs the hearts consider it? He who keeps your soul, doesn't he know it? Shall he not render to every man according to his work?

[87] The apparent contradiction between Matthew and Luke may be explained by saying Jesus traveled to the mountain (traditionally Mt. Hermon, which was about ten miles from Caesarea Philippi) with the twelve for six days and then spent two more days alone with Peter, James, and John on top of the mountain.

answered, and said to Jesus, "Lord, 5 Rabbi, 33 Master, it is good for us to be here. Let's make three tents: one for you, and one for Moses, and one for Elijah," not knowing what he said. 6 For he didn't know what to say, for they were very afraid.

5 While he was still speaking, behold, a bright cloud overshadowed them 34 and they were afraid as they entered into the cloud. 5 Behold, a voice came out of the cloud, saying, "This is My beloved Son, 35 My Chosen One 5 in Whom I am well pleased. Listen to Him!"[88]

6 When the disciples heard it, they fell on their faces, and were very afraid. 7 Jesus came and touched them and said, "Get up, and don't be afraid."

36 When the voice had ceased, 8 suddenly 8 lifting up their eyes, [and] 8 looking around, 8 they saw no one 8 with them any more, except Jesus only. 9 As they were coming down from the mountain, 9 Jesus commanded them, saying, "Don't tell anyone what you saw, until the Son of Man has risen from the dead."

10 They kept this saying to themselves, questioning what the "rising from the dead" meant. 36 But they kept quiet, and told no one in those days any of the things they had seen.

John the Baptist and Elijah

Matthew 17:10–13; Mark 9:11–13

10 His disciples asked Him, saying, "Then why do the scribes say that Elijah must come first?"

11 Jesus answered them, "Elijah indeed comes first, and will restore all things, 12 but I tell you that Elijah has come already,[89] and they didn't recognize him, but did to him whatever they wanted to 13 even as it is written about him. 12 How is it written about the Son of Man,

---

[88] **Deuteronomy 18:15** Yahweh your God will raise up to you a prophet from among you, of your brothers, like me. You shall listen to him. **Psalm 2:7** "I will tell of the decree. Yahweh said to me, 'You are my son. Today I have become your father.'"

[89] **Malachi 4:5–6** "Behold, I will send you Elijah the prophet before the great and terrible day of Yahweh comes. 6 He will turn the hearts of the fathers to the children, and the hearts of the children to their fathers, lest I come and strike the earth with a curse."

that He should suffer many things and be despised? 12 Even so the Son of Man will also suffer by them." 13 Then the disciples understood that He spoke to them of John the Baptizer.

Jesus Heals a Mute Boy and His Second Prediction of His Death

Luke 9:37–45; Mark 9:14–32; Matthew 17:14–23

37 On the next day, when they had come down from the mountain, a great multitude met Him.

14 Coming to the disciples, He saw a great multitude around them, and scribes questioning them.

15 Immediately all the multitude, when they saw Him, were greatly amazed, and running to Him greeted Him. 16 He asked the scribes, "What are you asking them?"

17 Then 38 behold, 17 one of the multitude, 38 a man from the crowd, 14 came to Him, kneeling down to Him, 38 called out, saying, [and] 17 answered 38 "Teacher, I beg You to look at my son, for he is my only child. 15 Lord, have mercy on my son, for he is epileptic, and suffers grievously; for he often falls into the fire, and often into the water. 17 Teacher, I brought to You my son, who has a mute spirit. 39 Behold, 18 wherever 39 a spirit takes him, 18 it seizes him, 39 he suddenly cries out, and it convulses him, 18 it throws him down, and he foams at the mouth, and grinds his teeth, and wastes away, 39 and it hardly departs from him, bruising him severely. 16 So I brought him to Your disciples, [and] 18 I asked [and] 40 begged Your disciples 18 to cast it out, and they weren't able 16 [to] cure him."

19 He answered him, "Unbelieving 17 and perverse 19 generation, how long shall I be with you? How long shall I bear with you? Bring him, 41 bring your son here 19 to Me."

20 They brought him to Him, and when he saw Him, 42 while he was still coming, 20 immediately the 42 demon 20 spirit 42 threw him down and 20 convulsed him, and he fell on the ground, wallowing and foaming at the mouth.

21 He asked his father, "How long has it been since this has come to him?"

He said, "From childhood. 22 Often it has cast him both into the fire and into the water, to destroy him. But if You can do anything, have compassion on us, and help us."

23 Jesus said to him, "If you can believe, all things are possible to him who believes."

24 Immediately the father of the child cried out with tears, "I believe. Help my unbelief!"

25 When Jesus saw that a multitude came running together, He rebuked the unclean spirit, saying to him, "You mute and deaf spirit, I command you, come out of him, and never enter him again!"

26 Having cried out, and convulsed greatly, it came out of him. The boy became like one dead; so much that most of them said, "He is dead."

But Jesus took him by the hand, and raised him up; 42 and healed the boy. 27 He arose 42 and [Jesus] gave him back to his father 18 and the boy was cured from that hour. 43 They were all astonished at the majesty of God.

But while all were marveling at all the things which Jesus did, He said to His disciples, 44 "Let these words sink into your ears, for the Son of Man will be delivered up into the hands of men." 45 But they didn't understand this saying. It was concealed from them, that they should not perceive it, and they were afraid to ask Him about this saying.

28 When He had come into the house, 19 the disciples came to Jesus privately, and 28 asked Him privately, "Why couldn't we cast it out?"

29 He said to them, 20 "Because of your unbelief. For most certainly I tell you, if you have faith as a grain of mustard seed, you will tell this mountain, 'Move from here to there,' and it will move; and nothing will be impossible for you. 21 But this kind doesn't go out. 29 This kind can come out by nothing, except by prayer and fasting."

30 They went out from there, and passed through Galilee.

He didn't want anyone to know it. 22 While they were staying in Galilee, Jesus said to them, 31 for He was teaching His disciples, and said to them, "The Son of Man is 22 about to be delivered up [and] 31 handed over to the hands of men, and they will kill Him; and when He is killed, on the third day He will rise again."

23 They were exceedingly sorry. 32 But they didn't understand the saying, and were afraid to ask Him.

Who Is the Greatest?

Luke 9:46–48; Mark 9:33–37; Matthew 18:1–6

46 There arose an argument among them about which of them was the greatest. 33 He came to Capernaum, and when He was in the house He asked them, "What were you arguing among yourselves on the way?"

34 But they were silent, for they had disputed one with another on the way about who was the greatest.

1 In that hour the disciples came to Jesus, saying, "Who then is greatest in the Kingdom of Heaven?"

47 Jesus, perceiving the reasoning of their hearts, 2 called a little child to Himself, 35 He sat down, 47 took a little child 2 and set him in the middle of them, 47 and set him by His side 35 and called the twelve; 48 and said to them, "Whoever receives this little child in My name receives Me. Whoever receives Me receives Him who sent Me. For whoever is least among you all, this one will be great."

3 And said, "Most certainly I tell you, unless you turn, and become as little children, you will in no way enter into the Kingdom of Heaven.

35 And He said to them, "If any man wants to be first, he shall be last of all, and servant of all."

36 Taking him in his arms, He said to them, 4 "Whoever therefore humbles himself as this little child, the same is the greatest in the Kingdom of Heaven. 37 Whoever receives one such little child in My name, receives Me, and whoever receives Me, doesn't receive Me, but Him who sent Me. 48 For whoever is least among you all, this one will be great, 6 but whoever causes one of these little ones who believe in me to stumble, it would be better for him that a huge millstone should be hung around his neck, and that he 42 were thrown into the sea [and] sunk in the depths of the sea."

Jesus Warns of Offenses

Matthew 18:7–11; Mark 9:42–50

7 "Woe to the world because of occasions of stumbling! For it must be that the occasions come, but woe to that person through whom the occasion comes! 8 If your hand or your foot causes you to stumble, cut it off, and cast it from you. It is better for you to enter into life maimed or crippled, rather than having two hands or two feet to be cast into the eternal fire, 43 into the unquenchable fire,[90] 44 'where their worm doesn't die, and the fire is not quenched.'[91]

45 "If your foot causes you to stumble, cut it off. It is better for you to enter into life lame, rather than having your two feet to be cast into Gehenna, into the fire that will never be quenched—46 'where their worm doesn't die, and the fire is not quenched.'[92] 9 If your eye causes you to stumble, pluck it out, and cast it from you. It is better for you to enter into life with one eye, rather than having two eyes to be cast into the Gehenna of fire, 48 where 'their worm does not die and the fire is not quenched.'[93]

49 "For everyone will be seasoned with fire, and every sacrifice will be seasoned with salt.[94] 50 Salt is good, but if the salt has lost its saltiness, with what will you season it? Have salt in yourselves, and be at peace with one another.

10 "See that you don't despise one of these little ones, for I tell you that in heaven their angels always see the face of My Father Who is in heaven. 11 For the Son of Man came to save that which was lost."

---

[90] **Isaiah 66:24** "They will go out, and look at the dead bodies of the men who have transgressed against me; for their worm will not die, nor will their fire be quenched, and they will be loathsome to all mankind."

[91] Ibid.

[92] Ibid.

[93] Ibid.

[94] **Leviticus 2:13** Every offering of your meal offering you shall season with salt. You shall not allow the salt of the covenant of your God to be lacking from your meal offering. With all your offerings you shall offer salt. **Ezekiel 43:24** You shall bring them near to Yahweh, and the priests shall cast salt on them, and they shall offer them up for a burnt offering to Yahweh.

The Parable of the Lost Sheep

Matthew 18:12–14

12 What do you think? If a man has one hundred sheep, and one of them goes astray, doesn't he leave the ninety-nine, go to the mountains, and seek that which has gone astray? 13 If he finds it, most certainly I tell you, he rejoices over it more than over the ninety-nine which have not gone astray. 14 Even so it is not the will of your Father Who is in heaven that one of these little ones should perish.

A Man Casts Out Demons in Jesus's Name

Mark 9:38–41; Luke 9:49–50

38 John said to Him, "Teacher, we saw someone who doesn't follow us casting out demons in Your name; and we forbade him, because he doesn't follow 49 with us."

39 But Jesus said 50 to him, 39 "Don't forbid him, for there is no one who will do a mighty work in My name, and be able quickly to speak evil of Me. 40 For whoever is not against us is 50 for us, 40 on our side. 41 For whoever will give you a cup of water to drink in My name, because you are Christ's, most certainly I tell you, he will in no way lose his reward.

Jesus Pays Taxes

Matthew 17:24–27

24 When they had come to Capernaum, those who collected the didrachma coins came to Peter, and said, "Doesn't your Teacher pay the didrachma?"

25 He said, "Yes."

When he came into the house, Jesus anticipated him, saying, "What do you think, Simon? From whom do the kings of the earth receive toll or tribute? From their children or from strangers?"

26 Peter said to him, "From strangers."

Jesus said to him, "Therefore the children are exempt. 27 But, lest we cause them to stumble, go to the sea, cast a hook, and take up the first fish that comes up. When you have opened its mouth, you will find a stater coin. Take that, and give it to them for Me and you."

Dealing with a Sinning Brother

Matthew 18:15–17

15 "If your brother sins against you, go, show him his fault between you and him alone. If he listens to you, you have gained back your brother. 16 But if he doesn't listen, take one or two more with you, that 'at the mouth of two or three witnesses every word may be established.'[95] 17 If he refuses to listen to them, tell it to the assembly. If he refuses to hear the assembly also, let him be to you as a Gentile or a tax collector.

Binding and Loosing

Matthew 18:18–20

18 "Most certainly I tell you, whatever things you bind on earth will have been bound in heaven, and whatever things you release on earth will have been released in heaven. 19 Again, assuredly I tell you, that if two of you will agree on earth concerning anything that they will ask, it will be done for them by My Father who is in heaven. 20 For where two or three are gathered together in My name, there I am in the middle of them."

The Parable of the Unforgiving Servant

Matthew 18:21–35

21 Then Peter came and said to him, "Lord, how often shall my brother sin against me, and I forgive him? Until seven times?"

22 Jesus said to him, "I don't tell you until seven times, but, until seventy times seven.[96] 23 Therefore the Kingdom of Heaven is like a

---

[95] **Deuteronomy 19:15** One witness shall not rise up against a man for any iniquity, or for any sin, in any sin that he sins. At the mouth of two witnesses, or at the mouth of three witnesses, shall a matter be established.

[96] **Genesis 4:24** "If Cain will be avenged seven times, truly Lamech seventy-seven times."

certain king, who wanted to reconcile accounts with his servants. 24
When he had begun to reconcile, one was brought to him who owed
him ten thousand talents. 25 But because he couldn't pay, his lord
commanded him to be sold, with his wife, his children, and all that he
had, and payment to be made.

26 "The servant therefore fell down and knelt before him, saying,
'Lord, have patience with me, and I will repay you all!' 27 The lord
of that servant, being moved with compassion, released him, and
forgave him the debt.

28 "But that servant went out, and found one of his fellow servants,
who owed him one hundred denarii, and he grabbed him, and took
him by the throat, saying, 'Pay me what you owe!'

29 "So his fellow servant fell down at his feet and begged him, saying,
'Have patience with me, and I will repay you!' 30 He would not, but
went and cast him into prison, until he should pay back that which was
due. 31 So when his fellow servants saw what was done, they were
exceedingly sorry, and came and told to their lord all that was done.

32 "Then his lord called him in, and said to him, 'You wicked servant!
I forgave you all that debt, because you begged me. 33 Shouldn't you
also have had mercy on your fellow servant, even as I had mercy on
you?' 34 His lord was angry, and delivered him to the tormentors,
until he should pay all that was due to him. 35 So My heavenly Father
will also do to you, if you don't each forgive your brother from your
hearts for his misdeeds."

Jesus Leaves Galilee for Jerusalem

Matthew 19:1; Mark 10:1; Luke 9:51–62

1 When Jesus had finished these words, 1 He arose from there [and]
1 He departed from Galilee.

It came to pass, when the days were near that He should be taken up,
He intently set His face to go to Jerusalem, 52 and sent messengers
before His face. They went, and entered into a village of the
Samaritans, so as to prepare for Him. 53 They didn't receive Him,
because He was traveling with His face set towards Jerusalem. 54
When His disciples, James and John, saw this, they said, "Lord, do

you want us to command fire to come down from the sky, and destroy them, just as Elijah did?"[97]

55 But He turned and rebuked them, "You don't know of what kind of spirit you are. 56 For the Son of Man didn't come to destroy men's lives, but to save them."

They went to another village. 57 As they went on the way, a certain man said to Him, "I want to follow You wherever You go, Lord."

58 Jesus said to him, "The foxes have holes, and the birds of the sky have nests, but the Son of Man has no place to lay His head."

59 He said to another, "Follow Me!"

But he said, "Lord, allow me first to go and bury my father."

60 But Jesus said to him, "Leave the dead to bury their own dead, but you go and announce God's kingdom."

61 Another also said, "I want to follow You, Lord, but first allow me to say good-bye to those who are at my house."

62 But Jesus said to him, "No one, having put his hand to the plow, and looking back, is fit for God's kingdom."[98]

The Seventy Sent Out

Luke 10:1–20

1 Now after these things, the Lord also appointed seventy others, and sent them two by two ahead of Him into every city and place, where He was about to come.

2 Then He said to them, "The harvest is indeed plentiful, but the laborers are few. Pray therefore to the Lord of the harvest, that He may

---

[97] **2 Kings 1:10** Elijah answered to the captain of fifty, "If I am a man of God, then let fire come down from the sky, and consume you and your fifty!" Then fire came down from the sky, and consumed him and his fifty.

[98] **1 Kings 19:20–21** Elisha left the oxen, and ran after Elijah, and said, "Let me please kiss my father and my mother, and then I will follow you." He said to him, "Go back again; for what have I done to you?" 21 He returned from following him, and took the yoke of oxen, and killed them, and boiled their flesh with the instruments of the oxen, and gave to the people, and they ate. Then he arose, and went after Elijah, and served him.

send out laborers into His harvest.

4 "Go your ways. Behold, I send you out as lambs among wolves. 4 Carry no purse, nor wallet, nor sandals. Greet no one on the way. 5 Into whatever house you enter, first say, 'Peace be to this house.' 6 If a son of peace is there, your peace will rest on him; but if not, it will return to you. 7 Remain in that same house, eating and drinking the things they give, for the laborer is worthy of his wages. Don't go from house to house.

8 "Into whatever city you enter, and they receive you, eat the things that are set before you. 9 Heal the sick who are therein, and tell them, 'God's kingdom has come near to you.'

10 "But into whatever city you enter, and they don't receive you, go out into its streets and say, 11 'Even the dust from your city that clings to us, we wipe off against you. Nevertheless know this, that God's kingdom has come near to you.' 12 I tell you, it will be more tolerable in that day for Sodom than for that city."

13 "Woe to you, Chorazin! Woe to you, Bethsaida! For if the mighty works had been done in Tyre and Sidon which were done in you, they would have repented long ago, sitting in sackcloth and ashes. 14 But it will be more tolerable for Tyre and Sidon in the judgment than for you.

15 "You, Capernaum, who are exalted to heaven, will be brought down to Hades. 16 Whoever listens to you listens to Me, and whoever rejects you rejects Me. Whoever rejects Me rejects Him who sent Me."

17 The seventy returned with joy, saying, "Lord, even the demons are subject to us in Your name!"

18 He said to them, "I saw Satan having fallen like lightning from heaven.[99] 19 Behold, I give you authority to tread on serpents and scorpions, and over all the power of the enemy. Nothing will in any way hurt you. 20 Nevertheless, don't rejoice in this, that the spirits are subject to you, but rejoice that your names are written in heaven."

---

[99] **Isaiah 14:12** How you have fallen from heaven, morning star, son of the dawn! How you are cut down to the ground, who laid the nations low!

Jesus Rejoices in Spirit

Luke 10:21–24

21 In that same hour Jesus rejoiced in the Holy Spirit, and said, "I thank you, O Father, Lord of heaven and earth, that You have hidden these things from the wise and understanding, and revealed them to little children. Yes, Father, for so it was well-pleasing in Your sight."

22 Turning to the disciples, He said, "All things have been delivered to Me by My Father. No one knows Who the Son is, except the Father, and Who the Father is, except the Son, and He to whomever the Son desires to reveal Him."

23 Turning to the disciples, He said privately, "Blessed are the eyes
which see the things that you see, 24 for I tell you that many prophets
and kings desired to see the things which you see, and didn't see them, and to hear the things which you hear, and didn't hear them."

The Parable of the Good Samaritan

Luke 10:25–42

25 Behold, a certain lawyer stood up and tested Him, saying, "Teacher, what shall I do to inherit eternal life?"

26 He said to him, "What is written in the law? How do you read it?"

27 He answered, "You shall love the Lord your God with all your heart, with all your soul, with all your strength, and with all your mind;[100] and your neighbor as yourself."[101]

28 He said to him, "You have answered correctly. Do this, and you will live."

29 But he, desiring to justify himself, asked Jesus, "Who is my neighbor?"

30 Jesus answered, "A certain man was going down from Jerusalem to Jericho, and he fell among robbers, who both stripped him and beat

---

[100] **Deuteronomy 6:5** You shall love Yahweh your God with all your heart, with all your soul, and with all your might.

[101] **Leviticus 19:18** You shall not take vengeance, nor bear any grudge against the children of your people; but you shall love your neighbor as yourself. I am Yahweh.

him, and departed, leaving him half dead. 31 By chance a certain priest was going down that way. When he saw him, he passed by on the other side.[102]

32 “In the same way a Levite also, when he came to the place, and saw him, passed by on the other side.[103]

33 “But a certain Samaritan, as he traveled, came where he was. When he saw him, he was moved with compassion, 34 came to him, and bound up his wounds, pouring on oil and wine. He set him on his own animal, and brought him to an inn, and took care of him.[104] 35 On the next day, when he departed, he took out two denarii, and gave them to the host, and said to him, ‘Take care of him. Whatever you spend beyond that, I will repay you when I return.’

36 “Now which of these three do you think seemed to be a neighbor to him who fell among the robbers?”

37 He said, “He who showed mercy on him.”

Then Jesus said to him, “Go and do likewise.”

Jesus’s Last Feast of Tabernacles
The Feast of Tabernacles

John 7:2–13

2 Now the feast of the Jews, the Feast of Booths, was at hand.[105] 3 His brothers therefore said to him, “Depart from here, and go into Judea,

---

[102] **Leviticus 21:1** Yahweh said to Moses, “Speak to the priests, the sons of Aaron, and say to them, ‘A priest shall not defile himself for the dead among his people.’”
[103] **Numbers 19:11** “He who touches the dead body of any man shall be unclean seven days.”
[104] **2 Chronicles 28:15** The men who have been mentioned by name rose up, and took the captives, and with the plunder clothed all who were naked among them, dressed them, gave them sandals, and gave them something to eat and to drink, anointed them, carried all the feeble of them on donkeys, and brought them to Jericho, the city of palm trees, to their brothers. Then they returned to Samaria.
[105] **Leviticus 23:33–36** Yahweh spoke to Moses, saying, 34 “Speak to the children of Israel, and say, ‘On the fifteenth day of this seventh month is the feast of tents for seven days to Yahweh. 35 On the first day shall be a holy convocation: you shall do no regular work. 36 Seven days you shall offer an offering made by fire to Yahweh. On the eighth day shall be a holy convocation to you; and you shall offer an offering made by fire to Yahweh. It is a solemn assembly; you shall do no regular work.’”

that Your disciples also may see Your works which You do. 4 for no one does anything in secret, and himself seeks to be known openly. If You do these things, reveal Yourself to the world." 5 For even His brothers didn't believe in Him.

6 Jesus therefore said to them, "My time has not yet come, but your time is always ready. 7 The world can't hate you, but it hates Me, because I testify about it, that its works are evil. 8 You go up to the feast. I am not yet going up to this feast, because My time is not yet fulfilled."

9 Having said these things to them, He stayed in Galilee. 10 But when His brothers had gone up to the feast, then He also went up, not publicly, but as it were in secret. 11 The Jews therefore sought Him at the feast, and said, "Where is He?"

12 There was much murmuring among the multitudes concerning Him. Some said, "He is a good Man." Others said, "Not so, but He leads the multitude astray." 13 Yet no one spoke openly of Him for fear of the Jews.

At the Home of Mary and Martha

Luke 10:38–42

38 As they went on their way, He entered into a certain village, and a certain woman named Martha received Him into her house. 39 She had a sister called Mary, who also sat at Jesus's feet, and heard His word. 40 But Martha was distracted with much serving, and she came up to Him, and said, "Lord, don't you care that my sister left me to serve alone? Ask her therefore to help me."

41 Jesus answered her, "Martha, Martha, you are anxious and troubled about many things, 42 but one thing is needed. Mary has chosen the good part, which will not be taken away from her."

Jesus Teaches at the Feast

John 7:14–53; 8:1

14 But when it was now the middle of the feast, Jesus went up into the temple and taught. 15 The Jews therefore marveled, saying, "How does this Man know letters, having never been educated?"

16 Jesus therefore answered them, "My teaching is not Mine, but His who sent Me. 17 If anyone desires to do His will, he will know about the teaching, whether it is from God, or if I am speaking from Myself. 18 He who speaks from himself seeks his own glory, but he who seeks the glory of him who sent him is true, and no unrighteousness is in him. 19 Didn't Moses give you the law, and yet none of you keeps the law? Why do you seek to kill me?"

20 The multitude answered, "You have a demon! Who seeks to kill you?"

21 Jesus answered them, "I did one work, and you all marvel because of it. 22 Moses has given you circumcision (not that it is of Moses, but of the fathers),[106] and on the Sabbath you circumcise a boy. 23 If a boy receives circumcision on the Sabbath, that the law of Moses may not be broken, are you angry with Me, because I made a man completely healthy on the Sabbath? 24 Don't judge according to appearance, but judge righteous judgment."[107]

Is Jesus the Christ?

25 Therefore some of them of Jerusalem said, "Isn't this He whom they seek to kill? 26 Behold, He speaks openly, and they say nothing to Him. Can it be that the rulers indeed know that this is truly the Christ? 27 However we know where this Man comes from, but when the Christ comes, no one will know where He comes from."

28 Jesus therefore cried out in the temple, teaching and saying, "You both know Me, and know where I am from. I have not come of Myself, but He who sent Me is true, whom you don't know. 29 I know Him,

---

[106] **Genesis 17:9–11** God said to Abraham, "As for you, you will keep my covenant, you and your offspring after you throughout their generations. 10 This is my covenant, which you shall keep, between me and you and your offspring after you. Every male among you shall be circumcised. 11 You shall be circumcised in the flesh of your foreskin. It will be a token of the covenant between me and you." **Leviticus 12:3** In the eighth day the flesh of his foreskin shall be circumcised.

[107] **Isaiah 11:3–4** His delight will be in the fear of Yahweh. He will not judge by the sight of his eyes, neither decide by the hearing of his ears; 4 but with righteousness he will judge the poor, and decide with equity for the humble of the earth. He will strike the earth with the rod of his mouth; and with the breath of his lips he will kill the wicked.

because I am from Him, and He sent Me."

30 They sought therefore to take Him; but no one laid a hand on Him, because His hour had not yet come. 31 But of the multitude, many believed in Him. They said, "When the Christ comes, He won't do more signs than those which this Man has done, will he?" 32 The Pharisees heard the multitude murmuring these things concerning Him, and the chief priests and the Pharisees sent officers to arrest Him.

32 Then Jesus said, "I will be with you a little while longer, then I go to Him who sent Me. 34 You will seek Me, and won't find Me; and where I am, you can't come."

35 The Jews therefore said among themselves, "Where will this Man go that we won't find Him? Will He go to the Dispersion among the Greeks, and teach the Greeks? 36 What is this word that He said, 'You will seek Me, and won't find Me; and where I am, you can't come'?"

Jesus Teaches on the Last Great Day

37 Now on the last and greatest day of the feast,[108] Jesus stood and cried out, "If anyone is thirsty, let him come to Me and drink! 38 He who believes in Me, as the Scripture has said, from within him will flow rivers of living water."[109]

39 But He said this about the Spirit, which those believing in Him were to receive. For the Holy Spirit was not yet given, because Jesus

---

[108] **Leviticus 23:36** On the eighth day shall be a holy convocation to you; and you shall offer an offering made by fire to Yahweh. It is a solemn assembly; you shall do no regular work.

[109] **Isaiah 44:3** For I will pour water on him who is thirsty, and streams on the dry ground. I will pour my Spirit on your descendants, and My blessing on your offspring. **Jeremiah 2:13** "For My people have committed two evils: they have forsaken Me, the spring of living waters, and cut them out cisterns, broken cisterns, that can hold no water." **Jeremiah 17:13** Those who depart from Me shall be written in the earth, because they have forsaken Yahweh, the spring of living waters. **Proverbs 18:4** The words of a man's mouth are like deep waters. The fountain of wisdom is like a flowing brook. **Zechariah 14:8** It will happen in that day, that living waters will go out from Jerusalem; half of them toward the eastern sea, and half of them toward the western sea; in summer and in winter will it be. **Revelation 22:1** "For the Lamb who is in the middle of the throne shepherds them, and leads them to springs of waters of life. And God will wipe away every tear from their eyes."

wasn't yet glorified.

The People Dispute About Whether Jesus Is the Christ

40 Many of the multitude therefore, when they heard these words, said, "This is truly the prophet."[110] 41 Others said, "This is the Christ." But some said, "What, does the Christ come out of Galilee? 42 Hasn't the Scripture said that the Christ comes of the offspring of David, and from Bethlehem, the village where David was?"[111]

43 So there arose a division in the multitude because of Him. 44 Some of them would have arrested Him, but no one laid hands on Him.

The Unbelief of the Jewish Leaders

45 The officers therefore came to the chief priests and Pharisees, and they said to them, "Why didn't you bring Him?"

46 The officers answered, "No man ever spoke like this Man!"

47 The Pharisees therefore answered them, "You aren't also led astray, are you? 48 Have any of the rulers believed in Him, or of the Pharisees? 49 But this multitude that doesn't know the law is accursed."

50 Nicodemus (he who came to Him by night, being one of them) said to them, 51 "Does our law judge a man, unless it first hears from him personally and knows what he does?"

52 They answered him, "Are you also from Galilee? Search, and see that no prophet has arisen out of Galilee."

---

[110] **Deuteronomy 18:15** Yahweh your God will raise up to you a prophet from among you, of your brothers, like me. You shall listen to him.

[111] **2 Samuel 7:12–14** When your days are fulfilled, and you sleep with your fathers, I will set up your offspring after you, who will proceed out of your body, and I will establish his kingdom. 13 He will build a house for my name, and I will establish the throne of his kingdom forever. 14 I will be his father, and he will be my son. If he commits iniquity, I will chasten him with the rod of men, and with the stripes of the children of men. **Isaiah 11:1** A shoot will come out of the stock of Jesse, and a branch out of his roots will bear fruit. **Micah 5:2** But you, Bethlehem Ephrathah, being small among the clans of Judah, out of you one will come out to me that is to be ruler in Israel; whose goings out are from of old, from ancient times.

53 Everyone went to his own house, 1 but Jesus went to the Mount of Olives.

Jesus Teaches On Prayer

Luke 11:1–13

1 When He finished praying in a certain place, one of his disciples said to Him, “Lord, teach us to pray, just as John also taught his disciples.”

2 He said to them, “When you pray, say,

‘Our Father in heaven, may Your name be kept holy.

May Your Kingdom come.

May Your will be done on earth, as it is in heaven.

3 Give us day by day our daily bread.

4 Forgive us our sins, for we ourselves also forgive everyone who is indebted to us.

Bring us not into temptation, but deliver us from the evil one.’”

5 He said to them, ”Which of you, if you go to a friend at midnight, and tell him, ‘Friend, lend me three loaves of bread, 6 for a friend of mine has come to me from a journey, and I have nothing to set before him,’ 7 and he from within will answer and say, ‘Don’t bother me. The door is now shut, and my children are with me in bed. I can’t get up and give it to you’? 8 I tell you, although he will not rise and give it to him because he is his friend, yet because of his persistence, he will get up and give him as many as he needs.

9 “I tell you, keep asking, and it will be given you. Keep seeking, and you will find. Keep knocking, and it will be opened to you. 10 For everyone who asks receives. He who seeks, finds. To him who knocks it will be opened.

11 “Which of you fathers, if your son asks for bread, will give him a stone? Or if he asks for a fish, he won’t give him a snake instead of a fish, will he? 12 Or if he asks for an egg, he won’t give him a scorpion, will he? 13 If you then, being evil, know how to give good gifts to your children, how much more will your heavenly Father give the

Holy Spirit to those who ask Him?"

The Woman Caught in the Act of Adultery

John 8:2–11

2 Now very early in the morning, He came again into the temple, and
all the people came to Him. He sat down, and taught them. 3 The
scribes and the Pharisees brought a woman taken in adultery. Having
set her in the middle, 4 they told Him, "Teacher, we found this woman
in adultery, in the very act. 5 Now in our law, Moses commanded us
to stone such women.[112] What then do You say about her?" 6 They
said this testing Him, that they might have something to accuse Him
of.

But Jesus stooped down, and wrote on the ground with His finger. 7
But when they continued asking Him, He looked up and said to them,
"He who is without sin among you, let him throw the first stone at
her." 8 Again He stooped down, and with His finger wrote on the
ground.

9 They, when they heard it, being convicted by their conscience, went
out one by one, beginning from the oldest, even to the last. Jesus was
left alone with the woman where she was, in the middle. 10 Jesus,
standing up, saw her and said, "Woman, where are your accusers? Did
no one condemn you?"

11 She said, "No one, Lord."

Jesus said, "Neither do I condemn you. Go your way. From now on,
sin no more."

---

[112] **Leviticus 20:10** The man who commits adultery with another man's wife, even he who commits adultery with his neighbor's wife, the adulterer and the adulteress shall surely be put to death. **Deuteronomy 22:22–24** If a man is found lying with a woman married to a husband, then they shall both die, the man who lay with the woman and the woman. So you shall remove the evil from Israel. 23 If there is a young lady who is a virgin pledged to be married to a husband, and a man finds her in the city, and lies with her; 24 then you shall bring them both out to the gate of that city, and you shall stone them to death with stones; the lady, because she didn't cry, being in the city; and the man, because he has humbled his neighbor's wife. So you shall remove the evil from among you.

The Light of the World and the Validity of Jesus's Testimony

John 8:12–20

12 Again, therefore, Jesus spoke to them, saying, "I am the light of the world. He who follows Me will not walk in the darkness, but will have the light of life."

13 The Pharisees therefore said to Him, "You testify about Yourself. Your testimony is not valid."

14 Jesus answered them, "Even if I testify about Myself, My testimony is true, for I know where I came from, and where I am going; but you don't know where I came from, or where I am going.

15 You judge according to the flesh. I judge no one. 16 Even if I do
judge, my judgment is true, for I am not alone, but I am with the Father
who sent Me. 17 It's also written in your law that the testimony of two
people is valid.[113] 18 I am One who testifies about Myself, and the
Father who sent Me testifies about Me."

19 They said therefore to him, "Where is Your Father?"

Jesus answered, "You know neither Me, nor my Father. If you knew Me, you would know my Father also."

20 Jesus spoke these words in the treasury, as He taught in the temple. Yet no one arrested Him, because His hour had not yet come.

Jesus Predicts His Departure

John 8:21–29

21 Jesus said therefore again to them, "I am going away, and you will seek Me, and you will die in your sins. Where I go, you can't come."

22 The Jews therefore said, "Will He kill Himself, that He says, 'Where I am going, you can't come?'"

[113] **Deuteronomy 17:6** At the mouth of two witnesses, or three witnesses, he who is to die shall be put to death. At the mouth of one witness he shall not be put to death. **Deuteronomy 19:15** One witness shall not rise up against a man for any iniquity, or for any sin, in any sin that he sins. At the mouth of two witnesses, or at the mouth of three witnesses, shall a matter be established.

23 He said to them, "You are from beneath. I am from above. You are of this world. I am not of this world. 24 I said therefore to you that you will die in your sins; for unless you believe that I am He, you will die in your sins."

25 They said therefore to Him, "Who are You?"

Jesus said to them, "Just what I have been saying to you from the beginning. 26 I have many things to speak and to judge concerning you. However He who sent Me is true; and the things which I heard from Him, these I say to the world."

27 They didn't understand that He spoke to them about the Father.

28 Jesus therefore said to them, "When you have lifted up the Son of Man, then you will know that I am He, and I do nothing of Myself, but as My Father taught Me, I say these things. 29 He who sent Me is with Me. The Father hasn't left Me alone, for I always do the things that are pleasing to Him."

Truth, Freedom, and the Children of Abraham

John 8:30–47

30 As he spoke these things, many believed in Him. 31 Jesus therefore said to those Jews who had believed Him, "If you remain in My word, then you are truly My disciples. 32 You will know the truth, and the truth will make you free."[114]

33 They answered Him, "We are Abraham's offspring, and have never been in bondage to anyone. How do You say, 'You will be made free?'"

34 Jesus answered them, "Most certainly I tell you, everyone who commits sin is the bondservant of sin. 35 A bondservant doesn't live in the house forever. A son remains forever. 36 If therefore the Son makes you free, you will be free indeed.

37 "I know that you are Abraham's offspring, yet you seek to kill Me, because My word finds no place in you. 38 I say the things which I have seen with My Father; and you also do the things which you have

[114] **Psalm 119:45** I will walk in liberty, for I have sought your precepts.

seen with your father."

39 They answered Him, "Our father is Abraham."

Jesus said to them, "If you were Abraham's children, you would do the works of Abraham.[115] 40 But now you seek to kill Me, a Man who has told you the truth, which I heard from God. Abraham didn't do this. 41 You do the works of your father."

They said to him, "We were not born of sexual immorality. We have one Father, God."

42 Therefore Jesus said to them, "If God were your father, you would love Me, for I came out and have come from God. For I haven't come of Myself, but He sent Me. 43 Why don't you understand My speech? Because you can't hear My word.

44 You are of your father, the devil, and you want to do the desires of your father. He was a murderer from the beginning, and doesn't stand in the truth, because there is no truth in him. When he speaks a lie, he speaks on his own; for he is a liar, and its father.

45 But because I tell the truth, you don't believe Me. 46 Which of you convicts Me of sin? If I tell the truth, why do you not believe Me? 47

---

[115] **Genesis 12:1–4** Now Yahweh said to Abram, "Leave your country, and your relatives, and your father's house, and go to the land that I will show you. 2 I will make of you a great nation. I will bless you and make your name great. You will be a blessing. 3 I will bless those who bless you, and I will curse him who curses you. All the families of the earth will be blessed through you." 4 So Abram went, as Yahweh had told him. Lot went with him. Abram was seventy-five years old when he departed from Haran. **Genesis 17:1–8** When Abram was ninety-nine years old, Yahweh appeared to Abram, and said to him, "I am God Almighty. Walk before Me, and be blameless. 2 I will make My covenant between Me and you, and will multiply you exceedingly." 3 Abram fell on his face. God talked with him, saying, 4 "As for Me, behold, My covenant is with you. You will be the father of a multitude of nations. 5 Your name will no more be called Abram, but your name will be Abraham; for I have made you the father of a multitude of nations. 6 I will make you exceedingly fruitful, and I will make nations of you. Kings will come out of you. 7 I will establish My covenant between me and you and your offspring after you throughout their generations for an everlasting covenant, to be a God to you and to your offspring after you. 8 I will give to you, and to your offspring after you, the land where you are traveling, all the land of Canaan, for an everlasting possession. I will be their God." **Genesis 26:5** "Because Abraham obeyed my voice, and kept My requirements, My commandments, My statutes, and My laws."

He who is of God hears the words of God. For this cause you don't hear, because you are not of God."

Jesus Before Abraham

John 8:48–59

48 Then the Jews answered Him, "Don't we say well that You are a Samaritan, and have a demon?"

49 Jesus answered, "I don't have a demon, but I honor My Father, and
you dishonor Me. 50 But I don't seek My own glory. There is One
who seeks and judges. 51 Most certainly, I tell you, if a person keeps
My word, he will never see death."

52 Then the Jews said to Him, "Now we know that You have a demon.
Abraham died, and the prophets; and You say, 'If a man keeps My
word, he will never taste of death.' 53 Are You greater than our father,
Abraham, who died? The prophets died. Who do You make Yourself
out to be?"

54 Jesus answered, "If I glorify Myself, My glory is nothing. It is My
Father who glorifies Me, of Whom you say that He is Our God. 55
You have not known Him, but I know Him. If I said, 'I don't know
Him,' I would be like you, a liar. But I know Him, and keep His word.
56 Your father Abraham rejoiced to see My day. He saw it, and was
glad."

57 The Jews therefore said to Him, "You are not yet fifty years old, and have You seen Abraham?"

58 Jesus said to them, "Most certainly, I tell you, before Abraham came into existence, I AM."

59 Therefore they took up stones to throw at Him, but Jesus was hidden, and went out of the temple, having gone through the middle of them, and so passed by.

Jesus Heals a Man Born Blind

John 9:1–12

1 As He passed by, He saw a man blind from birth. 2 His disciples
asked Him, "Rabbi, who sinned, this man or his parents, that he was

born blind?"

3 Jesus answered, "Neither did this man sin, nor his parents; but, that the works of God might be revealed in him. 4 I must work the works of Him who sent Me, while it is day. The night is coming, when no one can work. 5 While I am in the world, I am the light of the world."

6 When He had said this, He spat on the ground, made mud with the saliva, anointed the blind man's eyes with the mud, 7 and said to him, "Go, wash in the pool of Siloam" (which means "Sent"). So he went away, washed, and came back seeing.

8 The neighbors therefore, and those who saw that he was blind before, said, "Isn't this he who sat and begged?" 9 Others were saying, "It is he." Still others were saying, "He looks like him."

He said, "I am he." 10 They therefore were asking him, "How were your eyes opened?"

11 He answered, "A man called Jesus made mud, anointed my eyes, and said to me, 'Go to the pool of Siloam, and wash.' So I went away and washed, and I received sight."

12 Then they asked him, "Where is He?"

He said, "I don't know."

The Pharisees Throw Out the Healed Man

John 9:13–34

13 They brought him who had been blind to the Pharisees. 14 It was a Sabbath when Jesus made the mud and opened his eyes. 15 Again therefore the Pharisees also asked him how he received his sight. He said to them, "He put mud on my eyes, I washed, and I see."

16 Some therefore of the Pharisees said, "This Man is not from God, because He doesn't keep the Sabbath." Others said, "How can a Man Who is a sinner do such signs?"

There was division among them. 17 Therefore they asked the blind man again, "What do you say about Him, because He opened your eyes?"

He said, "He is a prophet."

18 The Jews therefore did not believe concerning him, that he had been blind, and had received his sight, until they called the parents of him who had received his sight, 19 and asked them, “Is this your son, whom you say was born blind? How then does he now see?”

20 His parents answered them, “We know that this is our son, and that he was born blind; 21 but how he now sees, we don’t know; or who opened his eyes, we don’t know. He is of age. Ask him. He will speak for himself.”

22 His parents said these things because they feared the Jews; for the Jews had already agreed that if any man would confess Him as Christ, he would be put out of the synagogue. 23 Therefore his parents said, “He is of age. Ask him.”

24 So they called the man who was blind a second time, and said to him, “Give glory to God. We know that this Man is a sinner.”

25 He therefore answered, “I don’t know if He is a sinner. One thing I do know: that though I was blind, now I see.”

26 They said to him again, “What did He do to you? How did He open your eyes?”

27 He answered them, “I told you already, and you didn’t listen. Why do you want to hear it again? You don’t also want to become His disciples, do you?”

28 They insulted him and said, “You are His disciple, but we are disciples of Moses. 29 We know that God has spoken to Moses. But as for this Man, we don’t know where He comes from.”

30 The man answered them, “How amazing! You don’t know where He comes from, yet He opened my eyes. 31 We know that God doesn’t listen to sinners, but if anyone is a worshiper of God, and does His will, He listens to him.[116] 32 Since the world began it has never been heard of that anyone opened the eyes of someone born blind. 33 If this Man were not from God, He could do nothing.”

---

[116] **Psalm 66:18** If I cherished sin in my heart, the Lord wouldn’t have listened. **Proverbs 15:29** Yahweh is far from the wicked, but he hears the prayer of the righteous. **Proverbs 28:9** He who turns away his ear from hearing the law, even his prayer is an abomination.

34 They answered him, “You were altogether born in sins, and do you teach us?” They threw him out.

Jesus Preaches on True Vision and True Blindness

John 9:35–41

35 Jesus heard that they had thrown him out, and finding him, He said, “Do you believe in the Son of God?”

36 He answered, “Who is He, Lord, that I may believe in Him?”

37 Jesus said to him, “You have both seen Him, and it is He who speaks with you.”

38 He said, “Lord, I believe!” and he worshiped Him.

39 Jesus said, “I came into this world for judgment, that those who don’t see may see; and that those who see may become blind.”

40 Those of the Pharisees who were with him heard these things, and said to him, “Are we also blind?”

41 Jesus said to them, “If you were blind, you would have no sin; but now you say, ‘We see.’ Therefore your sin remains.

The Parable of the Shepherd and His Flock

John 10:1–21

1 “Most certainly, I tell you, one who doesn’t enter by the door into the sheep fold, but climbs up some other way, the same is a thief and a robber. 2 But one who enters in by the door is the shepherd of the sheep. 3 The gatekeeper opens the gate for him, and the sheep listen to his voice. He calls his own sheep by name, and leads them out. 4 Whenever he brings out his own sheep, he goes before them, and the sheep follow him, for they know his voice. 5 They will by no means follow a stranger, but will flee from him; for they don’t know the voice of strangers.” 6 Jesus spoke this parable to them, but they didn’t understand what he was telling them.

7 Jesus therefore said to them again, “Most certainly, I tell you, I am the sheep’s door. 8 All who came before Me are thieves and robbers, but the sheep didn’t listen to them. 9 I am the door. If anyone enters

in by Me, he will be saved, and will go in and go out, and will find pasture. 10 The thief only comes to steal, kill, and destroy. I came that they may have life, and may have it abundantly.

11 I am the good shepherd.[117] The good shepherd lays down his life for the sheep. 12 He who is a hired hand, and not a shepherd, who doesn't own the sheep, sees the wolf coming, leaves the sheep, and flees. The wolf snatches the sheep, and scatters them. 13 The hired hand flees because he is a hired hand, and doesn't care for the sheep. 14 I am the good shepherd. I know My own, and I'm known by My own; 15 even as the Father knows Me, and I know the Father. I lay down my life for the sheep.

16 I have other sheep, which are not of this fold.[118] I must bring them also, and they will hear My voice. They will become one flock with one shepherd. 17 Therefore the Father loves Me, because I lay down My life,[119] that I may take it again. 18 No one takes it away from Me, but I lay it down by Myself. I have power to lay it down, and I have power to take it again. I received this commandment from my Father."

Therefore a division arose again among the Jews because of these words. 20 Many of them said, "He has a demon, and is insane! Why do you listen to Him?"

21 Others said, "These are not the sayings of One possessed by a demon. It isn't possible for a demon to open the eyes of the blind, is

---

[117] **Isaiah 40:11** He will feed his flock like a shepherd. He will gather the lambs in his arm, and carry them in his bosom. He will gently lead those who have their young. **Ezekiel 34:11–12, 15, 22** For thus says the Lord Yahweh: Behold, I myself, even I, will search for my sheep, and will seek them out. 12 As a shepherd seeks out his flock in the day that he is among his sheep that are scattered abroad, so will I seek out my sheep; and I will deliver them out of all places where they have been scattered in the cloudy and dark day. 15 I myself will be the shepherd of my sheep, and I will cause them to lie down, says the Lord Yahweh, 22 therefore will I save my flock, and they shall no more be a prey; and I will judge between sheep and sheep.

[118] **Isaiah 56:8** The Lord Yahweh, who gathers the outcasts of Israel, says, "I will yet gather others to him, besides his own who are gathered."

[119] **Isaiah 53:7–8** He was oppressed, yet when he was afflicted he didn't open his mouth. As a lamb that is led to the slaughter, and as a sheep that before its shearers is silent, so he didn't open his mouth. 8 He was taken away by oppression and judgment; and as for his generation, who considered that he was cut off out of the land of the living and stricken for the disobedience of my people?

it?”[120]

Generation Seeking a Sign

Luke 11:29–54

29 When the multitudes were gathering together to Him, He began to say, “This is an evil generation. It seeks after a sign. No sign will be given to it but the sign of Jonah,[121] the prophet. 30 For even as Jonah became a sign to the Ninevites, so will also the Son of Man be to this generation.

31 “The Queen of the South will rise up in the judgment with the men of this generation, and will condemn them: for she came from the ends of the earth to hear the wisdom of Solomon; and behold, one greater than Solomon is here. 32 The men of Nineveh will stand up in the judgment with this generation, and will condemn it: for they repented at the preaching of Jonah, and behold, one greater than Jonah is here.

The Lamp of the Body

33 “No one, when he has lit a lamp, puts it in a cellar or under a basket, but on a stand, that those who come in may see the light. 34 The lamp of the body is the eye. Therefore when your eye is good, your whole body is also full of light; but when it is evil, your body also is full of darkness. 35 Therefore see whether the light that is in you isn’t darkness. 36 If therefore your whole body is full of light, having no part dark, it will be wholly full of light, as when the lamp with its bright shining gives you light.”

Woe to the Pharisees and Lawyers

37 Now as He spoke, a certain Pharisee asked Him to dine with him. He went in, and sat at the table. 38 When the Pharisee saw it, he marveled that He had not first washed Himself before dinner.

---

[120] **Exodus 4:11** Yahweh said to him, “Who made man’s mouth? Or who makes one mute, or deaf, or seeing, or blind? Isn’t it I, Yahweh?”

[121] **Jonah 1:17** Yahweh prepared a great fish to swallow up Jonah, and Jonah was in the belly of the fish three days and three nights.

Luke 11:39–54

39 The Lord said to him, "Now you Pharisees cleanse the outside of the cup and of the platter, but your inward part is full of extortion and wickedness. 40 You foolish ones, didn't He who made the outside make the inside also? 41 But give for gifts to the needy those things which are within, and behold, all things will be clean to you.

42 "But woe to you Pharisees! For you tithe mint and rue and every herb, but you bypass justice and the love of God. You ought to have done these, and not to have left the other undone.

43 "Woe to you Pharisees! For you love the best seats in the synagogues, and the greetings in the marketplaces. 44 Woe to you, scribes and Pharisees, hypocrites! For you are like hidden graves, and the men who walk over them don't know it."

45 One of the lawyers answered Him, "Teacher, in saying this You insult us also."

46 He said, "Woe to you lawyers also! For you load men with burdens that are difficult to carry, and you yourselves won't even lift one finger to help carry those burdens.

47 "Woe to you! For you build the tombs of the prophets, and your fathers killed them. 48 So you testify and consent to the works of your fathers. For they killed them, and you build their tombs.

49 "Therefore also the wisdom of God said, 'I will send to them prophets and apostles; and some of them they will kill and persecute,'[122] 50 that the blood of all the prophets, which was shed from the foundation of the world, may be required of this generation; 51 from the blood of Abel to the blood of Zachariah, who perished between the altar and the sanctuary.' Yes, I tell you, it will be required of this generation.

---

[122] **2 Chronicles 24:19** Yet He sent prophets to them, to bring them again to Yahweh; and they testified against them: but they would not give ear. **2 Chronicles 36:15–16** Yahweh, the God of their fathers, sent to them by His messengers, rising up early and sending, because He had compassion on His people, and on His dwelling place: 16 but they mocked the messengers of God, and despised His words, and scoffed at His prophets, until Yahweh's wrath arose against His people, until there was no remedy.

52 “Woe to you lawyers! For you took away the key of knowledge. You didn’t enter in yourselves, and those who were entering in, you hindered.”

53 As He said these things to them, the scribes and the Pharisees began to be terribly angry, and to draw many things out of Him; 54 lying in wait for Him, and seeking to catch Him in something He might say, that they might accuse Him.

Warnings and Encouragement

Luke 12:1–59

1 Meanwhile, when a multitude of many thousands had gathered together, so much so that they trampled on each other, He began to tell His disciples first of all, “Beware of the yeast of the Pharisees, which is hypocrisy. 2 But there is nothing covered up, that will not be revealed, nor hidden, that will not be known. 3 Therefore whatever you have said in the darkness will be heard in the light. What you have spoken in the ear in the inner rooms will be proclaimed on the housetops.

4 “I tell you, My friends, don’t be afraid of those who kill the body, and after that have no more that they can do. 5 But I will warn you whom you should fear. Fear Him, who after He has killed, has power to cast into Gehenna. Yes, I tell you, fear Him.

6 “Aren’t five sparrows sold for two assaria coins? Not one of them is forgotten by God. 7 But the very hairs of your head are all numbered. Therefore don’t be afraid. You are of more value than many sparrows.

8 “I tell you, everyone who confesses Me before men, him will the Son of Man also confess before the angels of God; 9 but he who denies Me in the presence of men will be denied in the presence of the angels of God. 10 Everyone who speaks a word against the Son of Man will be forgiven, but those who blaspheme against the Holy Spirit will not be forgiven. 11 When they bring you before the synagogues, the rulers, and the authorities, don’t be anxious how or what you will answer, or what you will say; 12 for the Holy Spirit will teach you in that same hour what you must say.”

The Parable of the Rich Fool

13 One of the multitude said to Him, “Teacher, tell my brother to
divide the inheritance with me.”

14 But He said to him, “Man, who made Me a judge or an arbitrator
over you?” 15 He said to them, “Beware! Keep yourselves from
covetousness, for a man’s life doesn’t consist of the abundance of the
things which he possesses.”

16 He spoke a parable to them, saying, “The ground of a certain rich
man produced abundantly. 17 He reasoned within himself, saying,
‘What will I do, because I don’t have room to store my crops?’ 18 He
said, ‘This is what I will do. I will pull down my barns, and build
bigger ones, and there I will store all my grain and my goods. 19 I will
tell my soul, “Soul, you have many goods laid up for many years. Take
your ease, eat, drink, and be merry.”’”

20 “But God said to him, ‘You foolish one, tonight your soul is
required of you. The things which you have prepared—whose will
they be?’ 21 So is he who lays up treasure for himself, and is not rich
toward God.”

Do Not Worry

22 He said to His disciples, “Therefore I tell you, don’t be anxious for
your life, what you will eat, nor yet for your body, what you will wear.
23 Life is more than food, and the body is more than clothing.

24 “Consider the ravens: they don’t sow, they don’t reap, they have
no warehouse or barn, and God feeds them. How much more valuable
are you than birds!

25 “Which of you by being anxious can add a cubit to his height? 26
If then you aren’t able to do even the least things, why are you anxious
about the rest?

27 “Consider the lilies, how they grow. They don’t toil, neither do
they spin; yet I tell you, even Solomon in all his glory was not arrayed
like one of these. 28 But if this is how God clothes the grass in the
field, which today exists, and tomorrow is cast into the oven, how
much more will He clothe you, O you of little faith?

29 "Don't seek what you will eat or what you will drink; neither be anxious. 30 For the nations of the world seek after all of these things, but your Father knows that you need these things. 31 But seek God's kingdom, and all these things will be added to you.

32 "Don't be afraid, little flock, for it is your Father's good pleasure to give you the Kingdom. 33 Sell that which you have, and give gifts to the needy. Make for yourselves purses which don't grow old, a treasure in the heavens that doesn't fail, where no thief approaches, neither moth destroys. 34 For where your treasure is, there will your heart be also.

The Parable of Servants at a Marriage Feast

35 "Let your waist be dressed and your lamps burning. 36 Be like men watching for their lord, when he returns from the marriage feast; that, when he comes and knocks, they may immediately open to him.

37 "Blessed are those servants, whom the lord will find watching when he comes. Most certainly I tell you, that he will dress himself, and make them recline, and will come and serve them. 38 They will be blessed if he comes in the second or third watch, and finds them so. 39 But know this, that if the master of the house had known in what hour the thief was coming, he would have watched, and not allowed his house to be broken into. 40 Therefore be ready also, for the Son of Man is coming in an hour that you don't expect Him."

41 Peter said to him, "Lord, are you telling this parable to us, or to everybody?"

Parable of Servants Waiting for Their Master

42 The Lord said, "Who then is the faithful and wise steward, whom his lord will set over his household, to give them their portion of food at the right times?

43 "Blessed is that servant whom his lord will find doing so when he comes. 44 Truly I tell you, that he will set him over all that he has. 45 But if that servant says in his heart, 'My lord delays his coming,' and begins to beat the menservants and the maidservants, and to eat and drink, and to be drunken, 46 then the lord of that servant will come in

a day when he isn't expecting him, and in an hour that he doesn't know, and will cut him in two, and place his portion with the unfaithful.

47 "That servant, who knew his lord's will, and didn't prepare, nor do what he wanted, will be beaten with many stripes, 48 but who didn't know, and did things worthy of stripes, he will be beaten with few stripes. To whomever much is given, of him will much be required; and to whom much was entrusted, of him more will be asked.

Not Peace but Division

49 "I came to throw fire on the earth. I wish it were already kindled. 50 But I have a baptism to be baptized with, and how distressed I am until it is accomplished!

51 "Do you think that I have come to give peace in the earth? I tell you, no, but rather division. 52 For from now on, there will be five in one house divided, three against two, and two against three. 53 They will be divided, father against son, and son against father; mother against daughter, and daughter against her mother; mother-in-law against her daughter-in-law, and daughter-in-law against her mother-in-law."[123]

Interpreting the Time

54 He said to the multitudes also, "When you see a cloud rising from the west, immediately you say, 'A shower is coming,' and so it happens. 55 When a south wind blows, you say, 'There will be a scorching heat,' and it happens. 56 You hypocrites! You know how to interpret the appearance of the earth and the sky, but how is it that you don't interpret this time?

57 "Why don't you judge for yourselves what is right? 58 For when you are going with your adversary before the magistrate, try diligently on the way to be released from him, lest perhaps he drag you to the judge, and the judge deliver you to the officer, and the officer throw

[123] **Micah 7:6** For the son dishonors the father, the daughter rises up against her mother, the daughter-in-law against her mother-in-law; a man's enemies are the men of his own house.

you into prison. 59 I tell you, you will by no means get out of there, until you have paid the very last penny."

Accidental Death and Sin

Luke 13:1–35

1 Now there were some present at the same time who told Him about the Galileans, whose blood Pilate had mixed with their sacrifices.[124] 2 Jesus answered them, "Do you think that these Galileans were worse sinners than all the other Galileans, because they suffered such things? 3 I tell you, no, but unless you repent, you will all perish in the same way. 4 Or those eighteen, on whom the tower in Siloam fell, and killed them; do you think that they were worse offenders than all the men who dwell in Jerusalem?[125] 5 I tell you, no, but, unless you repent, you will all perish in the same way."

Parable of the Barren Fig Tree

6 He spoke this parable. "A certain man had a fig tree planted in his vineyard, and he came seeking fruit on it, and found none. 7 He said to the vine dresser, 'Behold, these three years I have come looking for fruit on this fig tree, and found none. Cut it down. Why does it waste the soil?'

8 "He answered, 'Lord, leave it alone this year also, until I dig around it, and fertilize it. 9 If it bears fruit, fine; but if not, after that, you can cut it down.'"[126]

---

[124] *Gill's Exposition on the Entire Bible* speculates: "These Galileans were very likely some of the some of the followers of Judas Gaulonitis, or Judas of Galilee (see Acts 5:37) who endeavored to draw off the Jews from the Roman government, and affirmed it was not lawful to give tribute to Caesar; at which Pilate being enraged, sent a band of soldiers, and slew these his followers; who were come up to the feast of the Passover, as they were offering their sacrifices in the temple, and so mixed their blood with the blood of the Passover lambs."

[125] David Burges, "The Tower in Siloam," *Testimony Magazine*, October 2009, http://www.testimony-magazine.org/back/oct2009/burges2.pdf.

[126] Jesus seems to refer to **Hosea 9:10**. "I found Israel like grapes in the wilderness; I saw your fathers as the first ripe in the fig tree at her first time: His ministry had continued for three years and just a little time was left for Israel to bear fruit." (Cheney)

Woman Healed of a Spirit of Infirmity

10 He was teaching in one of the synagogues on the Sabbath day. 11 Behold, there was a woman who had a spirit of infirmity eighteen years, and she was bent over, and could in no way straighten herself up. 12 When Jesus saw her, He called her, and said to her, "Woman, you are freed from your infirmity." 13 He laid his hands on her, and immediately she stood up straight, and glorified God.

14 The ruler of the synagogue, being indignant because Jesus had healed on the Sabbath, said to the multitude, "There are six days in which men ought to work. Therefore come on those days and be healed, and not on the Sabbath day!"

15 Therefore the Lord answered him, "You hypocrites! Doesn't each one of you free his ox or his donkey from the stall on the Sabbath, and lead him away to water? 16 Ought not this woman, being a daughter of Abraham, whom Satan had bound eighteen long years, be freed from this bondage on the Sabbath day?"

17 As He said these things, all His adversaries were disappointed, and all the multitude rejoiced for all the glorious things that were done by Him.

Parable of the Mustard Seed

18 He said, "What is God's kingdom like? To what shall I compare it?

19 "It is like a grain of mustard seed, which a man took, and put in his own garden. It grew, and became a large tree, and the birds of the sky live in its branches."[127]

---

[127] **Daniel 4:11–12** The tree grew, and was strong, and its height reached to the sky, and its sight to the end of all the earth. 12 The leaves of it were beautiful, and its fruit much, and in it was food for all: the animals of the field had shadow under it, and the birds of the sky lived in its branches, and all flesh was fed from it. **Ezekiel 31:5–6** Therefore its stature was exalted above all the trees of the field; and its boughs were multiplied, and its branches became long by reason of many waters, when it spread them out. 6 All the birds of the sky made their nests in its boughs;

Parable of Yeast

20 Again He said, "To what shall I compare God's kingdom?

21 "It is like yeast, which a woman took and hid in three measures[128] of flour, until it was all leavened."

The Narrow Way

22 He went on his way through cities and villages, teaching, and traveling on to Jerusalem. 23 One said to Him, "Lord, are they few who are saved?"

He said to them, 24 "Strive to enter in by the narrow door, for many, I tell you, will seek to enter in, and will not be able. 25 When once the master of the house has risen up, and has shut the door, and you begin to stand outside, and to knock at the door, saying, 'Lord, Lord, open to us!' then He will answer and tell you, 'I don't know you or where you come from.' 26 Then you will begin to say, 'We ate and drank in Your presence, and You taught in our streets.' 27 He will say, 'I tell you, I don't know where you come from. Depart from Me, all you workers of iniquity.'[129]

28 "There will be weeping and gnashing of teeth, when you see Abraham, Isaac, Jacob, and all the prophets, in God's kingdom, and yourselves being thrown outside. 29 They will come from the east, west, north, and south, and will sit down in God's kingdom. 30 Behold, there are some who are last who will be first, and there are some who are first who will be last."

31 On that same day, some Pharisees came, saying to Him, "Get out of here, and go away, for Herod wants to kill You."

32 He said to them, "Go and tell that fox, 'Behold, I cast out demons and perform cures today and tomorrow, and the third day I complete my mission. 33 Nevertheless I must go on My way today and tomorrow and the next day, for it can't be that a prophet perish outside

[128] **Genesis 18:6** Abraham hurried into the tent to Sarah, and said, "Quickly prepare three seahs of fine meal, knead it, and make cakes." [1 seah is about 7 liters or 1.9 gallons or 0.8 pecks]
[129] **Psalm 6:8** Depart from me, all you workers of iniquity, for Yahweh has heard the voice of my weeping.

of Jerusalem.'

Jesus Laments Over Jerusalem

34 "Jerusalem, Jerusalem, that kills the prophets, and stones those who are sent to her! How often I wanted to gather your children together, like a hen gathers her own brood under her wings, and you refused! 35 Behold, your house is left to you desolate. I tell you, you will not see Me, until you say, 'Blessed is He who comes in the Name of the Lord!'"[130]

Jesus Heals a Man with Dropsy on the Sabbath

Luke 14:1–14

1 When He went into the house of one of the rulers of the Pharisees on a Sabbath to eat bread, they were watching Him. 2 Behold, a certain man who had dropsy was in front of Him. 3 Jesus, answering, spoke to the lawyers and Pharisees, saying, "Is it lawful to heal on the Sabbath?"

4 But they were silent.

He took him, and healed him, and let him go. 5 He answered them, "Which of you, if your donkey or an ox fell into a well, wouldn't immediately pull him out on a Sabbath day?"

6 They couldn't answer Him regarding these things.

The Parable of Guests at a Wedding Feast

7 He spoke a parable to those who were invited, when He noticed how they chose the best seats, and said to them, 8 "When you are invited by anyone to a marriage feast, don't sit in the best seat, since perhaps someone more honorable than you might be invited by him, 9 and he who invited both of you would come and tell you, 'Make room for this person.' Then you would begin, with shame, to take the lowest place.

10 "But when you are invited, go and sit in the lowest place, so that

[130] **Psalm 118:26** Blessed is he who comes in Yahweh's name! We have blessed you out of Yahweh's house.

when he who invited you comes, he may tell you, 'Friend, move up higher.' Then you will be honored in the presence of all who sit at the table with you. 11 For everyone who exalts himself will be humbled, and whoever humbles himself will be exalted."

12 He also said to the one who had invited Him, "When you make a dinner or a supper, don't call your friends, nor your brothers, nor your kinsmen, nor rich neighbors, or perhaps they might also return the favor, and pay you back. 13 But when you make a feast, ask the poor, the maimed, the lame, or the blind; 14 and you will be blessed, because they don't have the resources to repay you. For you will be repaid in the resurrection of the righteous."

Acts 20:35

35 Remember the words of the Lord Jesus, that He Himself said, 'It is more blessed to give than to receive.'"

The Parable of the Great Supper

Luke 14:15–35

15 When one of those who sat at the table with him heard these things, he said to Him, "Blessed is he who will feast in God's kingdom!"

16 But He said to him, "A certain man made a great supper, and he invited many people. 17 He sent out his servant at supper time to tell those who were invited, 'Come, for everything is ready now.' 18 They all as one began to make excuses.

"The first said to him, 'I have bought a field, and I must go and see it. Please have me excused.'

19 "Another said, 'I have bought five yoke of oxen, and I must go try them out. Please have me excused.'

20 "Another said, 'I have married a wife, and therefore I can't come.'

21 "That servant came, and told his lord these things. Then the master of the house, being angry, said to his servant, 'Go out quickly into the streets and lanes of the city, and bring in the poor, maimed, blind, and lame.'

22 "The servant said, 'Lord, it is done as you commanded, and there is still room.'

23 "The lord said to the servant, 'Go out into the highways and hedges, and compel them to come in, that my house may be filled. 24 For I tell you that none of those men who were invited will taste of my supper.'"

Leaving All to Follow Christ

25 Now great multitudes were going with Him. He turned and said to them, 26 "If anyone comes to Me, and doesn't disregard his own father, mother, wife, children, brothers, and sisters, yes, and his own life also, he can't be My disciple. 27 Whoever doesn't bear his own cross, and come after Me, can't be My disciple.

The Parable of the Foolish Builder

28 "For which of you, desiring to build a tower, doesn't first sit down and count the cost, to see if he has enough to complete it? 29 Or perhaps, when he has laid a foundation, and is not able to finish, everyone who sees begins to mock him, 30 saying, 'This man began to build, and wasn't able to finish.'

The Parable of the King Going to War

31 "Or what king, as he goes to encounter another king in war, will not sit down first and consider whether he is able with ten thousand to meet him who comes against him with twenty thousand? 32 Or else, while the other is yet a great way off, he sends an envoy, and asks for conditions of peace.

33 "So therefore whoever of you who doesn't renounce all that he has, he can't be My disciple.

Tasteless Salt Is Worthless

34 "Salt is good, but if the salt becomes flat and tasteless, with what do you season it? 35 It is fit neither for the soil nor for the manure pile. It is thrown out. He who has ears to hear, let him hear."

Parable of the Lost Sheep

Luke 15:1–32

1 Now all the tax collectors and sinners were coming close to Him to hear Him. 2 The Pharisees and the scribes murmured, saying, "This Man welcomes sinners, and eats with them."

3 He told them this parable. 4 "Which of you men, if you had one hundred sheep, and lost one of them, wouldn't leave the ninety-nine in the wilderness, and go after the one that was lost, until he found it? 5 When he has found it, he carries it on his shoulders, rejoicing. 6 When he comes home, he calls together his friends and his neighbors, saying to them, 'Rejoice with me, for I have found my sheep which was lost!' 7 I tell you that even so there will be more joy in heaven over one sinner who repents, than over ninety-nine righteous people who need no repentance.

The Parable of the Lost Coin

8 "Or what woman, if she had ten drachma coins, if she lost one drachma coin, wouldn't light a lamp, sweep the house, and seek diligently until she found it? 9 When she has found it, she calls together her friends and neighbors, saying, 'Rejoice with me, for I have found the drachma which I had lost.'

10 "Even so, I tell you, there is joy in the presence of the angels of God over one sinner repenting."

The Parable of the Prodigal Son

11 He said, "A certain man had two sons. 12 The younger of them said to his father, 'Father, give me my share of your property.' He divided his livelihood between them.

13 "Not many days after, the younger son gathered all of this together and traveled into a far country. There he wasted his property with riotous living. 14 When he had spent all of it, there arose a severe famine in that country, and he began to be in need. 15 He went and joined himself to one of the citizens of that country, and he sent him into his fields to feed pigs. 16 He wanted to fill his belly with the husks that the pigs ate, but no one gave him any.

17 "But when he came to himself he said, 'How many hired servants of my father's have bread enough to spare, and I'm dying with hunger!

18 I will get up and go to my father, and will tell him, "Father, I have sinned against heaven, and in your sight. 19 I am no more worthy to be called your son. Make me as one of your hired servants."'

20 "He arose, and came to his father. But while he was still far off, his father saw him, and was moved with compassion, and ran, and fell on his neck, and kissed him. 21 The son said to him, 'Father, I have sinned against heaven, and in your sight. I am no longer worthy to be called your son.'

22 "But the father said to his servants, 'Bring out the best robe, and put it on him. Put a ring on his hand, and shoes on his feet. 23 Bring the fattened calf, kill it, and let us eat, and celebrate; 24 for this, my son, was dead, and is alive again. He was lost, and is found.' They began to celebrate.

25 "Now his elder son was in the field. As he came near to the house, he heard music and dancing. 26 He called one of the servants to him, and asked what was going on. 27 He said to him, 'Your brother has come, and your father has killed the fattened calf, because he has received him back safe and healthy.'

28 But he was angry, and would not go in. Therefore his father came out, and begged him. 29 But he answered his father, 'Behold, these many years I have served you, and I never disobeyed a commandment of yours, but you never gave me a goat, that I might celebrate with my friends. 30 But when this, your son, came, who has devoured your living with prostitutes, you killed the fattened calf for him.'

31 "He said to him, 'Son, you are always with me, and all that is mine is yours. 32 But it was appropriate to celebrate and be glad, for this, your brother, was dead, and is alive again. He was lost, and is found.'"

The Parable of the Unjust Steward

Luke 16:1–31

1 He also said to His disciples, "There was a certain rich man who had a manager. An accusation was made to him that this man was wasting his possessions. 2 He called him, and said to him, 'What is this that I hear about you? Give an accounting of your management, for you can no longer be manager.'

3 “The manager said within himself, ‘What will I do, seeing that my lord is taking away the management position from me? I don’t have strength to dig. I am ashamed to beg. 4 I know what I will do, so that when I am removed from management, they may receive me into their houses.’

5 “Calling each one of his lord’s debtors to him, he said to the first, ‘How much do you owe to my lord?’

6 “He said, ‘A hundred batos [104 gallons] of oil.’

“He said to him, ‘Take your bill, and sit down quickly and write fifty.’

7 “Then he said to another, ‘How much do you owe?’

“He said, ‘A hundred cors [600 bushels] of wheat.’

“He said to him, ‘Take your bill, and write eighty.’

8 “His lord commended the dishonest manager because he had done wisely, for the children of this world are, in their own generation, wiser than the children of the light.

9 “I tell you, make for yourselves friends by means of unrighteous mammon, so that when you fail, they may receive you into the eternal tents. 10 He who is faithful in a very little is faithful also in much. He who is dishonest in a very little is also dishonest in much. 11 If therefore you have not been faithful in the unrighteous mammon, who will commit to your trust the true riches? 12 If you have not been faithful in that which is another’s, who will give you that which is your own? 13 No servant can serve two masters, for either he will hate the one, and love the other; or else he will hold to one, and despise the other. You aren’t able to serve God and Mammon.”

The Pharisees Ridicule Jesus

14 The Pharisees, who were lovers of money, also heard all these things, and they scoffed at Him.

15 He said to them, “You are those who justify yourselves in the sight of men, but God knows your hearts. For that which is exalted among men is an abomination in the sight of God.

16 “The law and the prophets were until John. From that time, the good news of God’s kingdom is preached, and everyone is forcing his

way into it. 17 But it is easier for heaven and earth to pass away, than for one tiny stroke of a pen in the law to fall. 18 Everyone who divorces his wife, and marries another, commits adultery. He who marries one who is divorced from a husband commits adultery.

The Parable of the Rich Man and Lazarus

19 "Now there was a certain rich man, and he was clothed in purple and fine linen, living in luxury every day. 20 A certain beggar, named Lazarus, was laid at his gate, full of sores, 21 and desiring to be fed with the crumbs that fell from the rich man's table. Yes, even the dogs came and licked his sores.

22 "The beggar died, and he was carried away by the angels to Abraham's bosom. The rich man also died, and was buried.

23 "In Hades, he lifted up his eyes, being in torment, and saw Abraham far off, and Lazarus at his bosom. 24 He cried and said, 'Father Abraham, have mercy on me, and send Lazarus, that he may dip the tip of his finger in water, and cool my tongue! For I am in anguish in this flame.'

25 "But Abraham said, 'Son, remember that you, in your lifetime, received your good things, and Lazarus, in the same way, bad things. But now here he is comforted and you are in anguish. 26 Besides all this, between us and you there is a great gulf fixed, that those who want to pass from here to you are not able, and that no one may cross over from there to us.'

27 "He said, 'I ask you therefore, father, that you would send him to my father's house; 28 for I have five brothers, that he may testify to them, so they won't also come into this place of torment.'

29 "But Abraham said to him, 'They have Moses and the prophets. Let them listen to them.'

30 "He said, 'No, father Abraham, but if one goes to them from the dead, they will repent.'

31 "He said to him, 'If they don't listen to Moses and the prophets, neither will they be persuaded if one rises from the dead.'"

Sin, Faith, and Duty

Luke 17:1–37

1 He said to the disciples, "It is impossible that no occasions of stumbling should come, but woe to him through whom they come! 2 It would be better for him if a millstone were hung around his neck, and he were thrown into the sea, rather than that he should cause one of these little ones to stumble.

3 "Be careful. If your brother sins against you, rebuke him. If he repents, forgive him. 4 If he sins against you seven times in the day, and seven times returns, saying, 'I repent,' you shall forgive him."

5 The apostles said to the Lord, "Increase our faith."

6 The Lord said, "If you had faith like a grain of mustard seed, you would tell this sycamore tree, 'Be uprooted, and be planted in the sea,' and it would obey you.

7 "But who is there among you, having a servant plowing or keeping sheep, that will say, when he comes in from the field, 'Come immediately and sit down at the table,' 8 and will not rather tell him, 'Prepare my supper, clothe yourself properly, and serve me, while I eat and drink. Afterward you shall eat and drink?'

9 "Does he thank that servant because he did the things that were commanded? I think not. 10 Even so you also, when you have done all the things that are commanded you, say, 'We are unworthy servants. We have done our duty.'"

Jesus Heals Ten of Leprosy

11 As He was on His way to Jerusalem, He was passing along the borders of Samaria and Galilee. 12 As He entered into a certain village, ten men who were lepers met him, who stood at a distance. 13 They lifted up their voices, saying, "Jesus, Master, have mercy on us!"

14 When He saw them, He said to them, "Go and show yourselves to the priests."

As they went, they were cleansed. 15 One of them, when he saw that he was healed, turned back, glorifying God with a loud voice. 16 He fell on his face at Jesus's feet, giving Him thanks; and he was a

Samaritan.

17 Jesus answered, "Weren't the ten cleansed? But where are the nine? 18 Were there none found who returned to give glory to God, except this stranger?"

19 Then He said to him, "Get up, and go your way. Your faith has healed you."

The Coming of the Kingdom of God

20 Being asked by the Pharisees when God's kingdom would come, He answered them, "God's kingdom doesn't come with observation; 21 neither will they say, 'Look, here!' or, 'Look, there!' for behold, God's kingdom is among you."

22 He said to the disciples, "The days will come, when you will desire to see one of the days of the Son of Man, and you will not see it. 23 They will tell you, 'Look, here!' or 'Look, there!' Don't go away, nor follow after them, 24 for as the lightning, when it flashes out of the one part under the sky, shines to the other part under the sky; so will the Son of Man be in His day. 25 But first, He must suffer many things and be rejected by this generation.

26 "As it was in the days of Noah, even so will it be also in the days of the Son of Man. 27 They ate, they drank, they married, they were given in marriage, until the day that Noah entered into the ship, and the flood came, and destroyed them all.

28 "Likewise, even as it was in the days of Lot: they ate, they drank, they bought, they sold, they planted, they built; 29 but in the day that Lot went out from Sodom, it rained fire and sulfur from the sky, and destroyed them all. 30 It will be the same way in the day that the Son of Man is revealed.

31 "In that day, he who will be on the housetop, and his goods in the house, let him not go down to take them away. Let him who is in the field likewise not turn back. 32 Remember Lot's wife!

33 "Whoever seeks to save his life loses it, but whoever loses his life preserves it. 34 I tell you, in that night there will be two people in one bed. The one will be taken, and the other will be left. 35 There will be two grinding grain together. One will be taken, and the other will be

left. 36 Two will be in the field: the one taken, and the other left."

37 They, answering, asked him, "Where, Lord?"

He said to them, "Where the body is, there will the vultures also be gathered together."[131]

The Parable of the Persistent Widow

Luke 18:1–14

1 He also spoke a parable to them that they must always pray, and not give up, 2 saying, "There was a judge in a certain city who didn't fear God, and didn't respect man. 3 A widow was in that city, and she often came to him, saying, 'Defend me from my adversary!'

4 He wouldn't for a while, but afterward he said to himself, 'Though I neither fear God, nor respect man, 5 yet because this widow bothers me, I will defend her, or else she will wear me out by her continual coming.'"

6 The Lord said, "Listen to what the unrighteous judge says. 7 Won't God avenge His chosen ones, who are crying out to Him day and night, and yet He exercises patience with them? 8 I tell you that He will avenge them quickly. Nevertheless, when the Son of Man comes, will He find faith on the earth?"

The Parable of the Pharisee and the Tax Collector

9 He spoke also this parable to certain people who were convinced of their own righteousness, and who despised all others. 10 "Two men went up into the temple to pray; one was a Pharisee, and the other was a tax collector. 11 The Pharisee stood and prayed to himself like this: 'God, I thank you, that I am not like the rest of men, extortionists, unrighteous, adulterers, or even like this tax collector. 12 I fast twice a week. I give tithes of all that I get.'

13 "But the tax collector, standing far away, wouldn't even lift up his

---

[131] **Job 39:27** Does the eagle mount up at your command, And make its nest on high? **28** On the rock it dwells and resides, on the crag of the rock and the stronghold. **29** From there it spies out the prey; Its eyes observe from afar. **30** Its young ones suck up blood; and where the slain *are,* there it *is.*"

eyes to heaven, but beat his breast, saying, 'God, be merciful to me, a sinner!'

14 "I tell you, this man went down to his house justified rather than the other; for everyone who exalts himself will be humbled, but he who humbles himself will be exalted."

Jesus at the Feast of Dedication

John 10:22–39

22 It was the Feast of the Dedication[132] at Jerusalem. 23 It was winter, and Jesus was walking in the temple, in Solomon's porch. 24 The Jews therefore came around Him and said to Him, "How long will You hold us in suspense? If You are the Christ, tell us plainly."

25 Jesus answered them, "I told you, and you don't believe. The works that I do in my Father's name, these testify about Me. 26 But you don't believe, because you are not of My sheep, as I told you. 27 My sheep hear My voice, and I know them, and they follow Me. 28 I give eternal life to them. They will never perish, and no one will snatch them out of My hand. 29 My Father, who has given them to Me, is greater than all. No one is able to snatch them out of My Father's hand. 30 I and the Father are one."

31 Therefore Jews took up stones again to stone Him.

32 Jesus answered them, "I have shown you many good works from My Father. For which of those works do you stone Me?"

33 The Jews answered Him, "We don't stone You for a good work, but for blasphemy: because You, being a man, make Yourself God."

34 Jesus answered them, "Isn't it written in your law, 'I said, you are gods?'[133] 35 If He called them gods, to whom the word of God came (and the Scripture can't be broken), 36 do you say of Him Whom the Father sanctified and sent into the world, 'You blaspheme,' because I said, 'I am the Son of God?'

37 "If I don't do the works of My Father, don't believe Me. 38 But if

[132] The "Feast of the Dedication" is the Greek name for "Hanukkah," a celebration of the rededication of the Temple.
[133] **Psalm 82:6** I said, "You are gods, all of you are sons of the Most High."

I do them, though you don't believe Me, believe the works; that you may know and believe that the Father is in Me, and I in the Father."

39 They sought again to seize Him, and He went out of their hand.

Jesus Crosses the Jordan

John 10:40–42; Mark 10:1; Matthew 19:1–2

40 He went away again beyond the Jordan into 1 the borders of Judea and beyond the Jordan, 40 where John was baptizing at first, and there He stayed.

1 Multitudes came together to Him again, [and] 2 great multitudes followed Him, and He healed them there. 2 As He usually did, He was again teaching them. 41 Many came to Him, They said, "John indeed did no sign, but everything that John said about this Man is true." 42 Many believed in Him there.

Marriage and Divorce

Matthew 19:3–12; Mark 10:2–12

3 Pharisees came to him, testing Him, and saying, "Is it lawful for a man to divorce his wife for any reason?"

3 He answered, "What did Moses command you?"

4 They said, "Moses allowed a certificate of divorce to be written, and to divorce her."[134]

5 But Jesus said to them, "For your hardness of heart, he wrote you this commandment. 4 Haven't you read that He Who made them from the beginning 6 of the creation, God 4 'made them male and female,'[135] 5 and said, 'For this cause a man shall leave his father and

[134] **Deuteronomy 24:1** When a man takes a wife and marries her, then it shall be, if she finds no favor in his eyes, because he has found some unseemly thing in her, that he shall write her a bill of divorce, and put it in her hand, and send her out of his house.

[135] **Genesis 1:27** God created man in His own image. In God's image He created him; male and female he created them. **Genesis 5:2** He created them male and female, and blessed them. On the day they were created, He named them "Adam" ["Adam" and "Man" are spelled with the exact same consonants in Hebrew, so this can be correctly translated either way.]

mother, and shall join to his wife; and the two shall become one flesh?'[136] 6 So that they are no more two, but one flesh. What therefore God has joined together, don't let man tear apart."

7 They asked Him, "Why then did Moses command us to give her a bill of divorce, and divorce her?"

8 He said to them, "Moses, because of the hardness of your hearts, allowed you to divorce your wives, but from the beginning it has not been so.

10 In the house, His disciples asked Him again about the same matter.

11 He said to them, 9 "I tell you that whoever divorces his wife, except for sexual immorality, and marries another, commits adultery; and he who marries her when she is divorced commits adultery. 12 If a woman herself divorces her husband, and marries another, she commits adultery."

10 His disciples said to him, "If this is the case of the man with his wife, it is not expedient to marry."

11 But He said to them, "Not all men can receive this saying, but those to whom it is given. 12 For there are eunuchs who were born that way from their mother's womb, and there are eunuchs who were made eunuchs by men; and there are eunuchs who made themselves eunuchs for the Kingdom of Heaven's sake. He who is able to receive it, let him receive it."

Jesus Blesses Little Children

Luke 18:15–17; Mark 10:13–16; Matthew 19:13–15

15 They were also bringing their babies to Him, [and] 13 little children, that He 15 might touch them, 13 lay his hands on them and pray. 15 But when the disciples saw it, they rebuked them, 13 those who were bringing them.

14 But when Jesus saw it, he was moved with indignation. 16 Jesus summoned them, 14 and said to them, 16 saying, "Allow the little children to come to me, and don't hinder them, for God's kingdom

---

[136] **Genesis 2:24** Therefore a man will leave his father and his mother, and will join with his wife, and they will be one flesh.

belongs to such as these. 17 Most certainly, I tell you, whoever doesn't receive God's kingdom like a little child, he will in no way enter into it." 16 He took them in His arms, and blessed them, laying His hands on them, 15 and departed from there.

The Death of Lazarus

John 11:1–54

1 Now a certain man was sick, Lazarus from Bethany, of the village of Mary and her sister, Martha. 2 It was that Mary who had anointed the Lord with ointment, and wiped His feet with her hair, whose brother, Lazarus, was sick. 3 The sisters therefore sent to Him, saying, "Lord, behold, he for whom You have great affection is sick."

4 But when Jesus heard it, he said, "This sickness is not to death, but for the glory of God, that God's Son may be glorified by it."

5 Now Jesus loved Martha, and her sister, and Lazarus. 6 When therefore He heard that he was sick, He stayed two days in the place where He was. 7 Then after this He said to the disciples, "Let's go into Judea again."

8 The disciples told him, "Rabbi, the Jews were just trying to stone You, and are You going there again?"

9 Jesus answered, "Aren't there twelve hours of daylight? If a man walks in the day, he doesn't stumble, because he sees the light of this world. 10 But if a man walks in the night, he stumbles, because the light isn't in him."

11 He said these things, and after that, He said to them, "Our friend, Lazarus, has fallen asleep, but I am going so that I may awake him out of sleep."

12 The disciples therefore said, "Lord, if he has fallen asleep, he will recover."

13 Now Jesus had spoken of his death, but they thought that He spoke of taking rest in sleep. 14 So Jesus said to them plainly then, "Lazarus is dead. 15 I am glad for your sakes that I was not there, so that you may believe. Nevertheless, let's go to him."

16 Thomas therefore, who is called Didymus, said to his fellow

disciples, "Let's go also, that we may die with Him."

I am the Resurrection and the Life

17 So when Jesus came, He found that he had been in the tomb four
days already. 18 Now Bethany was near Jerusalem, about fifteen
stadia [1.7 miles] away. 19 Many of the Jews had joined the women
around Martha and Mary, to console them concerning their brother.
20 Then when Martha heard that Jesus was coming, she went and met
Him, but Mary stayed in the house.

21 Therefore Martha said to Jesus, "Lord, if You would have been
here, my brother wouldn't have died. 22 Even now I know that,
whatever You ask of God, God will give You."

23 Jesus said to her, "Your brother will rise again."

24 Martha said to Him, "I know that he will rise again in the
resurrection at the last day."

25 Jesus said to her, "I am the resurrection and the life. He who
believes in Me will still live, even if he dies. 26 Whoever lives and
believes in Me will never die. Do you believe this?"

27 She said to him, "Yes, Lord. I have come to believe that You are
the Christ, God's Son, He who comes into the world."

28 When she had said this, she went away, and called Mary, her sister,
secretly, saying, "The Teacher is here, and is calling you."

29 When she heard this, she arose quickly, and went to Him. 30 Now
Jesus had not yet come into the village, but was in the place where
Martha met him. 31 Then the Jews who were with her in the house,
and were consoling her, when they saw Mary, that she rose up quickly
and went out, followed her, saying, "She is going to the tomb to weep
there."

32 Therefore when Mary came to where Jesus was, and saw Him, she
fell down at his feet, saying to him, "Lord, if You would have been
here, my brother wouldn't have died."

33 When Jesus therefore saw her weeping, and the Jews weeping who
came with her, He groaned in the spirit, and was troubled, 34 and said,
"Where have you laid him?"

They told Him, "Lord, come and see."

35 Jesus wept.

36 The Jews therefore said, "See how much affection He had for him!"

37 Some of them said, "Couldn't this man, who opened the eyes of him who was blind, have also kept this man from dying?"

38 Jesus therefore, again groaning in Himself, came to the tomb. Now it was a cave, and a stone lay against it. 39 Jesus said, "Take away the stone."

Martha, the sister of him who was dead, said to Him, "Lord, by this time there is a stench, for he has been dead four days."

40 Jesus said to her, "Didn't I tell you that if you believed, you would see God's glory?"

41 So they took away the stone from the place where the dead man was lying. Jesus lifted up his eyes, and said, "Father, I thank You that You listened to Me. 42 I know that You always listen to Me, but because of the multitude that stands around I said this, that they may believe that You sent Me." 43 When he had said this, He cried with a loud voice, "Lazarus, come out!"

44 He who was dead came out, bound hand and foot with wrappings, and his face was wrapped around with a cloth.

Jesus said to them, "Free him, and let him go."

The Plot to Kill Jesus

45 Therefore many of the Jews, who came to Mary and saw what Jesus did, believed in Him. 46 But some of them went away to the Pharisees, and told them the things which Jesus had done. 47 The chief priests therefore and the Pharisees gathered a council, and said, "What are we doing? For this Man does many signs. 48 If we leave Him alone like this, everyone will believe in Him, and the Romans will come and take away both our place and our nation."

49 But a certain one of them, Caiaphas, being high priest that year, said to them, "You know nothing at all, 50 nor do you consider that it is advantageous for us that one man should die for the people, and that the whole nation not perish."

51 Now he didn't say this of himself, but being high priest that year, he prophesied that Jesus would die for the nation,[137] 52 and not for the nation only, but that He might also gather together into one the children of God who are scattered abroad.[138]

53 So from that day forward they took counsel that they might put Him to death. 54 Jesus therefore walked no more openly among the Jews, but departed from there into the country near the wilderness, to a city called Ephraim. He stayed there with his disciples.

Jesus Counsels the Rich Young Ruler

Mark 10:17–22; Matthew 19:16-22; Luke 18:18–23

17 As he was going out into the way, 18 a certain ruler 17 ran to him, knelt before Him, and asked Him, "Good Teacher, what 16 good thing 17 shall I do that I may inherit eternal life?"

18 Jesus said to him, "Why do you call me good? No one is good except one—God. 17 But if you want to enter into life, keep the commandments."

18 He said to him, "Which ones?"

Jesus said, "'You shall not murder.' 'You shall not commit adultery.' 'You shall not steal.' 'You shall not offer false testimony.' 19 'Honor your father and mother'[139] 19 And, 'You shall love your neighbor as

---

[137] **Isaiah 53:8** He was taken away by oppression and judgment; and as for His generation, who considered that He was cut off out of the land of the living and stricken for the disobedience of my people?

[138] **Isaiah 49:6** "Indeed," he says, "It is too light a thing that You should be My servant to raise up the tribes of Jacob, and to restore the preserved of Israel? I will also give you as a light to the nations, that You may be My salvation to the end of the earth."

[139] **Exodus 20:12–16** "Honor your father and your mother, that your days may be long in the land which Yahweh your God gives you. 13 You shall not murder. 14 You shall not commit adultery. 15 You shall not steal. 16 You shall not give false testimony against your neighbor." **Deuteronomy 5:16–20** "Honor your father and your mother, as Yahweh your God commanded you; that your days may be long, and that it may go well with you, in the land which Yahweh your God gives you. 17 You shall not murder. 18 You shall not commit adultery. 19 You shall not steal. 20 You shall not give false testimony against your neighbor."

yourself.'"[140]

20 The young man said to Him, 20 "Teacher, I have observed all these things from my youth. 20 What do I still lack?"

21 Jesus looking at him loved him, and 22 when Jesus heard these things, He said to him, 21 "One thing you 22 still lack. 21 If you want to be perfect, 21 go, sell whatever you have, and give to the poor, and you will have treasure in heaven; and come, follow Me, taking up the cross."

22 But when the young man heard the saying, he went away sad, [and] 23 very sorrowful, 22 for he was one who had great possessions, [and] 23 he was very rich.

With God All Things Are Possible

Luke 18:24–27; Mark 10:23–27; Matthew 19:23–26

24 Jesus, seeing that he became very sad, 23 Jesus looked around, and said to His disciples, "How difficult it is for those who have riches to enter into God's kingdom!"

24 The disciples were amazed at His words. But Jesus answered again, "Children, 23 most certainly I say to you, 24 how hard is it for 23 a rich man, 24 those who trust in riches to enter into God's kingdom! 24 Again I tell you, 25 it is easier for a camel to go through a needle's eye than for a rich man to enter into God's kingdom."

26 They were exceedingly astonished, 26 saying to Him, "Then who can be saved?"

27 Jesus, looking at them, said, "With men it is impossible, but not with God. 2 The things which are impossible with men are possible with God 27 for all things are possible with God."[141]

---

[140] **Leviticus 19:18** "'You shall not take vengeance, nor bear any grudge against the children of your people; but you shall love your neighbor as yourself. I am Yahweh."
[141] **Genesis 18:14** "Is anything too hard for Yahweh? At the set time I will return to you, when the season comes round, and Sarah will have a son." **Jeremiah 32:17** Ah Lord Yahweh! Behold, you have made the heavens and the earth by your great power and by your outstretched arm; there is nothing too hard for you.

Possessions and the Kingdom of God

Matthew 19:27–30; Mark 10:28–31; Luke 18:24–30

Then Peter answered 28 [and] began to tell Him 27, "Behold, we have left everything, and followed You. What then will we have?"

28 Jesus 29 answered and 28 said to them, "Most certainly I tell you that you who have followed Me, in the regeneration when the Son of Man will sit on the throne of His glory, you also will sit on twelve thrones, judging the twelve tribes of Israel."

29 Jesus said, "Most certainly I tell you, there is no one who has left house, or brothers, or sisters, or father, or mother, or wife, or children, or land, for My sake, and for the sake of the good news, 29 for My name's sake, [and] 29 for God's kingdom's sake, 30 who shall not receive 30 many times more—30 one hundred times more now in this time—30 houses, brothers, sisters, mothers, children, and land, with persecutions; and in the age to come 29 will inherit eternal life. 30 But many will be last who are first; and first who are last.

The Parable of the Workers in the Vineyard

Matthew 20:1–16

1 "For the Kingdom of Heaven is like a man who was the master of a household, who went out early in the morning to hire laborers for his vineyard. 2 When he had agreed with the laborers for a denarius a day, he sent them into his vineyard. 3 He went out about the third hour,[9:00 a.m.] and saw others standing idle in the marketplace. 4 He said to them, 'You also go into the vineyard, and whatever is right I will give you.' So they went their way. 5 Again he went out about the sixth [noon] and the ninth hour, [3:00 p.m.] and did likewise. 6 About the eleventh hour [5:00 p.m.] he went out, and found others standing idle. He said to them, 'Why do you stand here all day idle?'

7 "They said to him, 'Because no one has hired us.'

"He said to them, 'You also go into the vineyard, and you will receive whatever is right.' 8 When evening had come, the lord of the vineyard said to his manager, 'Call the laborers and pay them their wages, beginning from the last to the first.'

9 "When those who were hired at about the eleventh hour came, they each received a denarius. 10 When the first came, they supposed that they would receive more; and they likewise each received a denarius. 11 When they received it, they murmured against the master of the household, 12 saying, 'These last have spent one hour, and you have made them equal to us, who have borne the burden of the day and the scorching heat!'

13 "But he answered one of them, 'Friend, I am doing you no wrong. Didn't you agree with me for a denarius? 14 Take that which is yours, and go your way. It is my desire to give to this last just as much as to you. 15 Isn't it lawful for me to do what I want to with what I own? Or is your eye evil, because I am good?' 16 So the last will be first, and the first last. For many are called, but few are chosen."

Jesus's Third Prediction of His Death

Mark 10:32–34; Matthew 20:17–19; Luke 18:31–34

32 They were on the way, going up to Jerusalem; and Jesus was going in front of them, and they were amazed; and those who followed were afraid. He again took the twelve 31 aside 17 and on the way He 32 began to tell them the things that were going to happen to Him.

31 He took the twelve aside and said to them, 33 "Behold, we are going up to Jerusalem 31 and all the things that are written through the prophets concerning the Son of Man will be completed. 32 For 33 the Son of Man will be 18 delivered to the chief priests and scribes, and they will condemn Him to death, 19 and will hand Him over to the Gentiles 34 They will mock Him, 32 treat [Him] shamefully, 34 spit on Him, scourge Him, 19 and crucify 34 and kill Him. 19 And 34 on the third day 19 He will be raised up 34 [and] He will rise again."

34 They understood none of these things. This saying was hidden from them, and they didn't understand the things that were said.

Greatness Is Serving

Matthew 20:20–28; Mark 10:35–45

35 Then the mother of the sons of Zebedee came to him with her sons, 35 James and John, 20 kneeling and asking a certain thing of Him.

35 The sons of Zebedee, came near to Him, saying, "Teacher, we want you to do for us whatever we will ask."

36 He said to them, "What do you want Me to do for you?"

37 They said to Him, "Grant to us that we may sit, one at Your right hand, and one at Your left hand, in Your glory."

21 He said to her, "What do you want?"

She said to Him, "Command that these, my two sons, may sit, one on Your right hand, and one on Your left hand, in Your Kingdom."

22 But Jesus answered, "You don't know what you are asking. Are you able to drink the cup that I am about to drink, and be baptized with the baptism that I am baptized with?"

They said to him, "We are able."

23 He said to them, "You will indeed drink My cup, and be baptized with the baptism that I am baptized with, but to sit on My right hand and on My left hand is not Mine to give; but it is for whom it has been prepared by My Father."

24 When the ten heard it, they were indignant with the two brothers,
41 James and John.

25 But Jesus summoned them, and said, "You know that the 42 they who are recognized as 25 rulers of the nations lord it over them, and their great ones exercise authority over them. 26 It shall not be so among you, but whoever desires to become great among you shall be your servant. 27 Whoever desires to be first among you shall be your bondservant, 28 even as the Son of Man came not to be served, but to serve, and to give His life as a ransom for many."

Jesus Approaching Jericho, Heals a Blind Beggar

Luke 18:35–43

35 As He came near Jericho, a certain blind man sat by the road, begging. 36 Hearing a multitude going by, he asked what this meant. 37 They told him that Jesus of Nazareth was passing by. 38 He cried out, "Jesus, You son of David, have mercy on me!" 39 Those who led the way rebuked him, that he should be quiet; but he cried out all the more, "You son of David, have mercy on me!"

40 Standing still, Jesus commanded him to be brought to Him. When he had come near, He asked him, 41 "What do you want Me to do?"

He said, "Lord, that I may see again."

42 Jesus said to him, "Receive your sight. Your faith has healed you."

43 Immediately he received his sight, and followed Him, glorifying God. All the people, when they saw it, praised God.

Jesus Comes to Zacchaeus's House

Mark 10:46; Luke 19:1–10

They came to Jericho 1 He entered and was passing through Jericho. 2 There was a man named Zacchaeus. He was a chief tax collector, and he was rich. 3 He was trying to see who Jesus was, and couldn't because of the crowd, because he was short. 4 He ran on ahead, and climbed up into a sycamore tree to see Him, for He was going to pass that way.

5 When Jesus came to the place, He looked up and saw him, and said to him, "Zacchaeus, hurry and come down, for today I must stay at your house."

6 He hurried, came down, and received Him joyfully.

7 When they saw it, they all murmured, saying, "He has gone in to lodge with a man who is a sinner."

8 Zacchaeus stood and said to the Lord, "Behold, Lord, half of my goods I give to the poor. If I have wrongfully exacted anything of anyone, I restore four times as much."

9 Jesus said to him, "Today, salvation has come to this house, because he also is a son of Abraham. 10 For the Son of Man came to seek and to save that which was lost."

The Parable of the Minas (Pounds)

Luke 19:11–28

11 As they heard these things, He went on and told a parable, because He was near Jerusalem, and they supposed that God's kingdom would be revealed immediately. 12 He said therefore, "A certain nobleman

went into a far country to receive for himself a kingdom, and to return. 13 He called ten servants of his, and gave them ten mina coins, and told them, 'Conduct business until I come.' 14 But his citizens hated him, and sent an envoy after him, saying, 'We don't want this man to reign over us.'

15 "When he had come back again, having received the kingdom, he commanded these servants, to whom he had given the money, to be called to him, that he might know what they had gained by conducting business. 16 The first came before him, saying, 'Lord, your mina has made ten more minas.'

17 "He said to him, 'Well done, you good servant! Because you were found faithful with very little, you shall have authority over ten cities.'

18 "The second came, saying, 'Your mina, Lord, has made five minas.'

19 "So he said to him, 'And you are to be over five cities.'

20 "Another came, saying, 'Lord, behold, your mina, which I kept laid away in a handkerchief, 21 for I feared you, because you are an exacting man. You take up that which you didn't lay down, and reap that which you didn't sow.'

22 "He said to him, 'Out of your own mouth will I judge you, you wicked servant! You knew that I am an exacting man, taking up that which I didn't lay down, and reaping that which I didn't sow. 23 Then why didn't you deposit my money in the bank, and at my coming, I might have earned interest on it?' 24 He said to those who stood by, 'Take the mina away from him, and give it to him who has the ten minas.'

25 "They said to him, 'Lord, he has ten minas!'

26 "'For I tell you that to everyone who has, will more be given; but from him who doesn't have, even that which he has will be taken away from him. 27 But bring those enemies of mine who didn't want me to reign over them here, and kill them before me.'"

28 Having said these things, He went on ahead, going up to Jerusalem.

Jesus Heals Two Blind Men as He Leaves Jericho

Mark 10:46–52; Matthew 20:29–34

46 As He went out from Jericho, with his disciples and a great 29 multitude followed Him. 30 Behold, two blind men sitting by the road, [One was] 46 the son of Timaeus, Bartimaeus, a blind beggar, was sitting by the road. 47 When he heard that it was Jesus the Nazarene, he began to cry out, and say, Jesus, You son of David, have mercy on me!" 30 When they heard that Jesus was passing by, cried out, "Lord, have mercy on us, You son of David!"

48 Many 31 [of the] multitude rebuked them, telling them that they should be quiet, but they cried out even more, "Lord, have mercy on us, You son of David! 48 "Have mercy on me!"

49 Jesus stood still, and said, "Call him."

They called the blind man, [men], 49 saying to him, [them], "Cheer up! Get up. He is calling you!" 50 [They] He, casting away his cloak, sprang up, and came to Jesus.

51 Jesus asked him, [them] "What do you want me to do for you?"

The blind man 33 They 51 said to Him, "Rabboni,[142] 33 "Lord, that our eyes may be opened [and we] 51 may see again."

34 Jesus, being moved with compassion, touched their eyes; 52 Jesus said to him [them as they] he received his sight, "Go your way. Your faith has made you well."

34 And immediately their eyes received their sight, and they followed 52 Jesus on the way.

---

[142] *Rabboni* is a transliteration of the Hebrew word for "great teacher."

The Last Passover of Jesus's Ministry

The Fourth Passover Approaches

John 11:55–57

55 Now the Passover[143] of the Jews was at hand. Many went up from the country to Jerusalem before the Passover, to purify themselves. 56 Then they sought for Jesus and spoke one with another, as they stood in the temple, "What do you think—that He isn't coming to the feast at all?"

57 Now the chief priests and the Pharisees had commanded that if anyone knew where He was, he should report it, that they might seize Him.

The Anointing at Bethany Nisan 9

John 12:1–8; Matthew 26:6–13; Mark 14:3–9

1 Then six days before the Passover, Jesus came to Bethany, where Lazarus was, who had been dead, whom he raised from the dead. 6 Now when Jesus was in Bethany, in the house of Simon the leper, 2 they made Him a supper there. Martha served, but Lazarus was one of those who sat at the table with Him.

3 As He sat at the table, a woman came 7 to Him 3 having an alabaster jar of ointment of 7 very expensive, 3 very costly 7 ointment, 3 pure

---

[143] **Exodus 12:3–6** 3 Speak to all the congregation of Israel, saying, 'On the tenth day of this month, they shall take to them every man a lamb, according to their fathers' houses, a lamb for a household; 4 and if the household is too little for a lamb, then he and his neighbor next to his house shall take one according to the number of the souls; according to what everyone can eat you shall make your count for the lamb. 5 Your lamb shall be without defect, a male a year old. You shall take it from the sheep, or from the goats: 6 and you shall keep it until the fourteenth day of the same month; and the whole assembly of the congregation of Israel shall kill it at evening.' **Leviticus 23:4-5** "'These are the set feasts of Yahweh, even holy convocations, which you shall proclaim in their appointed season. [5] In the first month, on the fourteenth day of the month in the evening, is Yahweh's Passover.

nard.

3 Then Mary took a pound of very costly oil of spikenard, 7 And she 3 broke the jar, and 7 poured it on His head as He sat at the table 3 and anointed the feet of Jesus, and wiped His feet with her hair. The house was filled with the fragrance of the ointment.

8 But when His disciples saw this, 4 there were some who were indignant among themselves, saying, "Why has this ointment been wasted? 8 Why this waste? 9 For this ointment might have been sold for much, 5 more than three hundred denarii, 9 and given to the poor." 5 They grumbled against her.

4 Then Judas Iscariot, Simon's son, one of his disciples, who would betray Him, said, 5 "Why wasn't this ointment sold for three hundred denarii, and given to the poor?"

6 Now he said this, not because he cared for the poor, but because he was a thief, and having the money box, used to steal what was put into it.

10 However, knowing this, Jesus said to them, 6 "Leave her alone. 10 Why do you trouble the woman? Because she has done a good work for Me. 11 For you always have the poor with you;7 and whenever you want to, you can do them good; 11 but you don't always have Me. 8 She has done what she could. She has anointed My body beforehand for the burying. 12 For in pouring this ointment on My body, she did it to prepare Me for burial. 13 Most certainly I tell you, wherever this good news is preached in the whole world, what this woman has done will also be spoken of as a memorial of her."

The Plot to Kill Lazarus

John 12:9–11

9 A large crowd therefore of the Jews learned that He was there, and they came, not for Jesus's sake only, but that they might see Lazarus also, whom He had raised from the dead. 10 But the chief priests conspired to put Lazarus to death also, 11 because on account of him many of the Jews went away and believed in Jesus.

Jesus's Triumphal Entry Into Jerusalem – Nisan 10

John 12:12–19; Matthew 21:1–16; Mark 11:1–14; Luke 19:29–48

12 On the next day 1 when they came near to Jerusalem, and came to
Bethphage, 1 and Bethany, 1 to the Mount of Olives, then Jesus sent
two disciples, 2 saying to them, "Go into the village that is opposite
you. 2 Immediately as you enter into it, 2 you will find a donkey tied,
and a colt 30 tied 2 with her, 2 on which no one has 30 ever yet sat 2
Untie them, and bring them to Me. 3 If anyone says anything to you,
[like] 3 'Why are you doing this?' 3 you shall say, 'The Lord needs
them,' and immediately he will send them 3 back here."

4 All this was done, that it might be fulfilled which was spoken
through the prophet, saying,

> 5 "Tell the daughter of Zion, 14 'Don't be afraid, daughter of
> Zion; 5 behold, your King comes to you, humble, and riding on a
> donkey, on a 15 donkey's 5 colt, the foal of a donkey.'"[144]

5 The disciples went 4 away, 6 and did just as Jesus commanded them,
32 and found things just as He had told them. [They] 4 found a young
donkey tied at the door outside in the open street, and they untied him.

33 As they were untying the colt, 5 some of those who stood there, 33
its owners, 5 asked them, "What are you doing? 33 Why are you
untying the colt, 5 the young donkey?"

6 They said to them just as Jesus had said, 34 "The Lord needs it," 6
and they let them go.

7 They brought the donkey and the colt, 7 to Jesus, 7 and laid their
clothes on them; and He sat on them, 7 and Jesus sat on 14 a young
donkey. 36 As He went, they [and] 8 a very great multitude spread
their clothes on the road. 36 spread their cloaks on the road. 8 Others
cut branches from the trees, and spread them on the road.

37 As he was now getting near, at the descent of the Mount of Olives,
the whole multitude of the disciples, 9 the multitudes who went in
front of him, and those who followed, [and] 12 a great multitude had

---

[144] **Zechariah 9:9** Rejoice greatly, daughter of Zion! Shout, daughter of Jerusalem! Behold, your King comes to you! He is righteous, and having salvation; lowly, and riding on a donkey, even on a colt, the foal of a donkey.

come to the feast. When they heard that Jesus was coming to Jerusalem, 13 they took the branches of the palm trees, and went out to meet him, and cried out, [and] kept shouting, [and] 37 began to rejoice and praise God with a loud voice for all the mighty works which they had seen, 38 saying,

13 "Hosanna![145] 9 Hosanna to the son of David! Blessed is he who comes in the name of the Lord![146] 13 the King of Israel[147] 38 Blessed is the King who comes in the name of the Lord![148] 10 Blessed is the kingdom of our father David that is coming in the name of the Lord! 38 Peace in heaven, and glory in the highest! 9 Hosanna in the highest!"

16 His disciples didn't understand these things at first, but when Jesus was glorified, then they remembered that these things were written about Him, and that they had done these things to Him.

17 The multitude therefore that was with Him when He called Lazarus out of the tomb, and raised him from the dead, was testifying about it. 18 For this cause also the multitude went and met Him, because they heard that He had done this sign.

39 Some of the Pharisees from the multitude said to Him, "Teacher, rebuke Your disciples!"

40 He answered them, "I tell you that if these were silent, the stones would cry out.

19 The Pharisees therefore said among themselves, "See how you accomplish nothing. Behold, the world has gone after Him."

41 When He came near, He saw the city and wept over it, 42 saying, "If you, even you, had known today the things which belong to your peace! But now, they are hidden from your eyes. 43 For the days will

---

[145] "Hosanna" means "save us" or "help us, we pray."

[146] **Psalm 118:26** Blessed is he who comes in Yahweh's name! We have blessed you out of Yahweh's house.

[147] **Isaiah 44:6** This is what Yahweh, the King of Israel, and his Redeemer, Yahweh of Armies, says: "I am the first, and I am the last; and besides me there is no God. **Zephaniah 3:15** Yahweh has taken away your judgments. He has thrown out your enemy. The King of Israel, Yahweh, is among you. You will not be afraid of evil any more.

[148] **Psalm 118:26** Ibid.

come on you, when your enemies will throw up a barricade against you, surround you, hem you in on every side, 44 and will dash you and your children within you to the ground. They will not leave in you one stone on another, because you didn't know the time of your visitation."

10 When He had come into Jerusalem, all the city was stirred up, saying, "Who is this?"

11 The multitudes said, "This is the prophet, Jesus from Nazareth, of Galilee."

Jesus Enters the Temple

Mark 11:10–11

They came to Jerusalem, and 11 Jesus entered into the temple in Jerusalem. When He had looked around at everything, it being now evening, He went out to Bethany with the twelve.

Jesus Curses the Fig Tree on Nisan 11

Mark 11:12–14; Matthew 21:18–19

12 The next day, 18 in the morning, 12 when they had come out from Bethany, 18 as He returned to the city, 12 He was hungry. 13 Seeing a fig tree afar off having leaves, 19 by the road, He came to it, 13 to see if perhaps He might find anything on it.[149] When He came to it, He found nothing 19 on it 13 but leaves, for it was not the season for figs. 14 Jesus told it, 19 "Let there be no fruit from you forever! [and] 14 May no one ever eat fruit from you again!" and His disciples heard it.

19 Immediately the fig tree withered away.

[149] Normally, unripe figs appear when the leaves appear. The unripe figs are edible. Since there were no unripe figs on the tree, the tree would bear no fruit that year. Jesus turned the tree into a symbol of Israel, a tree not bearing fruit. Its death was prophetic of the uprooting of Israel from the Promised Land.

Jesus Clears the Temple

Mark 11:15-19; Matthew 21:12–18; Luke 19:45–48

15They came to Jerusalem, and Jesus entered into the temple of God, and began to drive out 12 all of 15 those who sold and bought in the temple, and overthrew the money changers' tables and the seats of those who sold the doves. 16 He would not allow anyone to carry a container through the temple.

17 He taught, saying to them, "Isn't written, 'My house will be called a house of prayer for all the nations?'[150] But you have made it 'a den of robbers!'"[151]

18 The chief priests and the scribes heard it, and sought how they might destroy Him. For they feared Him, because all the multitude was astonished at His teaching.

14 The blind and the lame came to Him in the temple, and He healed them.

15 But when the chief priests and the scribes saw the wonderful things that He did, and the children who were crying in the temple and saying, "Hosanna to the son of David!" they were indignant, 16 and said to Him, "Do You hear what these are saying?"

16 Jesus said to them, "Yes. Did you never read, 'Out of the mouth of babes and nursing babies you have perfected praise?'"[152][153]

17 He left them and 19 when evening came, He went out of the city 17 to Bethany, and camped there.

47 He was teaching daily in the temple, but the chief priests and the scribes and the leading men among the people sought to destroy Him.

---

[150] **Isaiah 56:7** "I will bring these to My holy mountain, and make them joyful in My house of prayer. Their burnt offerings and their sacrifices will be accepted on My altar; for My house will be called a house of prayer for all peoples."

[151] **Jeremiah 7:11** "Has this house, which is called by My name, become a den of robbers in your eyes? Behold, I, even I, have seen it," says Yahweh.

[152] Jesus only quoted the first part of Psalm 8:2, so the Pharisees would remember the second part and be rebuked by it. This was a standard rabbinical technique at the time. (Spangler/Tverberg)

[153] **Psalm 8:2** From the lips of babes and infants You have established strength, because of Your adversaries, that You might silence the enemy and the avenger.

48 They couldn't find what they might do, for all the people hung on to every word that He said.

The Lesson of the Withered Fig Tree on Nisan 12

Mark 11:20–26; Matthew 21:20–22

20 As they passed by in the morning, they saw the fig tree withered away from the roots. 21 Peter, remembering, said to Him, "Rabbi, look! The fig tree which You cursed has withered away."

When the disciples saw it, they marveled, saying, "How did the fig tree immediately wither away?"

22 Jesus answered them, "Have faith in God. 23 For most certainly I tell you, 21 if you have faith, and don't doubt, you will not only do what was done to the fig tree, but even if you [or] 22 whoever 21 told this mountain, 'Be taken up and cast into the sea,' it would be done.

24 "Therefore I tell you, all things whatever you pray and ask for, believe that you have received them, 22 you will receive 24 and you shall have them.

25 "Whenever you stand praying, forgive, if you have anything against anyone; so that your Father, Who is in heaven, may also forgive you your transgressions. 26 But if you do not forgive, neither will your Father in heaven forgive your transgressions."

Jesus Foretells His Death for the Fifth Time

John 12:20–41

20 Now there were certain Greeks among those that went up to worship at the feast. 21 These, therefore, came to Philip, who was from Bethsaida of Galilee, and asked him, saying, "Sir, we want to see Jesus."

22 Philip came and told Andrew, and in turn, Andrew came with Philip, and they told Jesus.

23 Jesus answered them, "The time has come for the Son of Man to be glorified. 24 Most certainly I tell you, unless a grain of wheat falls into the earth and dies, it remains by itself alone. But if it dies, it bears much fruit.

25 "He who loves his life will lose it. He who hates his life in this world will keep it to eternal life. 26 If anyone serves me, let him follow Me. Where I am, there will My servant also be. If anyone serves Me, the Father will honor him.

27 "Now My soul is troubled. What shall I say? 'Father, save Me from this time?' But for this cause I came to this time. 28 Father, glorify Your name!"

Then there came a voice out of the sky, saying, "I have both glorified it, and will glorify it again."

29 The multitude therefore, who stood by and heard it, said that it had thundered. Others said, "An angel has spoken to Him."

30 Jesus answered, "This voice hasn't come for My sake, but for your sakes. 31 Now is the judgment of this world. Now the prince of this world will be cast out. 32 And I, if I am lifted up from the earth, will draw all people to Myself."

33 But He said this, signifying by what kind of death He should die.

34 The multitude answered him, "We have heard out of the law that the Christ remains forever.[154] How do You say, 'The Son of Man must be lifted up?' Who is this Son of Man?"

35 Jesus therefore said to them, "Yet a little while the light is with you. Walk while you have the light, that darkness doesn't overtake you. He who walks in the darkness doesn't know where he is going. 36 While you have the light, believe in the light, that you may become children of light."

Jesus said these things and He departed and hid Himself from them.

37 But though He had done so many signs before them, yet they didn't believe in Him, 38 that the word of Isaiah the prophet might be

---

[154] **Isaiah 9:7** Of the increase of His government and of peace there shall be no end, on David's throne, and on his kingdom, to establish it, and to uphold it with justice and with righteousness from that time on, even forever. The zeal of Yahweh of Armies will perform this. **Daniel 2:44** In the days of those kings shall the God of heaven set up a kingdom which shall never be destroyed, nor shall its sovereignty be left to another people; but it shall break in pieces and consume all these kingdoms, and it shall stand forever.

fulfilled, which he spoke,

> "Lord, who has believed our report? To whom has the arm of the Lord been revealed?"[155]

39 For this cause they couldn't believe, for Isaiah said again,

> 40 "He has blinded their eyes and He hardened their heart, lest they should see with their eyes, and perceive with their heart, and would turn, and I would heal them."[156]

41 Isaiah said these things when he saw His glory, and spoke of Him.

Jesus and His Disciples Return to the Temple on Nisan 12

Mark 11:27–33: Luke 20:1–8; Matthew 21:23-27

27 They came again to Jerusalem, and as He was walking in the temple, 1 as He was teaching the people in the temple and preaching the good news, the chief priests and scribes came to Him with the elders 23 of the people came to Him 23 as He was teaching, and said, "By what authority do You do these things? Who gave You this authority 28 to do these things?"

3 He answered them, "I also will ask you one question, 24 which if you tell Me, 29 answer Me, and 24 I likewise, 29 I will tell you by what authority I do these things. 4 The baptism of John, 25 —was it from heaven, or from men? Answer Me."

5 They reasoned with themselves, saying, "If we say, 'From heaven,' He will say, 'Why didn't you believe Him?' 6 but if we say, 'From men,'" 26—they feared the people, 6 "all the people will stone us, for they are persuaded that John was a prophet." 32 —for all held John to really be a prophet. 7 They answered that they didn't know where it was from. 33 They answered Jesus, "We don't know."

8 Jesus said to them, "Neither will I tell you by what authority I do these things."

---

[155] **Isaiah 53:1** Who has believed Our message? To whom has the arm of Yahweh been revealed?

[156] **Isaiah 6:10** "Make the heart of this people fat. Make their ears heavy, and shut their eyes; lest they see with their eyes, and hear with their ears, and understand with their heart, and turn again, and be healed."

The Parable of the Two Sons

Mark 12:1

1 He began to speak to them in parables.

Matthew 21:28–32

28 "But what do you think? A man had two sons, and he came to the first, and said, 'Son, go work today in my vineyard.' 29 He answered, 'I will not,' but afterward he changed his mind, and went. 30 He came to the second, and said the same thing. He answered, 'I go, sir,' but he didn't go. 31 Which of the two did the will of his father?"

They said to Him, "The first."

Jesus said to them, "Most certainly I tell you that the tax collectors and the prostitutes are entering into God's kingdom before you. 32 For John came to you in the way of righteousness, and you didn't believe him, but the tax collectors and the prostitutes believed him. When you saw it, you didn't even repent afterward, that you might believe him.

The Parable of the Vineyard

Luke 20:9–18; Matthew 21:33–44; Mark 12:1-11

He began to tell the people this parable.

33 "Hear another parable. There was a man who was a master of a household, who planted a vineyard, set a hedge about it, dug a wine press in it, built a tower, leased it out to farmers, and went into another country[157] 9 for a long time.

---

[157] **Isaiah 5:1–7** Let me sing for my well beloved a song of my beloved about his vineyard. My beloved had a vineyard on a very fruitful hill. 2 He dug it up, gathered out its stones, planted it with the choicest vine, built a tower in the middle of it, and also cut out a wine press therein. He looked for it to yield grapes, but it yielded wild grapes. 3 "Now, inhabitants of Jerusalem and men of Judah, please judge between me and my vineyard. 4 What could have been done more to my vineyard, that I have not done in it? Why, when I looked for it to yield grapes, did it yield wild grapes? 5 Now I will tell you what I will do to my vineyard. I will take away its hedge, and it will be eaten up. I will break down its wall of it, and it will be trampled down. 6 I will lay it a wasteland. It won't be pruned nor hoed, but it will grow briers and

34 When the season for the fruit came near, he sent his servants to the farmers, 2 to get from the farmer his share of the fruit of the vineyard. 3 They took him, beat him, and sent him away empty.

11 "He sent yet another servant, and they also beat him, and treated him shamefully, and sent him away empty.

4 "Again, he sent 12 yet 4 another servant to them; 12 a third, 4 and they threw stones at him, wounded him in the head, 12 and threw him out, 4 and sent him away shamefully treated.

5 "Again he sent another; and they killed him; and many others. 36 Again, he sent other servants more than the first: 5 beating some, and killing some.

13 "The lord of the vineyard said, 'What shall I do? 6 Therefore still having one, his beloved son, he sent him last 37 of all, 6 to them, saying, 13 'I will send my beloved son. It may be that seeing him, they will respect him. 6 They will respect my son.'

38 "But the farmers, when they saw the son, 14 they reasoned among themselves, saying, 'This is the heir. Come, let's kill him, 38 and seize his inheritance 7 and the inheritance will be ours.' 39 So they took him, 8 killed him, and cast him out of the vineyard.

40 "When therefore the lord of the vineyard comes, what he will do to those farmers?"

41 They told him, "He will miserably destroy those miserable men, and will lease out the vineyard to other farmers, who will give him the fruit in its season."

[Jesus said] 16 "He will come and destroy these farmers, and will give the vineyard to others."

When they heard it, they said, "May it never be!"

17 But He looked at them, and 42 Jesus said to them, "Did you never read in the Scriptures? 17 Then what is this that is written,

42 'The stone which the builders rejected, the same was made the

---

thorns. I will also command the clouds that they rain no rain on it. 7 For the vineyard of Yahweh of Armies is the house of Israel, and the men of Judah his pleasant plant: and he looked for justice, but, behold, oppression; for righteousness, but, behold, a cry of distress.

head of the corner. This was from the Lord; it is marvelous in our eyes.'[158]

43 "Therefore I tell you, God's kingdom will be taken away from you, and will be given to a nation producing its fruit. 44 He who falls on this stone will be broken to pieces;[159] but on whomever it will fall, it will scatter him as dust."[160]

The Priests and the Scribes Seek to Arrest Jesus

Matthew 21:45–46; Luke 20:19; Mark 12:12

45 When the chief priests and the Pharisees heard His parables, they perceived that He spoke about them. 19 The chief priests and the scribes sought to lay hands on Him that very hour, 12 to seize Him, but they feared the multitude; for they perceived that He spoke the parable against them. 46 When they sought to seize Him, they feared the multitudes, because they considered Him to be a prophet. 12 They left Him, and went away.

Some Rulers Believe

John 12:42–43

42 Nevertheless even of the rulers many believed in Him, but because of the Pharisees they didn't confess it, so that they wouldn't be put out

---

[158] **Psalm 118:22–23** The stone which the builders rejected has become the head of the corner. 23 This is Yahweh's doing. It is marvelous in our eyes. **Isaiah 28:16** Therefore thus says the Lord Yahweh, "Behold, I lay in Zion for a foundation a stone, a tried stone, a precious cornerstone of a sure foundation. He who believes shall not act hastily."

[159] **Isaiah 8:14–15** "He will be a sanctuary, but for both houses of Israel, he will be a trap and a snare for the inhabitants of Jerusalem. 15 Many will stumble over it, fall, be broken, be snared, and be captured."

[160] **Daniel 2:34, 44–45** 34 You saw until a stone was cut out without hands, which struck the image on its feet that were of iron and clay, and broke them in pieces. 44 In the days of those kings shall the God of heaven set up a kingdom which shall never be destroyed, nor shall its sovereignty be left to another people; but it shall break in pieces and consume all these kingdoms, and it shall stand forever. 45 Because you saw that a stone was cut out of the mountain without hands, and that it broke in pieces the iron, the brass, the clay, the silver, and the gold; the great God has made known to the king what shall happen hereafter: and the dream is certain, and its interpretation sure.

of the synagogue, 43 for they loved men's praise more than God's praise.

Belief In Jesus is Belief in God

John 12:44–50

44 Jesus cried out and said, "Whoever believes in Me, believes not in Me, but in Him who sent Me. 45 He who sees Me sees Him who sent Me. 46 I have come as a light into the world, that whoever believes in Me may not remain in the darkness. 47 If anyone listens to My sayings, and doesn't believe, I don't judge him. For I came not to judge the world, but to save the world.

48 He who rejects Me, and doesn't receive My sayings, has one who judges Him. The word that I spoke, the same will judge him in the last day. 49 For I spoke not from Myself, but the Father who sent Me, He gave Me a commandment, what I should say, and what I should speak. 50 I know that His commandment is eternal life. The things therefore which I speak, even as the Father has said to Me, so I speak."

The Parable of the Wedding Banquet

Matthew 22:1–14

1 Jesus answered and spoke again in parables to them, saying, 2 "The Kingdom of Heaven is like a certain king, who made a marriage feast for his son, 3 and sent out his servants to call those who were invited to the marriage feast, but they would not come. 4 Again he sent out other servants, saying, 'Tell those who are invited, "Behold, I have prepared my dinner. My cattle and my fatlings are killed, and all things are ready. Come to the marriage feast!"'

5 "But they made light of it, and went their ways, one to his own farm, another to his merchandise, 6 and the rest grabbed his servants, and treated them shamefully, and killed them.

7 "When the king heard that, he was angry, and sent his armies, destroyed those murderers, and burned their city.

8 "Then he said to his servants, 'The wedding is ready, but those who were invited weren't worthy. 9 Go therefore to the intersections of the highways, and as many as you may find, invite to the marriage feast.'

10 "Those servants went out into the highways, and gathered together as many as they found, both bad and good. The wedding was filled with guests.

11 " But when the king came in to see the guests, he saw there a man who didn't have on wedding clothing, 12 and he said to him, 'Friend, how did you come in here not wearing wedding clothing?' He was speechless. 13 Then the king said to the servants, 'Bind him hand and foot, take him away, and throw him into the outer darkness; there is where the weeping and grinding of teeth will be.'

14 "For many are called, but few chosen."

A Conspiracy to Trap Jesus with Paying Taxes

Matthew 22:15–22; Luke 20:20–26; Mark 12:13–17

15 Then the Pharisees went and took counsel how they might entrap Him in His talk. 20 They watched Him, and sent out spies, 13 some of the Pharisees 16 [and] they sent their disciples to Him, along with the Herodians, 20 who pretended to be righteous, 13 to trap Him with words, 20 that they might trap Him in something He said, so as to deliver Him up to the power and authority of the governor.

14 When they had come, they asked Him, 16 saying, "Teacher, we know that You are honest, and teach the way of God in truth. 21 You say and teach what is right,16 no matter whom You teach, for You aren't partial to anyone 21 but truly teach the way of God. 17 Tell us therefore, what do You think? Is it lawful 22 for us 17 to pay taxes to Caesar, or not? 15 Shall we give, or shall we not give?"

18 But Jesus perceived their wickedness, and 23 craftiness, and 15 knowing their hypocrisy, 23 said to them, "Why do you test Me 18 you hypocrites? 19 Show Me the tax money. 15 Bring Me a denarius, that I may see it."

19 They brought to Him a denarius.

20 He asked them, "Whose is this image and inscription?"

24 They answered [and] 21 said to Him, "Caesar's."

21 Then 17 Jesus answered them, 21 [and] He said to them, "Give therefore to Caesar the things that are Caesar's, and to God the things

that are God's."

22 When they heard it, they marveled, 17 greatly at Him. 26 They weren't able to trap him in His words before the people. They marveled at His answer, and were silent, 21 and left Him, and went away.

The Sadducees Question Jesus About the Resurrection

Matthew 22:23–33; Luke 20:27–40; Mark 12:18–27

23 On that day Sadducees (those who say that there is no resurrection) came to Him. They asked Him, 24 saying, 28 "Teacher, Moses wrote to us that if a man's brother dies having a wife, and he is childless, his brother should take the wife, and raise up children for his brother.[161] 29 There were therefore seven brothers. The first took a wife, and died childless [and] 25 left his wife to his brother. 30 The second took her as wife, and he died childless. 31 The third took her, and likewise the seven all left no children, and died. 32 Afterward the woman also died. 33 Therefore in the resurrection 23 when they rise, 33 whose wife of them will she be? For the seven had her as a wife."

34 Jesus 24 answered [and] 34 said to them, 24 "Isn't this because you are mistaken, not knowing the Scriptures, nor the power of God? 29 You are mistaken. 34 The children of this age marry, and are given in marriage. 35 But those who are considered worthy to attain to that age and the resurrection from the dead, neither marry, nor are given in marriage. 36 For they can't die any more for they are like 30 God's angels in heaven 36 and are children of God, being children of the resurrection.

26 But about the dead, 31 [and] concerning the resurrection of the dead, 37 that the dead are raised, 31 haven't you read that which was spoken to you by God, saying, 26 in the book of Moses, [as] 37 even Moses showed at the bush, when he called the Lord 'The God of Abraham, the God of Isaac, and the God of Jacob.'[162] 38 Now He is

---

[161] **Deuteronomy 25:5** If brothers dwell together, and one of them dies, and has no son, the wife of the dead shall not be married outside to a stranger. Her husband's brother shall go in to her, and take her as his wife, and perform the duty of a husband's brother to her.

[162] **Exodus 3:6** Moreover He said, "I am the God of your father, the God of

not the God of the dead, but of the living, for all are alive to Him. 27 You are therefore badly mistaken."

33 When the multitudes heard it, they were astonished at His teaching. 39 Some of the scribes answered, "Teacher, you speak well." 40 They didn't dare to ask Him any more questions.

The Pharisees Question Jesus

Matthew 22:34–40; Mark 12:28–34

34 But the Pharisees, when they heard that He had silenced the Sadducees gathered themselves together. 35 One of them, a lawyer, [and] 28 one of the scribes came, and heard them questioning together. Knowing that He had answered them well, asked Him, 35 asked Him a question, testing Him. 36 "Teacher, which is the greatest commandment in the law? 28 Which commandment is the greatest of all?"

29 Jesus answered [and] 37 said to him, "'The greatest is,

'Hear, Israel, the Lord our God, the Lord is one: 30 you shall love the Lord your God with all your heart, and with all your soul, and with all your mind, and with all your strength.'[163]

38 "This is the first and great commandment.

31 "The second is like this, 'You shall love your neighbor as yourself.'[164] There is no other commandment greater than these. 40 The whole law and the prophets depend on these commandments."

32 The scribe said to Him, "Truly, Teacher, You have said well that He is one, and there is none other but He, 33 and to love Him with all the heart, and with all the understanding, with all the soul, and with all the strength, and to love his neighbor as himself, is more important than all whole burnt offerings and sacrifices."[165]

Abraham, the God of Isaac, and the God of Jacob."

[163] **Deuteronomy 6:4–5** Hear, Israel: Yahweh is our God. Yahweh is one. 5 You shall love Yahweh your God with all your heart, with all your soul, and with all your might.

[164] **Leviticus 19:18** 'You shall not take vengeance, nor bear any grudge against the children of your people; but you shall love your neighbor as yourself. I am Yahweh.'

[165] **1 Samuel 15:22** Samuel said, "Has Yahweh as great delight in burnt offerings

34 When Jesus saw that he answered wisely, He said to him, "You are not far from God's kingdom."

Jesus Questions the Scribes and the Pharisees

Matthew 22:41–46; Mark 12:35–37; Luke 20:41–44

41 Now while the Pharisees were gathered together, 35 Jesus responded, as He taught in the temple. 41 Jesus asked them a question, 42 saying, "What do you think of the Christ? Whose son is he?"

They said to him, "Of David."

35 "How is it that the scribes say that the Christ is the son of David? 36 For David himself said in the Holy Spirit, 42 in the book of Psalms,

> 'The Lord said to my Lord, "Sit at my right hand, 42 until I make your enemies the footstool of your feet."'"[166]

37 "Therefore David himself calls Him Lord, so how can He be His son?" 46 No one was able to answer Him a word; neither did any man dare ask Him any more questions from that day forward. 37 The common people heard Him gladly.

Jesus Warns About the Scribes and Pharisees

Luke 20:45–47; Mark 12:38–40; Matthew 23:1–39

1 Then 45 in the hearing of all the people, 1 Jesus spoke to the multitudes and to His disciples, 38 In His teaching 2 saying, "The scribes and the Pharisees sit on Moses's seat. 3 All things therefore whatever they tell you to observe, observe and do, but don't do their works; for they say, and don't do.

4 "For they bind heavy burdens that are grievous to be borne, and lay them on men's shoulders; but they themselves will not lift a finger to

---

and sacrifices, as in obeying Yahweh's voice? Behold, to obey is better than sacrifice, and to listen than the fat of rams. Psalm 51:16–17 For you don't delight in sacrifice, or else I would give it. You have no pleasure in burnt offering. 17 The sacrifices of God are a broken spirit. A broken and contrite heart, O God, you will not despise.

[166] **Psalm 110:1** Yahweh says to my Lord, "Sit at my right hand, until I make your enemies your footstool for your feet."

help them. 5 But all their works they do to be seen by men.

38 “Beware of the scribes, who like to walk in long robes. 5 They make their phylacteries,[167] [168] broad, enlarge the fringes of their garments, 6 and love the place of honor at feasts, the best seats in the synagogues, 46 and love greetings 7 [and] salutations in the marketplaces, and to be called ‘Rabbi, Rabbi’ by men, 40 those who devour widows’ houses, and for a pretense make long prayers. These will receive greater condemnation.”

8 “But don’t you be called ‘Rabbi,’ for one is your teacher, the Christ, and all of you are brothers. 9 Call no man on the earth your father, for one is your Father, He who is in heaven. 10 Neither be called masters, for One is your Master, the Christ. 11 But he who is greatest among you will be your servant. 12 Whoever exalts himself will be humbled, and whoever humbles himself will be exalted.

13 “Woe to you, scribes and Pharisees, hypocrites! For you devour widows’ houses, and as a pretense you make long prayers. Therefore you will receive greater condemnation.

14 “But woe to you, scribes and Pharisees, hypocrites! Because you shut up the Kingdom of Heaven against men; for you don’t enter in yourselves, neither do you allow those who are entering in to enter.

15 “Woe to you, scribes and Pharisees hypocrites! For you travel around by sea and land to make one proselyte; and when he becomes one, you make him twice as much of a son of Gehenna as yourselves.

16 “Woe to you, you blind guides, who say, ‘Whoever swears by the temple, it is nothing; but whoever swears by the gold of the temple, he is obligated.’

17 “You blind fools! For which is greater, the gold, or the temple that sanctifies the gold? 18 ‘Whoever swears by the altar, it is nothing; but

[167] Phylacteries (*tefillin* in Hebrew) are small leather pouches that some Jewish men wear on the forehead and arm during prayer. They are used to carry a small scroll with some Scripture in it. See Deuteronomy 6:8.

[168] **Deuteronomy 6:6–8** These words, which I command you today, shall be on your heart; 7 and you shall teach them diligently to your children, and shall talk of them when you sit in your house, and when you walk by the way, and when you lie down, and when you rise up. 8 You shall bind them for a sign on your hand, and they shall be for frontlets between your eyes.

whoever swears by the gift that is on it, he is obligated?' 19 You blind fools! For which is greater, the gift, or the altar that sanctifies the gift? 20 He therefore who swears by the altar, swears by it, and by everything on it. 21 He who swears by the temple swears by it, and by Him who lives in it. 22 He who swears by heaven swears by the throne of God, and by Him who sits on it.

23 "Woe to you, scribes and Pharisees, hypocrites! For you tithe[169] mint, dill, and cumin,[170] and have left undone the weightier matters of the law: justice, mercy, and faith.[171] But you ought to have done these, and not to have left the other undone. 24 You blind guides, who strain out a gnat, and swallow a camel![172]

25 "Woe to you, scribes and Pharisees, hypocrites! For you clean the outside of the cup and of the platter, but within they are full of extortion and unrighteousness. 26 You blind Pharisee, first clean the inside of the cup and of the platter, that its outside may become clean also.

27 "Woe to you, scribes and Pharisees, hypocrites! For you are like whitened tombs, which outwardly appear beautiful, but inwardly are full of dead men's bones, and of all uncleanness. 28 Even so you also outwardly appear righteous to men, but inwardly you are full of hypocrisy and iniquity.

29 "Woe to you, scribes and Pharisees, hypocrites! For you build the tombs of the prophets, and decorate the tombs of the righteous, 30 and

---

[169] **Leviticus 27:30** "'All the tithe of the land, whether of the seed of the land or of the fruit of the trees, is Yahweh's. It is holy to Yahweh." **Numbers 18:21–24** "To the children of Levi, behold, I have given all the tithe in Israel for an inheritance, in return for their service which they serve, even the service of the Tent of Meeting. 22 Henceforth the children of Israel shall not come near the Tent of Meeting, lest they bear sin, and die. 23 But the Levites shall do the service of the Tent of Meeting, and they shall bear their iniquity. It shall be a statute forever throughout your generations. Among the children of Israel, they shall have no inheritance."

[170] Cumin is an aromatic seed from *Cuminum cyminum*, resembling caraway in flavor and appearance. It is used as a spice. (The implication is the Pharisees paid tithe by tiny seeds.)

[171] **Micah 6:8** He has shown you, O man, what is good. What does Yahweh require of you, but to act justly, to love mercy, and to walk humbly with your God?

[172] A gnat was a small unclean animal that might be in a cup while a camel was a large unclean animal.

say, 'If we had lived in the days of our fathers, we wouldn't have been partakers with them in the blood of the prophets.' 31 Therefore you testify to yourselves that you are children of those who killed the prophets. 32 Fill up, then, the measure of your fathers.

33 "You serpents, you offspring of vipers, how will you escape the judgment of Gehenna?

34 "Therefore behold, I send to you prophets, wise men, and scribes. Some of them you will kill and crucify; and some of them you will scourge in your synagogues, and persecute from city to city; 35 that on you may come all the righteous blood shed on the earth, from the blood of righteous Abel to the blood of Zachariah son of Barachiah, whom you killed between the sanctuary and the altar. 36 Most certainly I tell you, all these things will come upon this generation.

Jesus Laments Over Jerusalem

37 "Jerusalem, Jerusalem, who kills the prophets, and stones those who are sent to her! How often I would have gathered your children together, even as a hen gathers her chicks under her wings, and you would not! 38 Behold, your house is left to you desolate. 39 For I tell you, you will not see me from now on, until you say, 'Blessed is he who comes in the name of the Lord!'"[173]

The Widow's Offering

Mark 12:41–44; Luke 21:1–4

41 Jesus sat down opposite the treasury, 1 He looked up, 41 and saw how the multitude cast money into the treasury. Many who were rich cast in much. 42 A poor widow came, and she cast in two small brass coins, which equal a quadrans coin.

43 He called His disciples to Himself, and said to them, "Most certainly I tell you, this poor widow gave more than all those who are giving into the treasury, 44 for they all gave [and] 4 put in gifts for God 43 out of their abundance, but she, out of her poverty, gave all that she had to live on."

---

[173] **Psalm 118:26** Ibed

Jesus and His Disciples Leave the Temple Area

Matthew 24:1–2; Mark 13:1–2; Luke 21:5–6

1 Jesus went out from the temple, and was going on his way. 1 As He went out of the temple, 5 as some were talking about the temple and how it was decorated with beautiful stones and gifts, 1 one of His disciples said to Him, "Teacher, see what kind of stones and what kind of buildings!"

2 But 2 Jesus said [and] 2 answered them, "You see all of these things, 2 these great buildings, 2 don't you? Most certainly I tell you, there will not be left here one stone on another, that will not be thrown down."

The Olivet Prophecy

Matthew 24:3–28; Mark 13:3–23; Luke 21:7–24

3 As He sat on the Mount of Olives, 3 opposite the temple, 3 the disciples 3 Peter, James, John, and Andrew 3 came to Him privately [and] 7 they 3 asked Him 3 saying, 7 "Teacher, so 3 tell us, when will these things be? 7 What is the sign that these things are about to happen? 3 What is the sign of Your coming, and of the end of the age 4 when all these things will be fulfilled?"

4 Jesus, answering, began to tell them, "Be careful that no one leads you astray. 6 For many will come in My Name, saying, 6 'I am He!' 5 'I am the Christ,' 8 and, 'The time is at hand,' 6 and will lead many astray.[174] 8 Therefore don't follow them.

6 "You will hear of wars and rumors of wars 9 and disturbances. 6 See that you aren't troubled, [and] 9 don't be terrified, 6 for all this must happen 9 first, 6 but the end is not yet. 9 For these things must happen first, but the end won't come immediately."

10 Then He said to them, 7 "For nation will rise against nation, and

[174] **Revelation 6:1–2** I saw that the Lamb opened one of the seven seals, and I heard one of the four living creatures saying, as with a voice of thunder, "Come and see!" 2 And behold, a white horse, and He who sat on it had a bow. A crown was given to Him, and He came out conquering, and to conquer.

kingdom against kingdom;[175] and there will be famines, 8 and troubles,[176] 7 plagues,[177] and 11 great 7 earthquakes in various places. 11 There will be terrors and great signs from heaven.[178] 8 But all these things are the beginning of birth pains.

12 "But before all these things, 9 watch yourselves, for 12 they will lay their hands on you and will persecute you, delivering you up to synagogues and prisons, [and] 9 to councils. You will be beaten in synagogues. You will stand before rulers and kings 12 and governors for My name's sake. 13 It will turn out as a testimony for you [and] 9 for a testimony to them. 10 The good news must first be preached to all the nations.

---

[175] **Revelation 6:3–4** When he opened the second seal, I heard the second living creature saying, "Come!" 4 Another came out, a red horse. To him who sat on it was given power to take peace from the earth, and that they should kill one another. There was given to him a great sword.

[176] **Revelation 6:5–6** When he opened the third seal, I heard the third living creature saying, "Come and see!" And behold, a black horse, and he who sat on it had a balance in his hand. 6 I heard a voice in the middle of the four living creatures saying, "A choenix [quart] of wheat for a denarius, and three choenix of barley for a denarius! Don't damage the oil and the wine!"

[177] **Revelation 6:7–8** When he opened the fourth seal, I heard the fourth living creature saying, "Come and see!" 8 And behold, a pale horse, and he who sat on it, his name was Death. Hades followed with him. Authority over one fourth of the earth, to kill with the sword, with famine, with death, and by the wild animals of the earth was given to him.

[178] **Isaiah 13:10** For the stars of the sky and its constellations will not give their light. The sun will be darkened in its going out, and the moon will not cause its light to shine. **Joel 2:30–31** I will show wonders in the heavens and in the earth: blood, fire, and pillars of smoke. 31 The sun will be turned into darkness, and the moon into blood, before the great and terrible day of Yahweh comes. **Amos 8:9** "It will happen in that day," says the Lord Yahweh, "that I will cause the sun to go down at noon, and I will darken the earth in the clear day." **Revelation 6:12–17** I saw when he opened the sixth seal, and there was a great earthquake. The sun became black as sackcloth made of hair, and the whole moon became as blood. 13 The stars of the sky fell to the earth, like a fig tree dropping its unripe figs when it is shaken by a great wind. 14 The sky was removed like a scroll when it is rolled up. Every mountain and island were moved out of their places. 15 The kings of the earth, the princes, the commanding officers, the rich, the strong, and every slave and free person, hid themselves in the caves and in the rocks of the mountains. 16 They told the mountains and the rocks, "Fall on us, and hide us from the face of him who sits on the throne, and from the wrath of the Lamb, 17 for the great day of his wrath has come; and who is able to stand?"

9 "Then they will deliver you up to oppression, and will kill you. You will be hated by all of the nations for my name's sake.[179]

10 "Then many will stumble, and will deliver up one another, and will hate one another. 11 Many false prophets will arise, and will lead many astray. 12 Because iniquity will be multiplied, the love of many will grow cold.

11 "When they lead you away and deliver you up, 14 settle it therefore in your hearts not to 11 be anxious beforehand, or premeditate what you will say, [or] 14 to meditate beforehand how to answer, 15 for I will give you a mouth and wisdom which all your adversaries will not be able to withstand or to contradict. 11 But say whatever will be given you in that hour. For it is not you who speak, but the Holy Spirit.

16 "You will be handed over even by parents, brothers, relatives, and friends. They will cause some of you to be put to death. 12 Brother will deliver up brother to death and the father his child. Children will rise up against parents, and cause them to be put to death. 18 And not a hair of your head will perish.

19 "By your endurance you will win your lives.

13 "You will be hated by all men for My Name's sake, but he who endures to the end, the same will be saved.

14 "This good news of the Kingdom 10 must first 14 be preached in the whole world for a testimony to all the nations, and then the end will come.

15 "When, therefore, you see the abomination of desolation,[180] which

---

[179] **Revelation 6:9–11** When he opened the fifth seal, I saw underneath the altar the souls of those who had been killed for the Word of God, and for the testimony of the Lamb which they had. 10 They cried with a loud voice, saying, "How long, Master, the holy and true, until you judge and avenge our blood on those who dwell on the earth?" 11 A long white robe was given to each of them. They were told that they should rest yet for a while, until their fellow servants and their brothers, who would also be killed even as they were, should complete their course.

[180] **Daniel 9:27** He shall make a firm covenant with many for one week: and in the middle of the week he shall cause the sacrifice and the offering to cease; and on the wing of abominations shall come one who makes desolate; and even to the full end, and that determined, shall wrath be poured out on the desolate. **Daniel 11:31** Forces shall stand on his part, and they shall profane the sanctuary, even the fortress, and shall take away the continual burnt offering, and they shall set up the abomination

was spoken of through Daniel the prophet, standing in the holy place, 14 where it ought not," 15 (let the reader understand), [and] 20 "when you see Jerusalem surrounded by armies, then know that its desolation is at hand. 21 Then let those who are in Judea flee to the mountains. Let those who are in the middle of her depart. Let those who are in the country not enter therein. 17 Let him who is on the housetop not go down 15 nor enter in, to take anything out of his house, 17 to take out things that are in his house. 18 Let him who is in the field not return back to get his clothes. 22 For these are days of vengeance, that all things which are written may be fulfilled.

19 "But woe to those who are with child and to nursing mothers 23 who nurse infants 19 in those days! 20 Pray that your flight will not be in the winter, nor on a Sabbath, 23 For there will be great distress in the land, and wrath to this people. 24 They will fall by the edge of the sword, and will be led captive into all the nations. Jerusalem will be trampled down by the Gentiles, until the times of the Gentiles are fulfilled.

21 "For then 19 in those days 21 there will be great oppression, such as has not been from the beginning 19 of the creation 21 of the world 19 which God created 21 until now, no, nor ever will be.[181] 22 Unless those days had been shortened, [and] 20 the Lord had shortened the days, 22 no flesh would have been saved. But for the sake of the chosen ones, 20 the chosen ones, whom He picked out, He shortened the days. 22 Those days will be shortened.

23 "Then if any man tells you, 'Behold, here is the Christ,' 21 or, 'Look, there!' 23 don't believe it. 24 For there will arise false christs, and false prophets, and they will show great signs and wonders, so as to lead astray, if possible, even the chosen ones. 23 But you watch.

---

that makes desolate. **Daniel 12:11** From the time that the continual burnt offering shall be taken away, and the abomination that makes desolate set up, there shall be one thousand two hundred ninety days.

[181] **Jeremiah 30:7** Alas! for that day is great, so that none is like it: it is even the time of Jacob's trouble; but he shall be saved out of it. **Daniel 12:1** "At that time shall Michael stand up, the great prince who stands for the children of your people; and there shall be a time of trouble, such as never was since there was a nation even to that same time: and at that time your people shall be delivered, everyone who shall be found written in the book.

26 "Behold, I have told you 23 all things 25 beforehand. 26 If
therefore they tell you, 'Behold, He is in the wilderness,' don't go out;
'Behold, He is in the inner rooms,' [or] 21 'Look, here is the Christ!'
or, 'Look, there!' don't believe it. 27 For as the lightning flashes from
the east, and is seen even to the west, so will be the coming of the Son
of Man. 28 For wherever the carcass is, there is where the vultures
gather together.[182]

The Coming of the Son of Man

Mark 13:24–37; Matthew 24:29–31; Luke 21:25–28

24 "But in those days, 29 immediately after the oppression of those
days, 25 there will be signs in the sun, moon, and stars; 24 the sun will
be darkened, the moon will not give its light, 29 the stars will fall from
the sky, and the powers 25 that are in 29 the heavens will be shaken;[183]

---

[182] **Job 39:27** Does the eagle mount up at your command, And make its nest on high? [28] On the rock it dwells and resides, on the crag of the rock and the stronghold. [29] From there it spies out the prey; Its eyes observe from afar. [30] Its young ones suck up blood; and where the slain *are,* there it *is.*"

[183] **Isaiah 2:19–21** Men shall go into the caves of the rocks, and into the holes of the earth, from before the terror of Yahweh, and from the glory of His majesty, when He arises to shake the earth mightily. 20 In that day, men shall cast away their idols of silver, and their idols of gold, which have been made for themselves to worship, to the moles and to the bats; 21 To go into the caverns of the rocks, and into the clefts of the ragged rocks, from before the terror of Yahweh, and from the glory of His majesty, when He arises to shake the earth mightily. **Isaiah 13:10** For the stars of the sky and its constellations will not give their light. The sun will be darkened in its going out, and the moon will not cause its light to shine. **Isaiah 34:4** All of the army of the sky will be dissolved. The sky will be rolled up like a scroll, and all its armies will fade away, as a leaf fades from off a vine or a fig tree. **Joel 2:30–31** I will show wonders in the heavens and in the earth: blood, fire, and pillars of smoke. 31 The sun will be turned into darkness, and the moon into blood, before the great and terrible day of Yahweh comes. **Amos 8:9** "It will happen in that day," says the Lord Yahweh, "that I will cause the sun to go down at noon, and I will darken the earth in the clear day." **Revelation 6:12–17** I saw when He opened the sixth seal, and there was a great earthquake. The sun became black as sackcloth made of hair, and the whole moon became as blood. 13 The stars of the sky fell to the earth, like a fig tree dropping its unripe figs when it is shaken by a great wind. 14 The sky was removed like a scroll when it is rolled up. Every mountain and island were moved out of their places. 15 The kings of the earth, the princes, the commanding officers, the rich, the strong, and every slave and free person, hid themselves in the caves and in the rocks of the mountains. 16 They told the

25 and on the earth anxiety of nations, in perplexity for the roaring of the sea and the waves; 26 men fainting for fear, and for expectation of the things which are coming on the world: for the powers of the heavens will be shaken.

27 "Then they will see 30 the sign of the Son of Man[184] will appear in the sky. Then all the tribes of the earth will mourn, and they will see the Son of Man coming on the clouds of the sky with 26 great 30 power and great glory. 28 But when these things begin to happen, look up, and lift up your heads, because your redemption is near.

31 "He will send out His angels with a great sound of a trumpet,[185] and they will gather together His chosen ones from the four winds, from one end of the sky to the other, 27 from the ends of the earth to the ends of the sky.

The Parable of the Fig Tree

Luke 21:29–36; Matthew 24:32–44; Mark 13:28–37

---

mountains and the rocks, "Fall on us, and hide us from the face of Him who sits on the throne, and from the wrath of the Lamb, 17 for the great day of his wrath has come; and who is able to stand?"

[184] **Daniel 7:13–14** I saw in the night visions, and behold, there came with the clouds of the sky one like a son of man, and he came even to the ancient of days, and they brought him near before Him. 14 There was given Him dominion, and glory, and a kingdom that all the peoples, nations, and languages should serve Him: His dominion is an everlasting dominion, which shall not pass away, and His kingdom that which shall not be destroyed.

[185] **1 Corinthians 15:49–53** As we have borne the image of those made of dust, we will also bear the image of the heavenly. 50 Now I say this, brothers, that flesh and blood can't inherit God's Kingdom; neither does the perishable inherit imperishable. 51 Behold, I tell you a mystery. We will not all sleep, but we will all be changed, 52 in a moment, in the twinkling of an eye, at the last trumpet. For the trumpet will sound, and the dead will be raised incorruptible, and we will be changed. 53 For this perishable body must become imperishable, and this mortal must put on immortality. **1 Thessalonians 4:16–17** For the Lord Himself will descend from heaven with a shout, with the voice of the archangel, and with God's trumpet. The dead in Christ will rise first, 17 then we who are alive, who are left, will be caught up together with them in the clouds, to meet the Lord in the air. So we will be with the Lord forever. **Revelation 11:15** The seventh angel sounded, and great voices in heaven followed, saying, "The kingdom of the world has become the Kingdom of our Lord, and of his Christ. He will reign forever and ever!"

29 He told them a parable. “See the fig tree, and all the trees. 32 Now from the fig tree learn this parable. 30 When they are already budding, you see it and know. 32 When its branch has now become tender, and produces its leaves, you know 30 by your own selves that the summer is already near. 33 Even so you also, when you see all 31 these things happening, 29 coming to pass, 31 know that God’s kingdom is near, 33 even at the doors.

34 “Most certainly I tell you, this generation will not pass away, until all these things are accomplished [and] 30 happen. 35 Heaven and earth will pass away, but My words will not pass away.[186] 36 But no one knows of that day and hour, not even the angels of heaven, 32 nor the Son, 36 but my Father only.

34 “So be careful, or your hearts will be loaded down with carousing, drunkenness, and cares of this life, and that day will come on you suddenly. 35 For it will come like a snare on all those who dwell on the surface of all the earth. 36 Therefore be watchful all the time, praying that you may be counted worthy to escape all these things that will happen, and to stand before the Son of Man.”

33 “Watch, keep alert, and pray; for you don’t know when the time is.

The Parable of a Man on a Journey

34 “It is like a man, traveling to another country, having left his house, and given authority to his servants, and to each one his work, and also commanded the doorkeeper to keep watch. 35 Watch therefore, for you don’t know when the lord of the house is coming, whether at evening, or at midnight, or when the rooster crows, or in the morning; 36 lest coming suddenly he might find you sleeping. 37 What I tell you, I tell all: Watch.”

37 “As the days of Noah were, so will be the coming of the Son of Man.[187] 38 For as in those days which were before the flood they were

---

[186] **Isaiah 40:6–8** “All flesh is like grass, and all its glory is like the flower of the field. 7 The grass withers, the flower fades, because Yahweh’s breath blows on it. Surely the people are like grass. 8 The grass withers, the flower fades; but the word of our God stands forever.”

[187] **Genesis 6:1–2, 5–8, 11–13** When men began to multiply on the surface of the ground, and daughters were born to them, 2 God’s sons saw that men’s daughters

eating and drinking, marrying and giving in marriage, until the day that Noah entered into the ship, 39 and they didn't know until the flood came, and took them all away, so will be the coming of the Son of Man.

40 "Then two men will be in the field: one will be taken and one will be left; 41 two women grinding at the mill, one will be taken and one will be left. 42 Watch therefore, for you don't know in what hour your Lord comes. 43 But know this, that if the master of the house had known in what watch of the night the thief was coming, he would have watched, and would not have allowed his house to be broken into. 44 Therefore also be ready, for in an hour that you don't expect, the Son of Man will come.

The Parable of the Faithful Servant and the Evil Servant

Matthew 24:45–51

45 "Who then is the faithful and wise servant, whom his lord has set over his household, to give them their food in due season? 46 Blessed is that servant whom his lord finds doing so when he comes. 47 Most certainly I tell you that he will set him over all that he has.

47 "But if that evil servant should say in his heart, 'My lord is delaying his coming,' 49 and begins to beat his fellow servants, and eat and drink with the drunkards, 50 the lord of that servant will come in a day when he doesn't expect it, and in an hour when he doesn't know it, 51 and will cut him in pieces, and appoint his portion with the hypocrites. There is where the weeping and grinding of teeth will be."

---

were beautiful, and they took any that they wanted for themselves as wives. 5 Yahweh saw that the wickedness of man was great in the earth, and that every imagination of the thoughts of man's heart was continually only evil. 6 Yahweh was sorry that he had made man on the earth, and it grieved him in his heart. 7 Yahweh said, "I will destroy man whom I have created from the surface of the ground—man, along with animals, creeping things, and birds of the sky—for I am sorry that I have made them." 8 But Noah found favor in Yahweh's eyes. 11 The earth was corrupt before God, and the earth was filled with violence. 12 God saw the earth, and saw that it was corrupt, for all flesh had corrupted their way on the earth. 13 God said to Noah, "I will bring an end to all flesh, for the earth is filled with violence through them. Behold, I will destroy them and the earth."

The Parable of the Ten Virgins

Matthew 25:1–13

1 “Then the Kingdom of Heaven will be like ten virgins, who took their lamps, and went out to meet the bridegroom. 2 Five of them were foolish, and five were wise. 3 Those who were foolish, when they took their lamps, took no oil with them, 4 but the wise took oil in their vessels with their lamps.

5 “Now while the bridegroom delayed, they all slumbered and slept. 6 But at midnight there was a cry, ‘Behold! The bridegroom is coming! Come out to meet him!’ 7 Then all those virgins arose, and trimmed their lamps.

8 “The foolish said to the wise, ‘Give us some of your oil, for our lamps are going out.’

9 “But the wise answered, saying, ‘What if there isn’t enough for us and you? You go rather to those who sell, and buy for yourselves.’

10 “While they went away to buy, the bridegroom came, and those who were ready went in with him to the marriage feast, and the door was shut. 11 Afterward the other virgins also came, saying, ‘Lord, Lord, open to us.’

12 “But he answered, ‘Most certainly I tell you, I don’t know you.’

13 “Watch therefore, for you don’t know the day nor the hour in which the Son of Man is coming.

The Parable of the Talents

Matthew 25:14–30

14 “For it is like a man, going into another country, who called his own servants, and entrusted his goods to them. 15 To one he gave five talents, to another two, to another one; to each according to his own ability. Then he went on his journey.

16 “Immediately he who received the five talents went and traded with them, and made another five talents. 17 In the same way, he also who got the two gained another two. 18 But he who received the one talent went away and dug in the earth, and hid his lord’s money.

19 "Now after a long time the lord of those servants came, and
reconciled accounts with them. 20 He who received the five talents
came and brought another five talents, saying, 'Lord, you delivered to
me five talents. Behold, I have gained another five talents besides
them.'

21 "His lord said to him, 'Well done, good and faithful servant. You
have been faithful over a few things; I will set you over many things.
Enter into the joy of your lord.'

22 "He also who got the two talents came and said, 'Lord, you
delivered to me two talents. Behold, I have gained another two talents
besides them.'

23 "His lord said to him, 'Well done, good and faithful servant. You
have been faithful over a few things; I will set you over many things.
Enter into the joy of your lord.'

24 "He also who had received the one talent came and said, 'Lord, I
knew you that you are a hard man, reaping where you did not sow,
and gathering where you did not scatter. 25 I was afraid, and went
away and hid your talent in the earth. Behold, you have what is yours.'

26 "But his lord answered him, 'You wicked and slothful servant. You
knew that I reap where I didn't sow, and gather where I didn't scatter.
27 You ought therefore to have deposited my money with the bankers,
and at my coming I should have received back my own with interest.
28 Take away therefore the talent from him, and give it to him who
has the ten talents. 29 For to everyone who has will be given, and he
will have abundance, but from him who doesn't have, even that which
he has will be taken away. 30 Throw out the unprofitable servant into
the outer darkness, where there will be weeping and gnashing of
teeth.'

The Judgment of Nations

Matthew 25:31–46

31 "But when the Son of Man comes in his glory, and all the holy
angels with Him, then He will sit on the throne of His glory. 32 Before
Him all the nations will be gathered, and He will separate them one
from another, as a shepherd separates the sheep from the goats. 33 He

will set the sheep on his right hand, but the goats on the left.[188]

34 "Then the King will tell those on His right hand, 'Come, blessed of My Father, inherit the Kingdom prepared for you from the foundation of the world; 35 for I was hungry, and you gave Me food to eat. I was thirsty, and you gave Me drink. I was a stranger, and you took Me in. 36 I was naked, and you clothed Me. I was sick, and you visited Me. I was in prison, and you came to Me.'

37 "Then the righteous will answer Him, saying, 'Lord, when did we see You hungry, and feed You; or thirsty, and give You a drink? 38 When did we see You as a stranger, and take You in; or naked, and clothe You? 39 When did we see You sick, or in prison, and come to You?'

40 "The King will answer them, 'Most certainly I tell you, because you did it to one of the least of these My brothers, you did it to Me.'

41 "Then He will say also to those on the left hand, 'Depart from Me, you cursed, into the eternal fire which is prepared for the devil and his angels; 42 for I was hungry, and you didn't give Me food to eat; I was thirsty, and you gave Me no drink; 43 I was a stranger, and you didn't take Me in; naked, and you didn't clothe Me; sick, and in prison, and you didn't visit Me.'

44 "Then they will also answer, saying, 'Lord, when did we see You hungry, or thirsty, or a stranger, or naked, or sick, or in prison, and didn't help You?'

45 "Then He will answer them, saying, 'Most certainly I tell you, because you didn't do it to one of the least of these, you didn't do it to Me.' 46 These will go away into eternal punishment, but the righteous into eternal life."

The Plot to Kill Jesus Nisan 12

Matthew 26:1–2

1 When Jesus had finished all these words, He said to his disciples, 2 "You know that after two days the Passover is coming, and the Son of

---

[188] **Ezekiel 34:17** As for you, O my flock, thus says the Lord Yahweh: Behold, I judge between sheep and sheep, the rams and the male goats.

Man will be delivered up to be crucified."

Jesus Teaches Daily in the Temple

Luke 21:37–38; 22:1–2; Mark 14:1–5; Matthew 26:3-5

37 Every day Jesus was teaching in the temple, and every night He would go out and spend the night on the mountain that is called Olivet. 38 All the people came early in the morning to Him in the temple to hear Him.

1 Now the feast of unleavened bread, which is called the Passover, was approaching. 1 It was now two days before the feast of the Passover and the unleavened bread. 3 Then the chief priests, the scribes, and the elders of the people were gathered together in the court of the high priest, who was called Caiaphas. 4 They took counsel together that they might take Jesus by deceit, and kill him. 5 But they said, "Not during the feast, lest a riot occur among the people."

Judas Agrees to Betray Jesus

Luke 22:3–6; Mark 14:10–11; Matthew 26:14–16

3 Satan entered into Judas, who was also called Iscariot, who was numbered with the twelve. 4 He 10 went away to the chief priests, that he might deliver Him to them.

[He] 4 talked with the chief priests and captains about how he might deliver Him to them, 15 and said, "What are you willing to give me, that I should deliver Him to you?"

11 They, when they heard it, 5 were glad, and agreed 11 and promised to give him money. 15 They weighed out for him thirty pieces of silver.[189]

6 He consented, and 16 from that time 6 sought an opportunity 11 how he might conveniently 16 betray Him [and] 6 deliver Him to them in the absence of the multitude.

---

[189] **Zechariah 11:12** I said to them, "If you think it best, give me my wages; and if not, keep them." So they weighed for my wages thirty pieces of silver.

The Disciples Prepare for the Passover - Nisan 13

Luke 22:7–13; Mark 14:12–16; Matthew 26:17–19

7 The 12 first 7 day of unleavened bread came, 7 on which the Passover must be sacrificed.[190] 8 He sent Peter and John, saying, "Go and prepare the Passover for us, that we may eat."

9 They said to Him, "Where do You want us to prepare 17 for You, 12 that You may eat the Passover?"

10 He said to them, 13 "Go into the city, and 10 behold, when you have entered into the city, a man carrying a pitcher of water;[191] will meet you. Follow him into the house which he enters. 11 Tell the master of the house 14 he enters, 11 'The Teacher says to you, 18 "My time is at hand. I will keep the Passover at your house with My disciples. 11 Where is the guest room, where I may eat the Passover with My disciples?"' 12 He will show you a large, furnished 15 and ready 12 upper room. Make preparations there."

13 So 19 the disciples did as Jesus commanded them. 13 They went 16 out, and came into the city, 13 found things as He had told them, and they prepared the Passover.

The Footwashing - Nisan 14 after Sunset

John 13:1–17; Mark 14:17; Luke 22:14–18; Matthew 26:20

1 Now before the feast of the Passover, Jesus, knowing that His time had come that He would depart from this world to the Father, having loved His own who were in the world, He loved them to the end.

When it was evening He came with the twelve. 14 When the hour had come, He sat down 20 he was reclining at the table 14 with the twelve apostles. 15 He said to them, "I have earnestly desired to eat this

---

[190] This was not the Jewish Feast day, the first day of Unleavened Bread, which occurred after the Passover. (See Leviticus 23:5–6.) Rather it refers to the start of the season of unleavened bread. The Jews typically had all leaven out of their homes by the day before the Passover, Nisan 13, which is when the disciples prepared. Nisan 14, when they ate the Passover, began at sunset. The Passover lamb was sacrificed on Nisan 14, beginning in the afternoon.

[191] Ordinarily, only women carried water. [Cheney] Jesus had apparently arranged this signal for secrecy from the scribes and Pharisees.

Passover with you before I suffer, 16 for I tell you, I will no longer by any means eat of it until it is fulfilled in God's kingdom." 17 He received a cup, and when he had given thanks, He said, "Take this, and share it among yourselves, for I tell you, [from now on],[192] I will not drink at all again from the fruit of the vine, until God's kingdom comes."

2 During supper, the devil having already put into the heart of Judas Iscariot, Simon's son, to betray Him, 3 Jesus, knowing that the Father had given all things into His hands, and that He came from God, and was going to God, 4 arose from supper, and laid aside His outer garments. He took a towel, and wrapped a towel around His waist. 5 Then He poured water into the basin, and began to wash the disciples' feet, and to wipe them with the towel that was wrapped around him.

6 Then He came to Simon Peter. He said to Him, "Lord, do you wash my feet?"

7 Jesus answered him, "You don't know what I am doing now, but you will understand later."

8 Peter said to Him, "You will never wash my feet!"

Jesus answered him, "If I don't wash you, you have no part with Me."

9 Simon Peter said to Him, "Lord, not my feet only, but also my hands and my head!"

10 Jesus said to him, "Someone who has bathed only needs to have his feet washed, but is completely clean. You are clean, but not all of you."

11 For He knew him who would betray Him, therefore He said, "You are not all clean."

12 So when He had washed their feet, put His outer garment back on, and sat down again, He said to them, "Do you know what I have done to you? 13 You call Me, 'Teacher' and 'Lord.' You say so correctly, for so I am. 14 If I then, the Lord and the Teacher, have washed your

---

[192] The phrase "from now on" appears in the *Nestle Aland Greek New Testament* and in the *United Bible Societies' Third E*dition from the majority of Greek manuscripts. It is not in the Received Text of the Sinaiticus and the Vatican manuscripts.

feet, you also ought to wash one another's feet. 15 For I have given you an example, that you also should do as I have done to you.

16 "Most certainly I tell you, a servant is not greater than his lord, neither one who is sent greater than he who sent him. 17 If you know these things, blessed are you if you do them."

Judas Leaves to Betray Jesus

Matthew 26:21–25; Mark 14:18–21; John 13:18–32; Luke 22:21–23

As they 18 sat and 21 were eating, He said, 18 "I don't speak concerning all of you. I know whom I have chosen.

"But that the Scripture may be fulfilled, 'He who eats bread with Me has lifted up his heel against Me.'[193]

19 "From now on, I tell you before it happens, that when it happens, you may believe that I am He. 20 Most certainly I tell you, he who receives whomever I send, receives Me; and he who receives Me, receives Him who sent Me.

21 When Jesus had said this, He was troubled in spirit, and testified, "Most certainly I tell you that one of you will betray Me. 21 But behold, the hand of him who betrays Me is with Me on the table. 22 The Son of Man indeed goes, as it has been determined, but woe to that man through whom He is betrayed!"

22 The disciples looked at one another, perplexed about whom He spoke. 23 They began to question among themselves, which of them it was who would do this thing. 19 They began to be sorrowful. 22 They were exceedingly sorrowful, and each began to ask Him, 19 one by one, "Surely not I?" 22 "It isn't me, is it, Lord?" 19 And another said, "Surely not I?"

23 One of his disciples, whom Jesus loved, was at the table, leaning against Jesus's breast. 24 Simon Peter therefore beckoned to him, and said to him, "Tell us who it is of whom He speaks."

25 He, leaning back, as he was, on Jesus's breast, asked him, "Lord,

---

[193] **Psalm 41:9** Yes, my own familiar friend, in whom I trusted, who ate bread with Me, has lifted up his heel against Me.

who is it?"

26 Jesus therefore answered 20 them, "It is one of the twelve, he who dips 23 his hand 20 with Me in the dish, 23 the same will betray Me. 21 For the Son of Man goes, even as it is written about Him, but woe to that man by whom the Son of Man is betrayed! It would be better for that man if he had not been born."

25 Judas, who betrayed Him, answered, "It isn't me, is it, Rabbi?"

He said to him, "You said it."

[To John] 26 Jesus therefore answered, "It is he to whom I will give this piece of bread when I have dipped it." So when He had dipped the piece of bread, He gave it to Judas, the son of Simon Iscariot. 27 After the piece of bread, then Satan entered into him.

Then Jesus said to him, "What you do, do quickly."

28 Now no man at the table knew why He said this to him. 29 For some thought, because Judas had the money box, that Jesus said to him, "Buy what things we need for the feast," or that he should give something to the poor. 30 Therefore having received that morsel, he went out immediately. It was night.

31When he had gone out, Jesus said, "Now the Son of Man has been glorified, and God has been glorified in Him. 32 If God has been glorified in Him, God will also glorify Him in Himself, and He will glorify Him immediately."

The New Covenant Passover Symbols Instituted

Matthew 26:26–29; Luke 22:19–20; 1 Corinthians 11:24–25; Mark 14:22–25

26 As they were eating, Jesus took bread, gave thanks for it, and broke it, 19 and gave to them, saying, 24 "Take, eat. 19 This is My body which is given [and] 24 broken for you. Do this in memory of Me."

27 He 20 likewise 25 in the same way 27 took the cup, 20 after supper, 27 gave thanks, and gave to them, saying, "All of you drink it."

23 And when He had given thanks, He gave to them. They all drank of it. 24 He said to them, 25 "This cup is the new covenant in My blood. 28 For this is My blood of the new covenant, which is poured

out 20 for you [and] for many for the remission of sins. 25 Do this, as often as you drink, in memory of Me. 29 But I tell you that I will not drink of this fruit of the vine from now on, until that day when I drink it anew with you in My Father's Kingdom, 25 in God's kingdom."

The Disciples Argue About Greatness

Luke 22:24–30; John 13:33–35

24 There arose also a contention among them, which of them was considered to be greatest.

25 He said to them, "The kings of the nations lord it over them, and those who have authority over them are called 'benefactors.' 26 But not so with you. But one who is the greater among you, let him become as the younger, and one who is governing, as one who serves. 27 For who is greater, one who sits at the table, or one who serves? Isn't it he who sits at the table? But I am among you as One Who serves. 28 But you are those who have continued with Me in my trials. 29 I confer on you a kingdom, even as My Father conferred on Me, 30 that you may eat and drink at My table in my Kingdom. You will sit on thrones, judging the twelve tribes of Israel.

33 "Little children, I will be with you a little while longer. You will seek Me, and as I said to the Jews, 'Where I am going, you can't come,' so now I tell you. 34 A new commandment I give to you, that you love one another. Just as I have loved you, you also love one another. 35 By this everyone will know that you are My disciples, if you have love for one another."

Jesus Predicts Peter's Denial

John 13:36–38; Luke 22:31–34

36 Simon Peter said to him, "Lord, where are You going?"

Jesus answered, "Where I am going, you can't follow now, but you will follow afterwards."

37 Peter said to him, "Lord, why can't I follow You now? I will lay down my life for You."

31 The Lord said, "Simon, Simon, behold, Satan asked to have you,

that he might sift you as wheat, 32 but I prayed for you, that your faith wouldn't fail. You, when once you have turned again, establish your brothers."

33 He said to Him, "Lord, I am ready to go with You both to prison and to death!"

38 Jesus answered him, "Will you lay down your life for Me? Most certainly I tell you, 34 Peter, 38 the rooster won't crow 34 today 38 until you have denied 34 you know Me 38 three times."

The Way, the Truth, and the Life

John 14:1–14

1 "Don't let your heart be troubled. Believe in God. Believe also in Me. 2 In My Father's house are many homes. If it weren't so, I would have told you. I am going to prepare a place for you. 3 If I go and prepare a place for you, I will come again, and will receive you to Myself; that where I am, you may be there also. 4 Where I go, you know, and you know the way."

5 Thomas said to him, "Lord, we don't know where You are going. How can we know the way?"

6 Jesus said to him, "I am the Way, the Truth, and the Life. No one comes to the Father, except through Me. 7 If you had known Me, you would have known My Father also. From now on, you know Him, and have seen Him."

8 Philip said to Him, "Lord, show us the Father, and that will be enough for us."

9 Jesus said to him, "Have I been with you such a long time, and do you not know Me, Philip? He who has seen Me has seen the Father. How do you say, 'Show us the Father?' 10 Don't you believe that I am in the Father, and the Father in Me? The words that I tell you, I speak not from Myself; but the Father who lives in Me does His works. 11 Believe Me that I am in the Father, and the Father in me; or else believe Me for the very works' sake.

12 "Most certainly I tell you, he who believes in Me, the works that I do, he will do also; and he will do greater works than these, because I

am going to My Father. 13 Whatever you will ask in My Name, that will I do, that the Father may be glorified in the Son. 14 If you will ask anything in My Name, I will do it.

Promise of Another Helper

John 14:15–31; Matthew 26:30; Mark 14:26; Luke 22:35–39

15 "If you love Me, keep My commandments. 16 I will pray to the Father, and He will give you another Counselor,[194] that He may be with you forever, — 17 the Spirit of truth, Whom the world can't receive; for it doesn't see Him, neither knows Him. You know Him, for He lives with you, and will be in you.

18 "I will not leave you[195] orphans. I will come to you. 19 Yet a little while, and the world will see Me no more; but you will see Me. Because I live, you will live also. 20 In that day you will know that I am in My Father, and you in Me, and I in you. 21 One who has My commandments, and keeps them, that person is one who loves Me. One who loves Me will be loved by My Father, and I will love him, and will reveal Myself to him."

22 Judas (not Iscariot) said to Him, "Lord, what has happened that You are about to reveal Yourself to us, and not to the world?"

23 Jesus answered him, "If a man loves Me, he will keep My word. My Father will love him, and We will come to him, and make Our home with him. 24 He who doesn't love Me doesn't keep My words. The word which you hear isn't Mine, but the Father's Who sent Me.

25 "I have said these things to you, while still living with you. 26 But the Counselor, the Holy Spirit, Whom the Father will send in My name, He will teach you all things, and will remind you of all that I said to you.

27 "Peace I leave with you. My peace I give to you; not as the world

---

[194] Greek παρακλητον (*parakleton*): Counselor, Helper, Intercessor, Advocate, and Comforter. (Strong's Concordance.)

[195] **Hebrews 13:5** For he has said, "I will in no way leave you, neither will I in any way forsake you. **Deuteronomy 31:6** "Be strong and courageous. Don't be afraid or scared of them; for Yahweh your God Himself is Who goes with you. He will not fail you nor forsake you."

gives, give I to you. Don't let your heart be troubled, neither let it be fearful. 28 You heard how I told you, 'I go away, and I come to you.' If you loved Me, you would have rejoiced, because I said 'I am going to My Father;' for the Father is greater than I. 29 Now I have told you before it happens so that, when it happens, you may believe.

30 "I will no more speak much with you, for the prince of the world comes, and he has nothing in Me. 31 But that the world may know that I love the Father, and as the Father commanded Me, even so I do. Arise, let us go from here."

30 When they had sung a hymn, they went out to the Mount of Olives.

35 He said to them, "When I sent you out without purse, and wallet, and shoes, did you lack anything?"

They said, "Nothing."

36 Then He said to them, "But now, whoever has a purse, let him take it, and likewise a wallet. Whoever has none, let him sell his cloak, and buy a sword. 37 For I tell you that this which is written must still be fulfilled in Me:

> 'He was counted with transgressors.'[196]

For that which concerns me has an end."

38 They said, "Lord, behold, here are two swords."

He said to them, "That is enough."

39 He came out, and went, as His custom was, to the Mount of Olives. His disciples also followed Him.

Jesus Predicts All Will Stumble

Matthew 26:31–35: Mark 14:27–31

31 Then Jesus said to them, "All of you will be made to stumble because of Me tonight, for it is written,

---

[196] **Isaiah 53:12** Therefore will I give Him a portion with the great, and He will divide the plunder with the strong; because He poured out His soul to death, and was numbered with the transgressors; yet He bore the sin of many, and made intercession for the transgressors.

'I will strike the shepherd, and the sheep of the flock will be scattered.'[197]

32 But after I am raised up, I will go before you into Galilee."

33 But Peter answered him, "Even if all will be made to stumble 29 [and] all will be offended 33 because of You, 29 yet 33 I will never be made to stumble."

34 Jesus said to him, "Most certainly I tell you 30 today, even this night, before the rooster crows twice, 34 you will deny Me three times."[198]

31 But 35 Peter said to Him, [and] 31 he spoke all the more, 35 "Even if I must die with You, I will not deny You." All of the disciples also said 31 the same thing 35 likewise.

The True Vine

John 15:1–7

1 "I am the true vine, and My Father is the farmer. 2 Every branch in Me that doesn't bear fruit, He takes away. Every branch that bears fruit, He prunes, that it may bear more fruit. 3 You are already pruned clean because of the word which I have spoken to you.

4 "Remain in Me, and I in you. As the branch can't bear fruit by itself, unless it remains in the vine, so neither can you, unless you remain in Me.

5 "I am the vine. You are the branches. He who remains in Me, and I in him, the same bears much fruit, for apart from Me you can do nothing. 6 If a man doesn't remain in Me, he is thrown out as a branch, and is withered; and they gather them, throw them into the fire, and they are burned. 7 If you remain in Me, and My words remain in you, you will ask whatever you desire, and it will be done for you.

---

[197] **Zechariah 13:7** "Awake, sword, against My shepherd, and against the man who is close to Me," says Yahweh of Armies." Strike the shepherd, and the sheep will be scattered; and I will turn My hand against the little ones.

[198] "Before the cock crows" seems to be a regular way of saying "before early in the morning." According to Roman time reckoning, "cockcrow" was the third watch of the night, roughly from midnight to 3 a.m" (The Interpreter's Bible).

Love and Joy Perfected

John 15:8–16

8 “In this is My Father glorified, that you bear much fruit; and so you will be My disciples. 9 Even as the Father has loved Me, I also have loved you. Remain in My love. 10 If you keep My commandments, you will remain in My love; even as I have kept my Father’s commandments, and remain in His love. 11 I have spoken these things to you, that My joy may remain in you, and that your joy may be made full.

12 “This is My commandment, that you love one another, even as I have loved you. 13 Greater love has no one than this, that someone lay down his life for his friends. 14 You are My friends, if you do whatever I command you.

15 “No longer do I call you servants, for the servant doesn’t know what his lord does. But I have called you friends, for everything that I heard from My Father, I have made known to you. 16 You didn’t choose Me, but I chose you, and appointed you, that you should go and bear fruit, and that your fruit should remain; that whatever you will ask of the Father in My name, He may give it to you.

The World’s Hatred

John 15:17–27

17 “I command these things to you, that you may love one another.

18 “If the world hates you, you know that it has hated Me before it hated you. 19 If you were of the world, the world would love its own. But because you are not of the world, since I chose you out of the world, therefore the world hates you. 20 Remember the word that I said to you: ‘A servant is not greater than his lord.’[199] If they persecuted Me, they will also persecute you. If they kept My word, they will keep yours also. 21 But all these things will they do to you for My name’s sake, because they don’t know Him who sent Me.

---

[199] **Matthew 10:24** “A disciple is not above his teacher, nor a servant above his lord.” **John 13:16** Most certainly I tell you, a servant is not greater than his lord, neither one who is sent greater than he who sent him.

22 "If I had not come and spoken to them, they would not have had sin; but now they have no excuse for their sin. 23 He who hates Me, hates My Father also. 24 If I hadn't done among them the works which no one else did, they wouldn't have had sin. But now have they seen and also hated both Me and My Father. 25 But this happened so that the word may be fulfilled which was written in their law, 'They hated Me without a cause.'[200]

26 "When the Counselor has come, Whom I will send to you from the Father, the Spirit of truth, Who proceeds from the Father, He will testify about Me. 27 You will also testify, because you have been with Me from the beginning.

The Coming Persecution

John 16:1–33

1 "These things have I spoken to you, so that you wouldn't be caused to stumble. 2 They will put you out of the synagogues. Yes, the time comes that whoever kills you will think that he offers service to God. 3 They will do these things to you because they have not known the Father, nor Me. 4 But I have told you these things, so that when the time comes, you may remember that I told you about them. I didn't tell you these things from the beginning, because I was with you.

The Work of the Holy Spirit

5 "But now I am going to Him who sent Me, and none of you asks Me, 'Where are you going?' 6 But because I have told you these things, sorrow has filled your heart. 7 Nevertheless I tell you the truth: It is to your advantage that I go away, for if I don't go away, the Counselor won't come to you. But if I go, I will send Him to you.

8 "When He has come, He will convict the world about sin, about righteousness, and about judgment; 9 about sin, because they don't believe in Me; 10 about righteousness, because I am going to My

[200] **Psalm 69:4** Those who hate me without a cause are more than the hairs of my head. Those who want to cut me off, being my enemies wrongfully, are mighty. I have to restore what I didn't take away. **Psalm 35:19** Don't let those who are my enemies wrongfully rejoice over me; neither let those who hate me without a cause wink their eyes.

Father, and you won't see Me any more; 11 about judgment, because the prince of this world has been judged.

12 "I have yet many things to tell you, but you can't bear them now. 13 However when He, the Spirit of truth, has come, He will guide you into all truth, for He will not speak from Himself; but whatever He hears, He will speak. He will declare to you things that are coming. 14 He will glorify Me, for He will take from what is Mine, and will declare it to you. 15 All things whatever the Father has are Mine; therefore I said that He will take of Mine, and will declare it to you.

Sorrow Will Turn to Joy

16 "A little while, and you will not see Me. Again a little while, and you will see Me."

17 Some of His disciples therefore said to one another, "What is this that He says to us, 'A little while, and you won't see Me, and again a little while, and you will see Me;' and, 'Because I go to the Father'?" 18 They said therefore, "What is this that He says, 'A little while?' We don't know what He is saying."

19 Therefore Jesus perceived that they wanted to ask Him, and He said to them, "Do you inquire among yourselves concerning this, that I said, 'A little while, and you won't see Me, and again a little while, and you will see Me?'

20 "Most certainly I tell you, that you will weep and lament, but the world will rejoice. You will be sorrowful, but your sorrow will be turned into joy.

21 "A woman, when she gives birth, has sorrow, because her time has come. But when she has delivered the child, she doesn't remember the anguish any more, for the joy that a human being is born into the world. 22 Therefore you now have sorrow, but I will see you again, and your heart will rejoice, and no one will take your joy away from you.

23 "In that day you will ask Me no questions. Most certainly I tell you, whatever you may ask of the Father in My Name, He will give it to you. 24 Until now, you have asked nothing in My Name. Ask, and you will receive, that your joy may be made full.

Jesus Christ Has Overcome the World

25 "I have spoken these things to you in figures of speech. But the time is coming when I will no more speak to you in figures of speech, but will tell you plainly about the Father. 26 In that day you will ask in My name; and I don't say to you, that I will pray to the Father for you, 27 for the Father Himself loves you, because you have loved Me, and have believed that I came from God. 28 I came from the Father, and have come into the world. Again, I leave the world, and go to the Father."

29 His disciples said to Him, "Behold, now You speak plainly, and speak no figures of speech. 30 Now we know that You know all things, and don't need for anyone to question You. By this we believe that You came from God."

31 Jesus answered them, "Do you now believe? 32 Behold, the time is coming, yes, and has now come, that you will be scattered, everyone to his own place, and you will leave Me alone. Yet I am not alone, because the Father is with Me. 33 I have told you these things, that in Me you may have peace. In the world you have oppression; but cheer up! I have overcome the world."

Jesus Prays

John 17:1–26

1 Jesus said these things, and lifting up His eyes to heaven, He said, "Father, the time has come. Glorify Your Son, that Your Son may also glorify You; 2 even as You gave Him authority over all flesh, He will give eternal life to all whom You have given Him.

3 "This is eternal life, that they should know You, the only true God, and Him Whom you sent, Jesus Christ. 4 I glorified You on the earth. I have accomplished the work which You have given Me to do. 5 Now, Father, glorify Me with Your Own Self with the glory which I had with You before the world existed.

Jesus Prays for His Disciples

6 "I revealed Your name to the people whom You have given Me out

of the world. They were Yours, and You have given them to Me. They
have kept Your word. 7 Now they have known that all things whatever
You have given Me are from You, 8 for the words which You have
given Me I have given to them, and they received them, and knew for
sure that I came from You, and they have believed that You sent Me.

9 "I pray for them. I don't pray for the world, but for those whom You
have given Me, for they are Yours. 10 All things that are Mine are
Yours, and Yours are Mine, and I am glorified in them. 11 I am no
more in the world, but these are in the world, and I am coming to You.

"Holy Father, keep them through Your name which You have given
Me, that they may be one, even as We are. 12 While I was with them
in the world, I kept them in Your name. Those whom You have given
Me I have kept. None of them is lost except the son of destruction,
that the Scripture might be fulfilled.

13 "But now I come to You, and I say these things in the world, that
they may have My joy made full in themselves. 14 I have given them
Your word. The world hated them, because they are not of the world,
even as I am not of the world. 15 I pray not that You would take them
from the world, but that You would keep them from the evil one. 16
They are not of the world even as I am not of the world.

17 "Sanctify them in Your truth. Your word is truth.[201] 18 As You sent
Me into the world, even so I have sent them into the world. 19 For
their sakes I sanctify Myself, that they themselves also may be
sanctified in truth.

Jesus Prays for All Believers

20 " Not for these only do I pray, but for those also who believe in Me
through their word, 21 that they may all be one; even as You, Father,
are in Me, and I in You, that they also may be one in Us; that the world
may believe that You sent Me. 22 The glory which You have given
Me, I have given to them; that they may be one, even as We are one;
23 I in them, and You in Me, that they may be perfected into one; that
the world may know that You sent Me, and loved them, even as You

---

[201] **Psalm 119:142** Your righteousness is an everlasting righteousness. Your law is truth.

loved Me.

24 “Father, I desire that they also whom You have given Me be with Me where I am, that they may see My glory, which You have given Me, for You loved Me before the foundation of the world. 25 Righteous Father, the world hasn’t known You, but I knew You; and these knew that You sent Me. 26 I made known to them Your name, and will make it known; that the love with which You loved Me may be in them, and I in them.”

The Prayer in the Garden – Nisan 14, 9:00 p.m.[202]

John 18:1–24; Matthew 26:36–46; Luke 22:40–46; Mark 14:32–42

1 After Jesus had said these things, He went out with His disciples across the Kidron Valley, where there was a garden, and He and His disciples went into it.

36 Then Jesus went with His disciples to a place called Gethsemane.

40 When He reached the place, He told 36 the disciples, “Sit here [and] 40 pray that you may not fall into temptation, 36 while I go over there and pray.”

37 Taking along Peter and the two sons of Zebedee, 33 James, and John with Him, 37 He began to be sorrowful, 33 greatly troubled and distressed 38 He said to them, “I am deeply grieved to the point of death. Remain here and stay awake with Me.”

39 Going a little farther, 41 then He withdrew from them about a stone’s throw, knelt down, and began to pray. 39 He fell facedown 35 to the ground, and prayed that if it were possible, the hour might pass from Him. 36 And He said, “Abba, Father! All things are possible for You.

39 “My Father, if it is possible, 42 Father, if You are willing, take this cup away from Me— 39 let this cup pass from Me. Yet not as I will, but as You will, [let it] 42 be done.”

40 Then He came to the disciples and found them sleeping. He asked Peter, 37 “Simon, are you sleeping? 40 So, couldn’t you stay awake

[202] All time estimates are my own and are *not* inspired. Others may have different times.

with Me one hour? 41 Stay awake and pray, so that you won't enter
into temptation. The spirit is willing, but the flesh is weak."

42 Again, a second time, He went away and prayed, 39 saying the
same thing. 42 "My Father, if this cup cannot pass from Me unless I
drink it, Your will be done."

43 And He came again and found them sleeping, because they could
not keep their eyes open. 40 They did not know what to say to Him.
44 After leaving them, He went away again and prayed a third time,
saying the same thing once more.

43 Then an angel from heaven appeared to Him, strengthening Him.
44 Being in anguish, He prayed more fervently, and His sweat became
like drops of blood falling to the ground. 45 When He got up from
prayer and came to the disciples, He found them sleeping, exhausted
from their grief.

41 Returning the third time, He 45 said to them, "Are you still sleeping
and resting? 46 Why are you sleeping?" He asked them. 41 "Enough!
6 Get up and pray, so that you won't fall into temptation. 45 See, the
time is near, 41 the hour has come, [and] 45 The Son of Man is
betrayed into the hands of sinners. 46 Get up; let's go. See, My
betrayer is near."

Jesus's Arrest, Trial, Death, and Resurrection

Betrayal and Arrest in Gethsemane – Nisan 14, midnight

John 18:2–11; Matthew 26:47–56; Luke 22:47–53; Mark 14:43–52

2 Judas, who betrayed Him, also knew the place, because Jesus often met there with His disciples. 3 So Judas took a company of soldiers and some officials from the chief priests and the Pharisees and came there with lanterns, torches, and weapons.

47 While He was still speaking, 47 one of the Twelve named Judas [and] 47 a large mob with swords and clubs was with him 43 suddenly arrived. 47 Judas was leading them. [They came] 47 from the chief priests 43 the scribes, 47 and elders of the people.

48 His betrayer had given them a sign: "The one I kiss, He's the one; arrest Him 44 and take Him away under guard." 45 So when he came, 49 immediately he went up to Jesus.

47 He came near Jesus to kiss Him, 45 and said, "Rabbi!"

48 But Jesus said to him, "Judas, are you betraying the Son of Man with a kiss?"

[Judas] 49 said, "Hail, Rabbi!" and kissed Him.

50 Jesus said to him, "Friend, why are you here?"

4 Then Jesus, knowing everything that was about to happen to Him, went out and said to them, "Who is it that you're seeking?"

5 "Jesus of Nazareth," they answered.

"I AM," Jesus told them.

Judas, who betrayed Him, was also standing with them. 6 When Jesus told them, "I am," they stepped back and fell to the ground.

7 Then He asked them again, "Who is it that you're seeking?"

"Jesus of Nazareth," they said.

8 "I told you I am He," Jesus replied. "So if you're looking for Me,

let these men go." 9 This was to fulfill the words He had said: "I have not lost one of those You have given Me."[203]

49 When those around Him saw what was going to happen, they asked, "Lord, should we strike with the sword?"

51 Then they came up, took hold of Jesus, and arrested Him.

51 At that moment one of those with Jesus 47 who stood by, 10 Simon Peter, who had a sword, 51 reached out his hand and drew his sword, 10 struck the high priest's servant, and cut off his right ear. (The servant's name was Malchus.)

11 At that, Jesus said to Peter, "Put your sword away 52 in its place because all who take up the sword will perish by the sword. 11 Am I not to drink the cup the Father has given Me? 53 Or do you think that I cannot call on My Father, and He will provide Me here and now with more than twelve legions of angels? 54 How, then, would the Scriptures be fulfilled that say it must happen this way?" 51 Jesus responded, "No more of this!" And touching his ear, He healed him.

52 Then 55 at that time Jesus said to the crowds, 52 to the chief priests, temple police, and the elders who had come for Him, "Have you come out with swords and clubs as if I were a criminal?[204] 53 Every day while I was with you in the temple, you never laid a hand on Me 49 and you didn't arrest Me. 53 But this is your hour —and the dominion of darkness. 56 But all this has happened so that the writings of the prophets would be fulfilled. 49 The Scriptures must be fulfilled."

56 Then all the disciples deserted Him and ran away.

51 Now a certain young man, wearing nothing but a linen cloth, was following Him. They caught hold of him, 52 but he left the linen cloth behind and ran away naked.

---

[203] **John 17:12** While I was with them, I was protecting them by your name that you have given me. I guarded them and not one of them is lost, except the son of destruction, so that the Scripture may be fulfilled. **John 6:39** This is the will of him who sent me: that I should lose none of those he has given me but should raise them up on the last day.

[204] **Matthew 26:55** and **Luke 22:52** "The word translated robber is used by Josephus to describe those revolutionaries who combined banditry and violent nationalism (e.g., Antiquities XX. 8. 5)" [Interpreter's] Literally, as against a thief or a bandit.

Before Annas the High Priest – Nisan 14, 12:30 a.m.

John 18:12–14; Matthew 26:57; Luke 22:54; Mark 14:53

12 Then the company of soldiers, the commander, and the Jewish officials arrested Jesus and tied Him up.

57 Those who had arrested Jesus, 54 seized Him, led Him away, 57 to Caiaphas the high priest, 54 and brought Him into the high priest's house 57 where the teachers of the law 53 and all the chief priests, 57 scribes and the elders had assembled.

13 First they led Him to Annas, since he was the father- in-law of Caiaphas, who was high priest that year. 14 Caiaphas was the one who had advised the Jews that it would be better for one man to die for the people.

Peter's First Denial - Nisan 14, 12:30 a.m.

John 18:15–18; Matthew 26:58; 69–70; Mark 14:54-68; Luke 22:55–57

15 Simon Peter was following Jesus, 58 at a distance 54 right into the high priest's courtyard, 15 as [did] another disciple. That disciple was an acquaintance of the high priest; so he went with Jesus into the high priest's courtyard. 16 But Peter remained standing outside by the door. So the other disciple, the one known to the high priest, went out and spoke to the girl who was the doorkeeper and brought Peter in.

55 They lit a fire in the middle of the courtyard and sat down together, and Peter 58 went in and was sitting with the servants to see the outcome, 54 warming himself by the fire.

66 While Peter 69 was sitting outside 66 in the courtyard below, one of the high priest's maidservants came. 17 Then the servant girl who was the doorkeeper 56 saw him sitting in the light, and looked closely at him, she said, 17 to Peter, "You aren't one of this Man's disciples too, are you? 56 This man was with Him too. 67 You also were with Jesus, the Man from Nazareth, 69 the Galilean too."

57 But he denied it, 70 in front of everyone: 17 "I am not." he said. 57 "Woman, I don't know Him. 68 I neither know, nor understand what you are saying." 68 He went out on the porch, and the rooster crowed.

18 Now the servants and the officials had made a charcoal fire, because it was cold. They were standing there warming themselves, and Peter was standing with them, warming himself.

Jesus Is Questioned by Annas the High Priest, 1:00 a.m.

John 18:19–24

19 The high priest then asked Jesus about His disciples, and about His teaching.

20 Jesus answered him, "I have talked so that anyone who wanted to could hear Me. I have always taught in the meeting houses and in the temple. That is where the Jews always go. I have not said anything in a secret way.

21 Why do you ask Me? The people heard Me talk. Ask them what I told them. They know what I said."

22 When He had said this, one of the officers who stood there hit Jesus. He said, "Is that the way You answer the high priest?"

23 Jesus answered him, "If I have said anything bad, tell Me plainly what wrong thing I have said. If I have told the truth, why do you hit Me?"

24 Jesus was still tied up. Annas sent Him over to Caiaphas the high priest.

Peter's Second Denial, 2:00 a.m.

John 18:25–27; Matthew 26:71–72; Luke 22:58; Mark 14:69–70

25 Simon Peter stayed by the fire and stood warming himself. 71
When he had gone out onto the porch, 58 after a little while 69 the
maid saw him, and began again, to tell 71 to those who were there, 69
who stood by, "This is one of them. 71 This man also was with Jesus
of Nazareth." 25 They said to him, "You aren't one of His disciples
too, are you?"

72 Again he denied it with an oath, 58 But Peter answered, "Man, I
am not! 72 I don't know the Man."

Jesus Is Led to Caiaphas the High Priest, 1:45 a.m.

Mark 14:53–59; Matthew 26:59–62

53 They led Jesus away to the high priest. All the chief priests, the elders, and the scribes came together with Him.

59 Now the chief priests, the elders, and the whole council sought false testimony against Jesus, that they might put Him to death; 60 and they found none. Even though many false witnesses came forward, they found none. 56 For many gave false testimony against Him, and their testimony didn't agree with each other.

60 But at last two false witnesses 57 stood up, 60 came forward, 57 and gave false testimony against Him, 61 and said, "This Man said, 'I am able to destroy the temple of God, and to build it in three days.'"

[And the other witness was] 57 saying, 58 "We heard Him say, 'I will destroy this temple that is made with hands, and in three days I will build another made without hands.'" 59 Even so, their testimony did not agree.

Jesus Is Condemned to Death

Matthew 26:62–68; Mark 14:60–65; Luke 22:63–65

60 Then the high priest stood up before them and asked Jesus, 62 and said to Him, "Have you no answer? What is this that these testify against You?"

63 But Jesus held His peace 61 and answered nothing. 63 The high priest answered Him, 61 again the high priest asked Him, 63 "I adjure You by the living God, that you tell us whether you are the Christ, 61 the Son of the Blessed, 63 the Son of God?"

64 Jesus said to him, 62 "I am. 64 You have said it. Nevertheless, I tell you, after this you will see the Son of Man sitting at the right hand of Power, and coming on the clouds of the sky." [205]

65 Then the high priest tore his clothing, saying, "He has spoken

---

[205] **Daniel 7:13** I saw in the night visions, and behold, there came with the clouds of the sky one like a son of man, and he came even to the ancient of days, and they brought him near before him.

blasphemy! Why do we need any more witnesses? Behold, now you have heard His blasphemy. 66 What do you think?"

They answered, "He is worthy of death!" 64 They all condemned Him to be worthy of death.

63 The men who held Jesus mocked Him and beat Him.67 Then 65 some began to spit on Him, and to cover His face, 67 they spit in His face and beat Him with their fists. 64 Having blindfolded Him, they struck Him on the face 67 and some slapped Him, 64 and asked Him, 68 saying, "Prophesy to us, you Christ! Who hit you?" 65 And the guards took Him and beat Him.[206]

65 They spoke many other things against Him, insulting Him.

Peter's Third Denial, 3:00 a.m.

Matthew 26:73–75; Luke 22:59–62; John 18:27; Mark 14:70-72

73 After a little while, 59 after about one hour passed, 73 those who stood by came [and] 59 another confidently affirmed, saying, "Truly this man also was with Him, for he is a Galilean!" 70 Again those who stood by said to Peter, "You truly are one of them, for you are a Galilean, 73 Surely you are also one of them, for your speech makes you known 70 and your speech shows it."

26 One of the servants of the high priest, being a relative of him whose ear Peter had cut off, said, "Didn't I see you in the garden with Him?"

27 Peter therefore denied it again. 74 Then he began to curse and to swear, 60 "Man, I don't know what you are talking about! 74 I don't know the Man 71 of whom you speak!" 27 And immediately the rooster crowed 72 the second time. 61 The Lord turned, and looked at Peter.

72 Peter remembered the 61 Lord's word, 75 which Jesus had said to him, "Before the rooster crows 72 twice,[207] 75 you will deny Me three

---

[206] **Isaiah 50:6** I offered My back to those who beat Me, My cheeks to those who pulled out My beard; I did not hide My face from mocking and spitting.

[207] The Interpreter's Bible suggests a manuscript error accounts for the "twice" reference in Mark. Upon reflection, I think it more likely that Mark is correct. Of the three possible witnesses to the events (John, Peter, and Jesus), Peter is the one most likely to relate this detail. Since Mark was a companion to Peter, he is logically

times." 72 When he thought about that, 75 he went out and wept bitterly.

At Dawn, the Sanhedrin Condemns Jesus to Death, 5:30 a.m.

Mark 15:1; Matthew 27:1–2; Luke 22:66–71; 23:1–2

1 Immediately, 1 when morning had come, 66 as soon as it was day, 1 the chief priests, with the elders and scribes, 66 the assembly of the elders of the people was gathered together, 1 and the whole council, 1 took counsel against Jesus to put Him to death: 66 and they led Him away into their council, saying, 67 "If you are the Christ, tell us."

But He said to them, "If I tell you, you won't believe, 68 and if I ask, you will in no way answer Me or let Me go. 69 From now on, the Son of Man will be seated at the right hand of the power of God."[208]

70 They all said, "Are you then the Son of God?"

He said to them, 70 "You say it, because I am."

71 They said, "Why do we need any more witness? For we ourselves have heard from His own mouth!"

1 The whole company of them rose up 1 and bound Jesus, 2 and led 1 and carried Him away, 2 and brought Him before 1 and delivered Him up to 2 Pontius Pilate, the governor.

Judas Hangs Himself, 6:00 a.m.

Matthew 27:3–10; Acts 1:18–19

3 Then Judas, who betrayed Him, when he saw that Jesus was condemned, felt remorse, and brought back the thirty pieces of silver to the chief priests and elders, 4 saying, "I have sinned in that I betrayed innocent blood."

But they said, "What is that to us? You see to it."

5 He threw down the pieces of silver in the sanctuary, and departed.

---

correct. In the retelling of the Gospel, others might have glossed over this detail or been unaware of it.

[208] **Psalm 110:1** Yahweh says to my Lord, "Sit at My right hand, until I make Your enemies Your footstool for Your feet."

He went away and hanged himself 18 and falling headlong, his body burst open, and all his intestines gushed out.

6 The chief priests took the pieces of silver, and said, "It's not lawful to put them into the treasury, since it is the price of blood." 7 They took counsel, and bought the potter's field with them, to bury strangers in.

19 It became known to everyone who lived in Jerusalem that in their language that field was called 'Akeldama,' that is, 'The field of blood.' 8 Therefore that field was called "The Field of Blood" to this day. 9 Then that which was spoken through Jeremiah[209] the prophet was fulfilled, saying,

> "They took the thirty pieces of silver, the price of Him upon Whom a price had been set, Whom some of the children of Israel priced, 10 and they gave them for the potter's field, as the Lord commanded me."[210]

Jesus Handed Over to Pontius Pilate, 6:00 a.m.

Luke 23:1–3; John18:28–38; Matthew 27:11; Mark 15:2

1 The whole company of them rose up and 28 they led Jesus therefore from Caiaphas into the Praetorium 1 and brought Him before Pilate. It was early, and they themselves didn't enter into the Praetorium, that they might not be defiled, but might eat the Passover.

29 Pilate therefore went out to them, and said, "What accusation do you bring against this Man?"

30 They answered him, "If this Man weren't an evildoer, we wouldn't have delivered Him up to you."

2 They began to accuse Him, saying, "We found this Man perverting the nation, forbidding paying taxes to Caesar, and saying that He Himself is Christ, a king."

---

[209] This quote is found in Zechariah but may well have been spoken by Jeremiah and written by Zechariah.

[210] **Zechariah 11:13** Yahweh said to me, "Throw it to the potter, the handsome price that I was valued at by them!" I took the thirty pieces of silver, and threw them to the potter, in Yahweh's house.

31 Pilate therefore said to them, “Take Him yourselves, and judge Him according to your law.”

Therefore the Jews said to him, “It is not lawful for us to put anyone to death,” 32 that the word of Jesus might be fulfilled, which He spoke, signifying by what kind of death He should die.

33 Pilate therefore entered again into the Praetorium, [and] called Jesus.

11 Now Jesus stood before the governor: and the governor 3 Pilate 11 asked Him, saying, “Are You the King of the Jews?”

34 Jesus answered him, “Do you say this by yourself, or did others tell you about Me?”

35 Pilate answered, “I’m not a Jew, am I? Your own nation and the chief priests delivered You to me. What have You done?”

36 Jesus answered, “My Kingdom is not of this world. If My Kingdom were of this world, then My servants would fight, that I wouldn’t be delivered to the Jews. But now My Kingdom is not from here.”

37 Pilate therefore said to Him, “Are You a king then?”

37 Jesus answered, 37 “You say that I am a king. 2 So you say. 37 For this reason I have been born, and for this reason I have come into the world, that I should testify to the truth. Everyone who is of the truth listens to My voice.”

38 Pilate said to Him, “What is truth?”

Pilate Declares Christ’s Innocence

John 18:38; Luke 23:4–12; Mark 15:3-5; Matthew 27:12–14

38 When he had said this, he went out again to the Jews, and 4 Pilate said to the chief priests and the multitudes, “I find no basis for a charge against this Man.”

3 The chief priests accused Him of many things. 12 When He was accused by the chief priests and elders, He answered nothing.

13 Then Pilate said to Him, [and] 4 again asked Him, “Have You no answer? 13 Don’t you hear how many things they testify against You?”

5 But Jesus made no further answer, 14 not even one word, so that the governor 5 Pilate 14 marveled greatly.

5 But they insisted, saying, "He stirs up the people, teaching throughout all Judea, beginning from Galilee even to this place."

6 But when Pilate heard Galilee mentioned, he asked if the Man was a Galilean. 7 When he found out that He was in Herod's jurisdiction, he sent Him to Herod, who was also in Jerusalem during those days.

Jesus Sent to Herod, 6:30 a.m.

Luke 23:8–12

8 Now when Herod saw Jesus, he was exceedingly glad, for he had wanted to see Him for a long time, because he had heard many things about Him. He hoped to see some miracle done by Him. 9 He questioned Him with many words, but He gave no answers.

10 The chief priests and the scribes stood, vehemently accusing Him.

11 Herod with his soldiers humiliated Him and mocked Him. Dressing Him in luxurious clothing, they sent Him back to Pilate. 12 Herod and Pilate became friends with each other that very day, for before that they were enemies with each other.

Pilate Declares Jesus Innocent Again, 7:00 a.m.

Luke 23:13–17

13 Pilate called together the chief priests and the rulers and the people, 14 and said to them, "You brought this Man to me as One that perverts the people, and see, I have examined Him before you, and found no basis for a charge against this Man concerning those things of which you accuse Him. 15 Neither has Herod, for he sent Him back to us and see, nothing worthy of death has been done by Him. 16 I will therefore chastise Him and release Him." 17 Now he had to release one prisoner to them at the feast.

The People Demand Jesus's Crucifixion Instead of Barabbas

Matthew 27:15–26; Mark 15:6–15; Luke 23:18–25; John 18:39–40

18 But they all cried out together, saying, "Away with this man! Release to us Barabbas!"

15 Now at the feast the governor was accustomed to release to the multitude one prisoner, whom they desired, 6 whom they asked of him. 16 They had then a notable prisoner, called Barabbas. 19 who was thrown into prison for a certain revolt in the city, and for murder [and] 7 bound with his fellow insurgents, men who in the insurrection had committed murder.

17 When therefore they were gathered together, 8 the multitude, crying aloud, began to ask him [Pilate] to do as he always did for them.

20 Then Pilate spoke to them again, wanting to release Jesus [and] 17 said to them, 39 "But you have a custom, that I should release someone to you at the Passover. Therefore do you want me to release to you the King of the Jews? 17 Whom do you want me to release to you? Barabbas, or Jesus, who is called Christ?" 18 For he knew that because of envy they, 10 the chief priests, had delivered Him up.

19 While he was sitting on the judgment seat, his wife sent to him, saying, "Have nothing to do with that righteous Man, for I have suffered many things today in a dream because of Him."

Now the chief priests and the elders persuaded [and] 11 stirred up the multitude, that he should release Barabbas to them instead.

21 But the governor answered them, "Which of the two do you want me to release to you?"

40 Then cried they all again, saying, "Not this Man, but Barabbas." Now Barabbas was a robber.

12 Pilate again asked them, 22 "What then shall I do to Jesus, who is called Christ? 12 "What then should I do to Him whom you call the King of the Jews?"

They all 13 cried out again, 22 [and] said to him, "Let Him be crucified!" 13 "Crucify Him!" 21 "Crucify Him!!"

23 But the governor 14 Pilate said to them, 22 the third time, 14 "Why, what evil has He done? 22 What evil has this Man done? I have found no capital crime in Him. I will therefore chastise Him and release Him."

23 But they were urgent with loud voices, asking that He might be crucified. 23 But they cried out exceedingly, saying, "Let Him be crucified! 14 Crucify Him!" 23 Their voices and the voices of the chief priests prevailed.

24 So when Pilate saw that nothing was being gained, but rather that a disturbance was starting, he took water, and washed his hands before the multitude, saying, "I am innocent of the blood of this righteous person. You see to it."

25 All the people answered, "May His blood be on us, and on our children!"

15 Pilate, wishing to please the multitude, 24 decreed that what they asked for should be done. 26 Then he released to them Barabbas, 24 who had been thrown into prison for insurrection and murder, for whom they asked, 25 but he delivered Jesus up to their will, 15 when he had flogged Him, to be crucified.

The Soldiers Scourge and Mock Jesus, 7:30 a.m.

John 19:1–3; Matthew 27:26–30; Mark 15:16–19

1 So Pilate then took Jesus, and flogged Him. 26 Jesus he flogged and delivered to be crucified.

27 Then the governor's soldiers took Jesus [and] 16 led Him away within the court, which is 27 the Praetorium; 16 and they called together 27 and gathered 16 the whole cohort, 27 the whole garrison together against Him. 28 They stripped Him, and put a scarlet [and] 2 purple garment,[211] 28 robe on Him. 29 They braided a crown of thorns and put it on His head, and a reed in His right hand; and they kneeled down before Him, and mocked Him. 18 They began to salute Him, 29 saying, "Hail, King of the Jews!" 3 and they kept slapping Him.

30 They spat on Him, and took the reed and 19 they struck His head with a reed, and spat on Him, and bowing their knees, did homage to

[211] The Gospels John and Matthew give two different colors to the robe. Either there were two robes or one robe with two different colors, purple and scarlet. The robe probably came from Herod, who had dressed Him in a gorgeous robe. (See Luke 23:11.) One robe with two colors seems to be the more likely possibility.

Him.[212]

Pilate's Decision, 8:00 a.m.

John 19:4–16; Matthew 27:31; Mark 15:20

4 Then Pilate went out again, and said to them, "Behold, I bring Him out to you, that you may know that I find no basis for a charge against Him."

5 Jesus therefore came out, wearing the crown of thorns and the purple garment. Pilate said to them, "Behold, the Man!"

6 When therefore the chief priests and the officers saw Him, they shouted, saying, "Crucify! Crucify!"

Pilate said to them, "Take Him yourselves, and crucify Him, for I find no basis for a charge against Him."

7 The Jews answered him, "We have a law, and by our law He ought to die, because He made Himself the Son of God."

8 When therefore Pilate heard this saying, he was more afraid. 9 He
entered into the Praetorium again, and said to Jesus, "Where are You from?"

But Jesus gave him no answer.

10 Pilate therefore said to Him, "Aren't you speaking to me? Don't you know that I have power to release You, and have power to crucify You?"

11 Jesus answered, "You would have no power at all against Me, unless it were given to you from above. Therefore he who delivered Me to you has greater sin."

12 At this, Pilate was seeking to release Him, but the Jews cried out, saying, "If you release this Man, you aren't Caesar's friend! Everyone who makes himself a king speaks against Caesar!"

13 When Pilate therefore heard these words, he brought Jesus out, and sat down on the judgment seat at a place called "The Pavement," but

---

[212] **Isaiah 50:6** I offered My back to those who beat Me, My cheeks to those who pulled out My beard; I did not hide My face from mocking and spitting.

in Hebrew, "Gabbatha." 14 Now it was the Preparation Day of the Passover, at about the sixth hour [6:00 a.m.].[213]

He said to the Jews, "Behold, your King!"

15 They cried out, "Away with Him! Away with Him! Crucify Him!"

Pilate said to them, "Shall I crucify your King?"

The chief priests answered, "We have no king but Caesar!"

16 So then he delivered Him to them to be crucified.

31 When they had mocked Him, they took the 20 purple 31 robe off of Him, and put His clothes on Him, and led Him away to crucify Him.[214] 16 So they took Jesus and led Him away.

Jesus Led to Crucifixion, 8:30 a.m.

John 19:17–22; Matthew 27:32–38; Mark 15:21–28; Luke 23:26–34

17 He went out, bearing His cross, to the place called "The Place of a Skull," which is called in Hebrew, "Golgotha."

32 As they came out, they found [and] 21 compelled one passing by, 32 a man of Cyrene, Simon by name, 21 the father of Alexander and Rufus. 26 They grabbed 32 him to go with them that he might carry His cross. 26 When they led Him away, [they] laid on him the cross, to carry it after Jesus.

27 A great multitude of the people followed Him, including women who also mourned and lamented Him.

---

[213] "The sixth hour" would have been 6:00 a.m., according to the Roman timekeeping system or noon for the Jewish timekeeping system in use at the time. John uses the Roman clock, which runs from midnight. The other Gospels use the Jewish clock, which runs from dawn (6:00 a.m.). Thus, Jesus was crucified at the third hour on the Jewish clock but at the ninth hour on the Roman clock. The Synoptic Gospels use Jewish reckoning, which runs from dawn (6:00 a.m.) to dusk (6:00 p.m.). John's chronology of 6:00 a.m. just before Jesus is led away to the crucifixion is in conflict with the Synoptic Gospels, which put His crucifixion at 9:00 a.m. One possibility is that 6:00 a.m. refers to the start of the trial, not the end of it. (Pulpit Commentary)

[214] The Merged Gospels puts this before the scene with Pilate, but He appears with Pilate in the robe. MG splits v. 31 at the comma. But I cannot break a sentence like that.

28 But Jesus, turning to them, said, "Daughters of Jerusalem, don't weep for Me, but weep for yourselves and for your children. 29 For behold, the days are coming in which they will say, 'Blessed are the barren, the wombs that never bore, and the breasts that never nursed.' 30 Then they will begin to tell the mountains, 'Fall on us!' and tell the hills, 'Cover us!'"[215]

31 "For if they do these things in the green tree, what will be done in the dry?"

32 There were also others, two criminals, led with Him to be put to death.

Jesus Is Crucified, 9:00 a.m.

Matthew 27:33–38; Mark 15:22–28; John 19:20–24; Luke 23:33–34

33 They came to a place called 17 in Hebrew, 33 "Golgotha," that is to say, 22 being interpreted, 33 "The place of a skull." 23 They offered Him 33 sour wine 23 mixed with 34 gall[216] [and] 23 myrrh to drink, but He didn't take it. 34 When He had tasted it, He would not drink. 25 It was the third hour, and they crucified Him 33 there with the criminals, one on the right and the other on the left.

34 Jesus said, "Father, forgive them, for they don't know what they are doing."

23 Then the soldiers, when they had crucified Jesus, took His garments and made four parts, to every soldier a part; and also the coat. Now the coat was without seam, woven from the top throughout. 24 Then they said to one another, "Let's not tear it, but cast lots for it to decide whose it will be." 35 Casting lots, 24 that the Scripture might be fulfilled, 35 which was spoken by the prophet: 24 which says,

> "They parted my garments among them. For my cloak they cast lots."[217]

---

[215] **Hosea 10:8** The high places also of Aven, the sin of Israel, will be destroyed. The thorn and the thistle will come up on their altars. They will tell the mountains, "Cover us!" and the hills, "Fall on us!"

[216] **Psalm 69:21** They also gave Me gall for My food. In My thirst, they gave Me vinegar to drink.

[217] **Psalm 22:18** They divide My garments among them. They cast lots for My

24 Therefore the soldiers did these things 36 and they sat and watched Him there.

19 Pilate wrote a title also, and put it on the cross. 37 They set up over His head the accusation against Him written, 38 over Him in letters of Greek, Latin, and Hebrew:

> 37 "THIS IS JESUS, 19 OF NAZARETH, 37 THE KING OF THE JEWS."

The chief priests of the Jews therefore said to Pilate, "Don't write, 'The King of the Jews,' but, 'He said, I am King of the Jews.'"

22 Pilate answered, "What I have written, I have written."

38 Then 27 with Him they crucified 18 two others, 38 two robbers crucified with Him, 18 on either side, 38 one on His right hand and one on the left, 18 and Jesus in the middle. 28 The Scripture was fulfilled, which says,

> "He was numbered with transgressors."[218]

Jesus Is Mocked on the Cross, 9:30 a.m.–12:00 noon

Luke 23:35–44; Matthew 27:39–45; Mark 15:29–41

35 The people stood watching. 39 Those who passed by blasphemed Him, wagging their heads[219] 40 and saying, 29 "Ha! 40 You Who destroy the temple, and build it in three days, save Yourself 30 and come down from the cross! 40 If You are the Son of God, come down from the cross!"

35 The rulers with them also scoffed at Him. 41 Likewise the chief priests also mocking, with the scribes, the Pharisees, and the elders, 31 mocking among themselves with the scribes said, 42 "He saved others, but He can't save Himself. 35 Let Him save Himself, if this is the Christ of God, His chosen One! 43 If He is the King of Israel, let

---

clothing.

[218] **Isaiah 53:12** Therefore will I give Him a portion with the great, and He will divide the plunder with the strong; because He poured out His soul to death, and was numbered with the transgressors; yet He bore the sin of many, and made intercession for the transgressors.

[219] **Psalm 22:7** All those who see Me mock Me. They insult Me with their lips. They shake their heads.

Him come down from the cross now, and we will believe in Him. 32 Let the Christ, the King of Israel, now come down from the cross, that we may see and believe Him. 43 He trusts in God. Let God deliver Him now,[220] if He wants Him; for He said, 'I am the Son of God.'"

36 The soldiers also mocked Him, coming to Him and offering Him vinegar, 37 and saying, "If You are the King of the Jews, save Yourself!"

44 The robbers also who were crucified with Him cast on Him the same reproach. 39 One of the criminals who was hanged insulted Him, saying, "If You are the Christ, save Yourself and us!"

40 But the other answered, and rebuking him said, "Don't you even fear God, seeing you are under the same condemnation? 41 And we indeed justly, for we receive the due reward for our deeds, but this Man has done nothing wrong." 42 He said to Jesus, "Lord, remember me when You come into your Kingdom."

43 Jesus said to him, "Assuredly I tell you today you will be with Me in Paradise."

44 It was now about the sixth hour [noon]. 33 When the sixth hour had come, 44 darkness came over the whole land, until the ninth hour [3:00 p.m.].

Jesus Takes Care of His Mother, 12:00 noon

John 19:25–27

25 But there were standing by the cross of Jesus His mother, and His mother's sister, Mary the wife of Clopas, and Mary Magdalene.

26 Therefore when Jesus saw His mother, and the disciple whom He loved standing there, He said to His mother, "Woman, behold your son!"

27 Then He said to the disciple, "Behold, your mother!" From that hour, the disciple took her to his own home.

[220] **Psalm 22:8** "He trusts in Yahweh; let Him deliver Him. Let Him rescue Him, since He delights in Him."

Jesus Dies and His Side Is Pierced, 3:00 p.m.

John 19:28–37; Matthew 27:46–56; Mark 15:34–41; Luke 23:45–55

28 After this, 46 about the ninth hour Jesus cried with a loud voice, saying, "Eli, Eli, lama sabachthani?" That is, "My God, My God, why have You forsaken Me?"[221]

47 Some of them who stood there, when they heard it, said, 35 "Behold, 47 this Man is calling Elijah."

28 Jesus, knowing that all things were now finished, that the Scripture might be fulfilled, said, "I am thirsty."[222]

Now a vessel full of vinegar was set there. 48 Immediately one of them ran, and took a sponge, and filled it 36 full of 48 vinegar,[223] and put it on a 29 hyssop[224] 48 reed, 29 and held it at His mouth 48 and gave Him a drink. 49 The rest said, "Let Him be. Let's see whether Elijah comes 36 to take Him down 49 to save Him."

30 When Jesus therefore had received the vinegar, 46 Jesus, crying with a loud voice, said, "Father, into Your hands I commit my spirit!"[225] 50 Jesus cried again with a loud voice, [and] 30 He said, "It is finished." 46 Having said this, 30 He bowed his head, and 46 He breathed His last 50 and yielded up His spirit.

45 The sun was darkened, and 51 behold, the veil of the temple was torn in two from the top to the bottom. The earth quaked and the rocks were split. 52 The tombs were opened, and many bodies of the saints who had fallen asleep were raised; 53 and coming out of the tombs after His resurrection, they entered into the holy city and appeared to many.

---

[221] **Psalm 22:1** My God, my God, why have you forsaken Me? Why are you so far from helping Me, and from the words of My groaning?

[222] **Psalm 22:15** My strength is dried up like a potsherd. My tongue sticks to the roof of My mouth. You have brought Me into the dust of death.

[223] **Psalm 69:21** They also gave Me gall for my food. In My thirst, they gave Me vinegar to drink.

[224] **Exodus 12:22** You shall take a bunch of hyssop, and dip it in the blood that is in the basin, and strike the lintel and the two door posts with the blood that is in the basin; and none of you shall go out of the door of his house until the morning.

[225] **Psalm 31:5** Into Your hand I commend My spirit. You redeem Me, Yahweh, God of truth.

54 Now the centurion, 39 who stood by opposite Him, 54 and those who were with him watching Jesus, when they saw the earthquake, and the things that were done, 39 saw that He cried out like this and breathed His last, 54 feared exceedingly, saying, "Truly this was the Son of God." [And] 39 the centurion, 47 glorified God, saying, "Certainly this was a righteous Man. 39 Truly this Man was the Son of God!"

48 All the multitudes that came together to see this, when they saw the things that were done, returned home beating their breasts.

49 All His acquaintances, 55 many women were there watching from afar, who had followed 49 with 55 Jesus from Galilee, serving Him, 49 stood at a distance, watching these things. Among them were Mary Magdalene, Mary the mother of James 40 the less 56 and Joses, and the mother of the sons of Zebedee, 40 Salome; 41 who, when He was in Galilee, followed Him, and served Him; and many other women who came up with Him to Jerusalem.

31 Therefore the Jews, because it was the Preparation Day, so that the bodies wouldn't remain on the cross on the Sabbath (for that Sabbath was a special one), asked of Pilate that their legs might be broken, and that they might be taken away. 32 Therefore the soldiers came, and broke the legs of the first, and of the other who was crucified with Him; 33 but when they came to Jesus, and saw that He was already dead, they didn't break His legs. 34 However one of the soldiers pierced His side with a spear, and immediately blood and water came out.

35 He who has seen has testified, and his testimony is true. He knows that he tells the truth, that you may believe. 36 For these things happened, that the Scripture might be fulfilled,

> "A bone of Him will not be broken."[226]

37 Again another Scripture says, "They will look on Him Whom they

---

[226] **Exodus 12:46** It must be eaten In one house. You shall not carry any of the meat outside of the house. Do not break any of its bones. **Numbers 9:12** They shall leave none of it until the morning, nor break a bone of it. According to all the statute of the Passover they shall keep it. **Psalm 34:20** He protects all of His bones. Not one of them is broken.

pierced."[227]

Jesus Buried in Joseph's Tomb, 4:00–6:00 p.m.

John 19:38–42; Mark 15:42–47; Matthew 27:57–61; Luke 23:50–55

38 After these things, 57 when evening had come, 42 because it was
the Preparation Day, that is, the day before the Sabbath, 57 a rich man
from Arimathaea, 51 a city of the Jews, 57 named Joseph, came. [He
was] 43 a prominent council member [who] 51 had not consented to
their counsel and deed, 50 a good and upright man, 43 who also
himself was looking for God's kingdom, [and] 57 who himself was
also Jesus's disciple 38 but secretly for fear of the Jews. 43 He boldly
went in to Pilate, and asked for Jesus's body.

44 Pilate marveled if He were already dead; and summoning the
centurion, he asked him whether He had been dead long. 45 When he
found out from the centurion, he granted the body to Joseph. 58 Then
Pilate commanded the body to be given up. 38 Pilate gave him
permission. He came therefore and took away His body.

46 He bought a linen cloth, and took Him down. 39 Nicodemus, who
at first came to Jesus by night, also came bringing a mixture of myrrh
and aloes, about a hundred Roman pounds [72 pounds].

40 So 59 Joseph [and Nicodemus] 40 they took Jesus's body, and
bound it in 59 clean linen cloths, 40 with the spices, as the custom of
the Jews is to bury.

41 Now in the place where He was crucified there was a garden. In
the garden was a new tomb in which no man had ever yet been laid.
42 Then because of the Jews' Preparation Day (for the tomb was near
at hand) they laid Jesus there 60 and laid it in his own new tomb,
which he had cut out in the rock, 53 where no one had ever been laid.

---

[227] **Zechariah 12:10** "I will pour on David's house, and on the inhabitants of Jerusalem, the spirit of grace and of supplication; and they will look to Me Whom they have pierced; and they shall mourn for Him, as one mourns for his only son, and will grieve bitterly for Him, as one grieves for his firstborn." **Revelation 1:7** Behold, He is coming with the clouds, and every eye will see Him, including those who pierced Him. All the tribes of the earth will mourn over Him. Even so, Amen.

60 He rolled a great stone to the door of the tomb, and departed.[228]

54 It was the day of the Preparation, and the Sabbath was drawing near.

55 The women, who had come with Him out of Galilee, followed
after, 61 Mary Magdalene and the other Mary, 47 the mother of
Joses[229] 61 were sitting there opposite the tomb. [They] 55 saw the
tomb, and how 61 [and] 47 where 55 His body was laid.

Guards Are Placed at the Tomb on the Holy Day, Nisan 15

Matthew 27:62–66

62 Now on the next day, which was the day after the Preparation Day,
the chief priests and the Pharisees were gathered together to Pilate, 63
saying, "Sir, we remember what that deceiver said while He was still
alive: 'After three days I will rise again.' 64 Command therefore that
the tomb be made secure until the third day, lest perhaps His disciples come at night and steal Him away, and tell the people, 'He is risen from the dead;' and the last deception will be worse than the first."

65 Pilate said to them, "You have a guard. Go, make it as secure as you can."

66 So they went with the guard and made the tomb secure, sealing the stone.

Women Prepare Spices and Rest on the Weekly Sabbath, Nisan 15–17

Mark 16:1; Luke 23:56

1 When the Sabbath was past, Mary Magdalene, and Mary the mother
of James, and Salome, bought spices, that they might come and anoint
Him. 56 They returned, and prepared spices and ointments. On the

---

[228] **Isaiah 53:9** He was assigned a grave with the wicked, and with the rich in His death, though He had done no violence, nor was any deceit in His mouth.

[229] WEB and NKJV have 'Joses' which makes this Mary the mother of James the Less (Younger) and Joses. Note 'Joseph' is the Hebrew form of the name and 'Joses' is Greek translation.

Sabbath they rested according to the commandment.[230]

The Women Find the Empty Tomb, Nisan 18

Matthew 28:1–8; John 20:1–10; Luke 24:1–8; Mark 16:2–8

1 Now after the Sabbaths,[231] as it began to dawn on the first day of the week, Mary Magdalene and the other Mary 1 Mary the mother of James, 1 and some others, 1 and Salome, 1 came to the tomb, 1 to see the tomb. 1 [They] 1 went early, 2 very early on the first day of the week, 1 while it was still dark, 1 bringing the spices which they had prepared, 2 they came to the tomb when the sun had risen. 3 They were saying among themselves, "Who will roll away the stone from the door of the tomb for us?" 4 for it was very big.

2 Behold, there was a great earthquake, for an angel of the Lord descended from the sky, and came and rolled away the stone from the door, and sat on it. 3 His appearance was like lightning, and his clothing white as snow. 4 For fear of him, the guards shook, and became like dead men.

4 Looking up, they [the women] saw that the stone was rolled back, [and] 1 taken away from the tomb. 2 Therefore she [Mary Magdalene] ran.

3 They [the women] entered in, and didn't find the Lord Jesus's body.

5 Entering into the tomb, they saw a young man sitting on the right side, dressed in a white robe, and they were amazed.

4 While they were greatly perplexed about this, behold, two men stood by them in dazzling clothing. 5 Becoming terrified, they bowed their

---

[230] Putting the four Gospel accounts together, the women clearly had no time after Jesus's burial to purchase spices before the Sabbath. Mark 16:1 explicitly says they prepared spices after the Sabbath, and Luke 23:56 explicitly says they prepared spices before the Sabbath, "according to the commandment," that is, the Saturday Sabbath. Jesus was crucified in 30 or 31 AD. The Passover that year was on a Wednesday, the First Day of Unleavened Bread (a High Day Sabbath) (John 19:31) on Thursday, and the Sabbath on Saturday.

[231] In *Eberhard Nestle's Greek Text*, the word "sabbath" is plural, which is consistent with the evidence for two sabbaths in the week, and Jesus's time in the tomb, three days and three nights.

faces down to the earth.

They said to them, "Why do you seek the living among the dead?"

5 The angel answered the women, "Don't be afraid, [or] 6 amazed, 5 for I know that you seek Jesus, 6 Jesus, the Nazarene, 5 Who has been crucified. 6 He is not here, for He has risen, just like He said. 6 Remember what He told you when He was still in Galilee, 7 saying that the Son of Man must be delivered up into the hands of sinful men, and be crucified, and the third day rise again?[232] 6 Come, see the place where the Lord was lying. 6 He is not here. 6 Come, 6 behold, the place where they laid Him! 7 Go quickly and tell His disciples, 7 and Peter, 7 'He has risen from the dead, and behold, He goes before you into Galilee;[233] there you will see Him.' 7 as He said to you. 7 Behold, I have told you."

8 They remembered His words. 8 They went out, [and] 8 departed quickly from the tomb with fear and great joy, 8 and fled from the tomb, for trembling and astonishment had come on them. They said nothing to anyone; for they were afraid 8 and ran to bring His disciples word.

2 Therefore she [Mary Magdalene] ran and came to Simon Peter, and to the other disciple whom Jesus loved, and said to them, "They have taken away the Lord out of the tomb, and we don't know where they have laid Him!"

3 Therefore Peter and the other disciple went out, and they went toward the tomb. 12 But Peter got up and ran to the tomb.

4 They both ran together. The other disciple outran Peter, and came to the tomb first. 5 Stooping and looking in, he saw the linen cloths lying, yet he didn't enter in.

6 Then Simon Peter came, following him, 12 stooping and looking in,

---

[232] **Matthew 17:22–23** 22 While they were staying in Galilee, Jesus said to them, "The Son of Man is about to be delivered up into the hands of men, 23 and they will kill him, and the third day he will be raised up." They were exceedingly sorry. **Mark 9:31** For he was teaching his disciples, and said to them, "The Son of Man is being handed over to the hands of men, and they will kill him; and when he is killed, on the third day he will rise again."

[233] **Matthew 26:32** "But after I am raised up, I will go before you into Galilee." **Mark 14:28** "However, after I am raised up, I will go before you into Galilee."

6 and entered into the tomb. 7 He saw the linen cloths lying, 12 by themselves, 7 and the cloth that had been on His head, not lying with the linen cloths, but rolled up in a place by itself.

8 So then the other disciple who came first to the tomb also entered in, and he saw and believed. 9 For as yet they didn't know the Scripture,[234] that He must rise from the dead. 12 He [Peter] departed to his home, wondering what had happened. 10 So the disciples went away again to their own homes.

Mary Magdalene Sees the Risen Lord

Mark 16:9–11; John 20:11–18

9 Now when He [Jesus] had risen, early on the first day of the week, He appeared first to Mary Magdalene, from whom He had cast out seven demons.

11 But Mary was standing outside at the tomb weeping. So, as she wept, she stooped and looked into the tomb, 12 and she saw two angels in white sitting, one at the head, and one at the feet, where the body of Jesus had lain.

13 They told her, "Woman, why are you weeping?"

She said to them, "Because they have taken away my Lord, and I don't know where they have laid Him."

14 When she had said this, she turned around and saw Jesus standing, and didn't know that it was Jesus.

15 Jesus said to her, "Woman, why are you weeping? Who are you looking for?"

She, supposing Him to be the gardener, said to Him, "Sir, if You have carried Him away, tell me where You have laid him, and I will take Him away."

16 Jesus said to her, "Mary."

She turned and said to Him, "Rabboni!" which is to say, "Teacher!"

---

[234] **Psalm 16:10** For You will not leave My soul in Sheol, neither will You allow Your holy one to see corruption.

17 Jesus said to her, "Don't hold Me, for I haven't yet ascended to My Father; but go to My brothers, and tell them, 'I am ascending to My Father and your Father, to My God and your God.'"

Jesus Appears to the Women

Matthew 28:9–10

9 As they [the other Mary and the other women] went to tell his disciples, behold, Jesus met them, saying, "Rejoice!"

They came and took hold of His feet, and worshiped Him.

10 Then Jesus said to them, "Don't be afraid. Go tell My brothers that they should go into Galilee, and there they will see Me."

The Guards Report to the Pharisees

Matthew 28:11–15

11 Now while they were going, behold, some of the guards came into the city, and told the chief priests all the things that had happened.

12 When they were assembled with the elders, and had taken counsel,
they gave a large amount of silver to the soldiers, 13 saying, "Say that
His disciples came by night, and stole Him away while we slept. 14 If
this comes to the governor's ears, we will persuade him and make you
free of worry."

15 So they took the money and did as they were told. This saying was spread abroad among the Jews, and continues until today.

The Women Tell the Disciples of the Empty Tomb

Luke 24:8–12; John 20:11–18; Mark 16:10–11

8 They remembered His words, 9 returned from the tomb, and told all
these things to the eleven, and to all the rest. 10 Now they were Mary
Magdalene, Joanna, and Mary the mother of James. The other women
with them told these things to the apostles.

11 Mary Magdalene came and told the disciples 10 who had been with
Him, as they mourned and wept, 18 that she had seen the Lord, and
that He had said these things to her.

11 When they heard that He was alive, and had been seen by her, 11
these words seemed to them to be nonsense, and they didn't believe
them.

The Road to Emmaus

Mark 16:12–13; Luke 24:13–35; 1 Corinthians 15:5

12 After these things He was revealed in another form to two of them,
as they walked, on their way into the country.

13 Behold, two of them were going that very day to a village named
Emmaus, which was sixty stadia [seven miles] from Jerusalem. 14
They talked with each other about all of these things which had
happened. 15 While they talked and questioned together, Jesus
Himself came near, and went with them. 16 But their eyes were kept
from recognizing Him.

17 He said to them, "What are you talking about as you walk, and are
sad?"

18 One of them, named Cleopas, answered Him, "Are You the only
stranger in Jerusalem who doesn't know the things which have
happened there in these days?"

19 He said to them, "What things?"

They said to Him, "The things concerning Jesus, the Nazarene, Who
was a prophet mighty in deed and word before God and all the people;
20 and how the chief priests and our rulers delivered Him up to be
condemned to death, and crucified Him. 21 But we were hoping that
it was He who would redeem Israel. Yes, and besides all this, it is now
the third day since these things happened. 22 Also, certain women of
our company amazed us, having arrived early at the tomb; 23 and
when they didn't find His body, they came saying that they had also
seen a vision of angels, who said that He was alive. 24 Some of us
went to the tomb, and found it just like the women had said, but they
didn't see Him."

25 He said to them, "Foolish men, and slow of heart to believe in all
that the prophets have spoken! 26 Didn't the Christ have to suffer
these things and to enter into His glory?"

27 Beginning from Moses and from all the prophets, He explained to them in all the Scriptures the things concerning Himself. 28 They came near to the village, where they were going, and He acted like He would go further.

29 They urged Him, saying, "Stay with us, for it is almost evening, and the day is almost over."

30 He went in to stay with them. 30 When He had sat down at the table with them, He took the bread and gave thanks. Breaking it, He gave to them. 31 Their eyes were opened, and they recognized Him, and He vanished out of their sight.

32 They said to one another, "Weren't our hearts burning within us, while He spoke to us along the way, and while He opened the Scriptures to us?"

33 They rose up that very hour, 13 and they went [and] 33 returned to Jerusalem, and found the eleven gathered together, and those who were with them, 34 saying, "The Lord is risen indeed, and has appeared to Simon!"

5 (He was seen by Cephas, then by the twelve.)

35 They related 13 to the rest, 13 the things that happened along the way, and how He was recognized by them in the breaking of the bread.

13 They didn't believe them, either.

Jesus Appears to the Apostles Except for Thomas

Luke 24:36–49; John 20:19–23; Mark 16:14

36 As they said these things, 19 when therefore it was evening, on that day, the first day of the week, and when the doors were locked where the disciples were assembled, for fear of the Jews, 14 He was revealed to the eleven themselves as they sat at the table.

19 Jesus 36 Himself 19 came and stood 36 among them, 19 in the middle, and said to them, "Peace be to you."

37 But they were terrified and filled with fear, and supposed that they had seen a spirit.

38 He said to them, "Why are you troubled? Why do doubts arise in

your hearts? 39 See My hands and My feet, that it is truly Me. Touch Me and see, for a spirit doesn't have flesh and bones, as you see that I have."

20 When He had said this, He showed them His hands 40 and His feet 20 and His side. 41 While they still didn't believe for joy, and wondered, He said to them, "Do you have anything here to eat?"

42 They gave Him a piece of a broiled fish and some honeycomb. 43 He took them, and ate in front of them.

20 The disciples therefore were glad when they saw the Lord.

14 And He rebuked them for their unbelief and hardness of heart, because they didn't believe those who had seen Him after He had risen.

21 Jesus therefore said to them again, "Peace be to you. As the Father has sent Me, even so I send you." 22 When He had said this, He breathed on them, and said to them, "Receive the Holy Spirit! 23 If you forgive anyone's sins, they have been forgiven them. If you retain anyone's sins, they have been retained."

44 He said to them, "This is what I told you, while I was still with you, that all things which are written in the law of Moses, the prophets, and the psalms, concerning Me must be fulfilled."

45 Then He opened their minds, that they might understand the Scriptures. 46 He said to them, "Thus it is written, and thus it was necessary for the Christ to suffer and to rise from the dead the third day, 47 and that repentance and remission of sins should be preached in His name to all the nations, beginning at Jerusalem. 48 You are witnesses of these things. 49 Behold, I send out the promise of My Father on you. But wait in the city of Jerusalem until you are clothed with power from on high."

Jesus Teaches Thomas about Seeing and Believing, Nisan 26

John 20:24–31

24 But Thomas, one of the twelve, called Didymus, wasn't with them when Jesus came. 25 The other disciples therefore said to him, "We have seen the Lord!"

But he said to them, "Unless I see in His hands the print of the nails, and put My hand into His side, I will not believe."

26 After eight days again His disciples were inside, and Thomas was with them. Jesus came, the doors being locked, and stood in the middle, and said, "Peace be to you." 27 Then He said to Thomas, "Reach here your finger, and see My hands. Reach here your hand, and put it into My side. Don't be unbelieving, but believing."

28 Thomas answered Him, "My Lord and my God!"

29 Jesus said to him, "Because you have seen Me, Thomas, you have believed. Blessed are those who have not seen, and have believed."

30 Therefore Jesus did many other signs in the presence of His disciples, which are not written in this book; 31 but these are written, that you may believe that Jesus is the Christ, the Son of God, and that believing you may have life in His name.

Breakfast by the Sea

John 21:1–14

After these things, Jesus revealed himself again to the disciples at the sea of Tiberias. He revealed Himself this way. 2 Simon Peter, Thomas called Didymus,[235] Nathanael of Cana in Galilee, and the sons of Zebedee, and two others of his disciples were together.

3 Simon Peter said to them, "I'm going fishing."

They told him, "We are also coming with you."

They immediately went out, and entered into the boat. That night, they caught nothing. 4 But when day had already come, Jesus stood on the beach, yet the disciples didn't know that it was Jesus.

5 Jesus therefore said to them, "Children, have you anything to eat?"

They answered Him, "No."

6 He said to them, "Cast the net on the right side of the boat, and you will find some."

They cast it therefore, and now they weren't able to draw it in for the

---

[235] Thomas (Aramaic) and *Didymus* (Greek) both mean "twin."

multitude of fish. 7 That disciple therefore whom Jesus loved said to Peter, "It's the Lord!"

So when Simon Peter heard that it was the Lord, he wrapped his coat around him (for he was naked), and threw himself into the sea. 8 But the other disciples came in the little boat (for they were not far from the land, but about two hundred cubits away) [one hundred yards], dragging the net full of fish.

9 So when they got out on the land, they saw a fire of coals there, and fish laid on it, and bread. 10 Jesus said to them, "Bring some of the fish which you have just caught."

11 Simon Peter went up, and drew the net to land, full of great fish, one hundred fifty-three; and even though there were so many, the net wasn't torn.

12 Jesus said to them, "Come and eat breakfast."

None of the disciples dared inquire of Him, "Who are you?" knowing that it was the Lord.

13 Then Jesus came and took the bread, gave it to them, and the fish likewise. 14 This is now the third time that Jesus was revealed to His disciples, after He had risen from the dead.

Jesus Restores Peter

John 21:15–19

15 So when they had eaten their breakfast, Jesus said to Simon Peter, "Simon, son of Jonah, do you love Me more than these?"[236]

He said to him, "Yes, Lord; You know that I have affection for You." [as a brother][237]

He said to him, "Feed my lambs." 16 He said to him again a second time, "Simon, son of Jonah, do you love Me?"

He said to Him, "Yes, Lord; you know that I have affection for You." [as a brother].

---

[236] This is the New English Bible's translation. The Greek word used by Jesus is *agapas*, which means a love that implies commitment and devotion.

[237] The Greek word used by Peter is *philo*, which means a brotherly kind of love.

He said to him, "Tend My sheep." 17 He said to him the third time, "Simon, son of Jonah, do you have affection for Me?" [as a brother].

Peter was grieved because He asked him the third time, "Do you have affection for Me?" He said to Him, "Lord, You know everything. You know that I have affection for You."

Jesus said to him, "Feed My sheep. 18 Most certainly I tell you, when you were young, you dressed yourself, and walked where you wanted to. But when you are old, you will stretch out your hands, and another will dress you, and carry you where you don't want to go."

19 Now He said this, signifying by what kind of death he would glorify God. When He had said this, He said to him, "Follow Me."

The Beloved Disciple

John 21:20–24

20 Then Peter, turning around, saw a disciple following. This was the disciple whom Jesus loved, the one who had also leaned on Jesus's breast at the supper and asked, "Lord, who is going to betray You?"

21 Peter seeing him, said to Jesus, "Lord, what about this man?"

22 Jesus said to him, "If I desire that he stay until I come, what is that to you? You follow Me."

23 This saying therefore went out among the brothers, that this disciple wouldn't die. Yet Jesus didn't say to him that he wouldn't die, but, "If I desire that he stay until I come, what is that to you?"

24 This is the disciple who testifies about these things, and wrote these things. We know that his witness is true.

Jesus Meets the Apostles in Galilee

Matthew 28:16–20; Mark 16:15–20

16 But the eleven disciples went into Galilee, to the mountain where Jesus had sent them. 17 When they saw Him, they bowed down to Him, but some doubted.

Jesus came to them and spoke to them, saying, "All authority has been given to Me in heaven and on earth 15 "Go into all the world, and preach the good news to the whole creation. 16 He who believes and is baptized will be saved; but he who disbelieves will be condemned. 19 Go therefore, and make disciples of all nations, baptizing them in the Name of the Father and of the Son and of the Holy Spirit, 20 teaching them to observe all things that I commanded you.

17 "These signs will accompany those who believe: in My name they will cast out demons; they will speak with foreign languages;[238] 18 they will take up serpents; and if they drink any deadly thing, it will in no way hurt; them they will lay hands on the sick, and they will recover. 20 Behold, I am with you always, even to the end of the age." Amen.

The Great Commission Given

Acts 1:1–11 Luke 24:50–53; Mark 16:19; John 21:25

1 The first book I wrote, Theophilus, concerned all that Jesus began both to do and to teach, 2 until the day in which He was received up, after He had given commandment through the Holy Spirit to the apostles whom He had chosen. 3 To these He also showed Himself alive after He suffered, by many proofs, appearing to them over a period of forty days, and speaking about God's kingdom.

4 Being assembled together with them, He commanded them, "Don't depart from Jerusalem, but wait for the promise of the Father, which you heard from me. 5 For John indeed baptized in water, but you will be baptized in the Holy Spirit not many days from now."

6 Therefore when they had come together, they asked Him, "Lord, are You now restoring the kingdom to Israel?"

7 He said to them, "It isn't for you to know times or seasons which the Father has set within His own authority. 8 But you will receive power when the Holy Spirit has come upon you. You will be witnesses to me in Jerusalem, in all Judea and Samaria, and to the uttermost parts of the earth."

---

[238] This is the Goodspeed translation. It is more in accordance with the actual miracles of Pentecost and modern usage when the apostles spoke in tongues foreign (and new to them, as the New King James has) to them but familiar to the visiting Jews.

19 So then the Lord, after He had spoken to them, 50 He led them out
as far as Bethany, and He lifted up his hands, and blessed them.[239]

51 While He blessed them, He withdrew from them, and was carried
up into heaven. 9 When He had said these things, as they were
looking, He was taken up, and a cloud received Him out of their sight.
19 He . . . was received up into heaven, and sat down at the right hand
of God.

10 While they were looking steadfastly into the sky as He went,
behold, two men stood by them in white clothing, 11 who also said,
"You men of Galilee, why do you stand looking into the sky? This
Jesus, who was received up from you into the sky will come back in
the same way as you saw Him going into the sky."

52 They worshiped Him, and returned to Jerusalem with great joy, 53
and were continually in the temple, praising and blessing God. 20
They went out, and preached everywhere, the Lord working with
them, and confirming the word by the signs that followed.

25 There are also many other things which Jesus did, which if they
would all be written, I suppose that even the world itself wouldn't
have room for the books that would be written. 20 Amen.

---

[239] **Deuteronomy 33:1** This is the blessing that Moses the man of God pronounced on the Israelites before his death.

Bibliography

1. Brown, Francis, Driver, S. R., and Briggs, Charles A., *The Brown-Driver-Briggs Hebrew and English Lexicon* (Massachusetts: Hendrickson Publisher, 1996).

2. Cheney, Johnston M., *The Life of Christ in Stereo* (Portland: Western Baptist Seminary Press, 1969).

3. Coulter, Frederick R., *A Harmony of the Gospels in Modern English, The Life of Jesus Christ* (Los Angeles: York Publishing Company, 1974).

4. Crossland, Gary, *The Merged Gospels: The Ultimate Word-by-Word Gospel Harmony* (Soma Communications, 2011).

5. David Burges, "The Tower in Siloam," Testimony Magazine, October 2009, http://www.testimony-magazine.org/back/oct2009/burges2.pdf.

6. *Gill's Exposition of the Entire Bible*, "Luke 13:1," http://biblehub.com/commentaries/luke/13-1.htm.

7. Ginomai, "The KJV New Testament Greek Lexicon," Bible Study Tools, https://www.biblestudytools.com/lexicons/greek/kjv/ginomai.html.

8. *The Interpreter's Bible, Volume VII* (Nashville: Abingdon Press, 1951).

9. Myers, J. D., What's on Second? Who's on First? Deuteroprōtō in Luke 6:1, redeeminggod.com/wp-content/uploads/2010/12/Whats-on-Second-Whos-on-First-Luke-6-1.pdf.

10. *Pulpit Commentary*, "John 19," http://biblehub.com/commentaries/pulpit/john/19.htm.

11. Roman Timekeeping, Wikipedia, https://en.wikipedia.org/wiki/Roman_timekeeping

12. Spangler, Ann and Lois Tverberg, *Sitting at the Feet of Jesus* (Grand Rapids: Zondervan, 2009).

13. Strong, James, *The Exhaustive Concordance of the Bible* (Iowa Falls: Riverside Book and Bible House), https://www.biblestudytools.com/concordances/strongs-exhaustive-concordance/.

14. Testimony Magazine, "The Tower in Siloam," October 2009, http://www.testimony-magazine.org/back/oct2009/burges2.pdf.

15. *Twenty-Six Translations of the Bible, Volume 3* (Grand Rapids: The Zondervan Corporation, 1985).

16. Tverberg, Lois, *Walking in the Dust of Rabbi Jesus* (Grand Rapids: Zondervan, 2012).

17. T*he Zondervan Parallel New Testament in Greek and English* (Grand Rapids: Zondervan Bible Publishers, 1980).

18. *The Zondervan Interlinear and the Emphasized New Testament: A New Translation* by J. B. Rotherham (https://www.studylight.org/study-desk/interlinear.html?q1=John

Appendix A: Chart of Jesus's Last Week

Nisan 9	Nisan 10	Nisan 11	Nisan 12	Nisan 13	Nisan 14 The Passover	Nisan 15First Day of Feast	Nisan 16	Nisan 17	Nisan 18
Day **until sunset** Jesus comes to Bethany 6 days before Passover	Day Jesus sends Disciples to get donkey's foal, then enters Jerusalem amid cheers. Looks around	Day Jesus returns and curses fig tree. Then He cleanses the Temple. He heals the blind and lame. He teaches daily	Day The fig tree is withered. Jesus answers and asks questions. He gives parables and chief priests and Pharisees seek to arrest Him. Jesus gives woes, Olivet prophecy	Day Judas betrays Jesus Jesus sends disciples to prepare Passover.	Day Peter's 3 denials. Jesus sentenced to death. Taken to Pilate. Scourged, crucified. Nicodemus and Joseph bury Him before sunset.	Day Chief priests and Pharisees ask Pilate for a guard on the tomb, who gives it. 1st day	Day Mary Magdalene, Mary mother of James, and Salome bought spices and prepared them. 2nd day Mark 16:1, Luke 23:56	Day 7th day Sabbath rest 3rd day. Jesus resurrected at sunset after 3 days and nights in the tomb.	Day Women arrive to anoint Jesus, find tomb empty. Mary Magdalene runs to tell Peter and runs back. Mary meets Jesus. Women meet Jesus. Jesus appears to others.
Night Nisan 10 Mary of Bethany anoints Jesus for His burial. John 12:1-8	Night Nisan 11 Jesus returns to Bethany	Night Nisan 12 Jesus returns to Bethany	Night Nisan 13 Jesus returns to Bethany "After two days comes the Passover and My crucifixion" Mt 26:2	Night Nisan 14 Jesus washes feet. Judas leaves. Jesus begins New Covenant. Prayer in garden. Arrest.	Night Nisan 15 Women note the site then rest on high day sabbath, beginning at sunset. 1st night John 19:31	Night Nisan 16 2nd night	Night Nisan 17 Women rested on the Sabbath according to command-ment. 3rd night	Night Nisan 18 Earthquake before dawn. Angel opens tomb. Guards faint.	Night Nisan 19 Jesus appears to 11 without Thomas at night.

Appendix B: The Timing and Structure of Jesus's Ministry

There is uncertainty over which text to select for Luke 6:1. The Received Text has "on the second Sabbath after the first" (Greek: *deuteroproto sabboton*), whereas the Critical Text has "One Sabbath." I have selected the Received Text for these reasons:

1. The United Bible Society (UBS), authors of the Critical Text, themselves say they are unable to tell whether deuteroproto sabboton is the original or not in this text.

2. The more difficult reading is deuteroproto sabboton. One of the key principles of textual criticism is that a difficult reading is more likely the original per the theory that copyists are more likely to simplify instead of making the reading more difficult.

3. In the context of this verse, the Pharisees saw the disciples eating the grain and contested vigorously and Jesus replied, citing David and the priests. The selection of one reading over the other must better explain this context, and deuteroproto sabboton better explains the context. See reason 4.

4. Traditionally, the harvest took place on the Sabbath before Pentecost when the priests rubbed the grain heads. The priests may have felt that the disciples usurped what they saw as their rightful task. Jesus's answer implied His disciples were priests.

5. When Jesus answered, he tied David's men to the priests and also held that the priests were blameless for profaning the Sabbath. This pointed to His ancestry as David's son and implied He was Messiah and His followers were priests.

6. Jesus asserted His greatness over the temple. If priests could work in the temple on the Sabbath, His followers could work with Him on the Sabbath.

7. The timing of this event within the larger context of the Gospel is correct for the Days of Unleavened Bread and Pentecost.

I am very grateful to J.D. Myers for explaining the various interpretations of Luke 6:1 in his paper.

Appendix C: Currency

Matthew 6:26 – Penny, literally, *kodrantes*. A kodrantes was a small copper coin worth about two *lepta* (widow's mites)—not enough to buy much of anything.

Matthew 10:29 – An *assarion* was a small coin worth one-tenth of a *drachma* or a sixteenth of a *denarius*. An assarion was approximately the wages of one half-hour of agricultural labor.

Mark 6:37 – Two hundred *denarii* was about seven or eight months wages for an agricultural laborer.

Mark 12:42 – Two small brass coins, which equaled a *quadrans* coin, Greek; literally, lepta or widow's mites. Lepta were very small brass coins worth half a quadrans each, which was a quarter of the copper assarion. Lepta were worth less than 1 percent of an agricultural worker's daily wages. A quadrans is was a coin worth about 1/64 of a denarius.

Matthew 17:24 – A *didrachma* is a Greek silver coin worth two drachmas, about as much as two Roman denarii or about two days' wages. It was commonly used to pay the half-shekel temple tax because two drachmas were worth one half shekel of silver. A shekel was about ten grams or about 0.35 ounces, usually in the form of a silver coin. Note: Jesus gives a word of knowledge to Peter that He knew the tax collector had talked with him. This miracle may have given him faith to follow Jesus's incredible instruction.

Matthew 17:27 – Greek *stater*, the exact amount to pay the temple tax for two (didrachma). A stater was a silver coin equivalent to four Attic or two Alexandrian drachmas or a Jewish shekel: exactly enough to cover the half-shekel temple tax for two people.

Matthew 18:24 – Ten thousand talents (about three hundred metric tons of silver) represented an extremely large sum of money, equivalent to about sixty million denarii, where one denarius was typical of one day's wages for agricultural labor. This is close to twenty thousand years of average wages.

Matthew 18:28 – One hundred denarii was about one-sixtieth of a talent or about five hundred grams (1.1 pounds) of silver (about one hundred days' wages).

Matthew 25:15 – A talent was about thirty kilograms or sixty-six pounds, usually used to weigh silver unless otherwise specified.

Luke 15:8 – A drachma coin was worth about two days' wages for an agricultural laborer.

Matthew 20:2 – A denarius was a silver Roman coin worth 1/25th of a Roman *aureus*. This was a common wage for a day of farm labor.

Luke 19:13 – In Hebrew, *maneh* or *mina* was equal to fifty holy shekels, about 1.26 pounds. Composed of silver, at six dollars per ounce, this was about $120. Ten minas was more than three years' wages for an agricultural laborer.

Mark 14:5 – Three hundred denarii was about a year's wages for an agricultural laborer.

John 19:39 – One hundred Roman pounds of twelve ounces each or about seventy-two pounds or thirty-three kilograms.

Appendix D: Measurements

Mark 4:21 – A *modion*, a dry measuring basket containing about a peck (about nine liters).

Matthew 13:33 – Three *sata* or about thirty-nine liters, a bit more than a bushel. In Hebrew, *se'ah* equals one-third *ephah* or 12.148 liters (10.696 quarts) (from Brown-Driver-Briggs).

John 6:19 – Twenty-five to thirty *stadia* was about five to six kilometers or about three to four miles.

John 11:18 – Fifteen stadia was about 2.8 kilometers or 1.7 miles.

Luke 24:13 – Sixty stadia equaled about eleven kilometers or about seven miles.

John 21:8 – Two hundred cubits was about one hundred yards or about ninety-one meters.

Appendix E: Time Table

Jewish Time	Roman Time	Our Time
0 hour	6th hour	6:00 AM
1st	7th	7:00 AM
2nd	8th	8:00 AM
3rd	9th	9:00 AM
4th	10th	10:00 AM
5th	11th	11:00 AM
6th	12th	12:00 PM
7th	1st hour	1:00 PM
8th	2nd	2:00 PM
9th	3rd	3:00 PM
10th	4th	4:00 PM
11th	5th	5:00 PM
12th	6th	6:00 PM
1st hour	7th	7:00 PM
2nd	8th	8:00 PM
3rd	9th	9:00 PM
4th	10th	10:00 PM
5th	11th	11:00 PM
6th	12th	12:00 AM
7th	1st hour	1:00 AM
8th	2nd hour	2:00 AM
9th	3rd hour	3:00 AM
10th	4th hour	4:00 AM
11th	5th hour	5:00 AM
12th	6th hour	6:00 AM

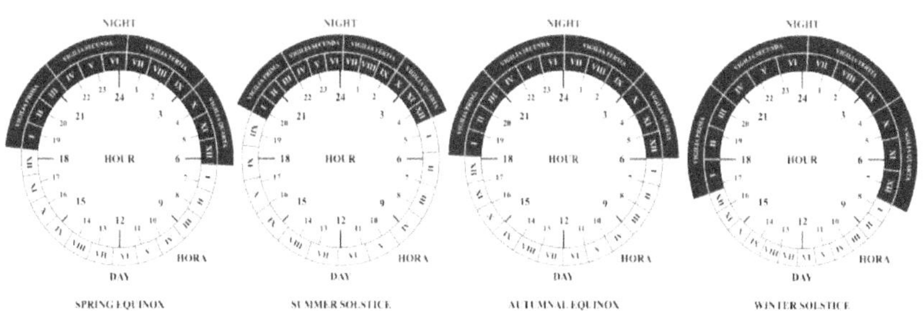

Appendix F: Translation Decisions

Bible Versions Mentioned

1. *King James Version* (KJV)

2. Weymouth translation from *Twenty-Six Translations of the Bible, Volume III*

3. New English Bible (NEB), alternate reading, NU manuscript

4. Complete Jewish Bible (CJB).

5. From *New King James Version* (NKJV), *Good News Translation* (GNT), *Common English Bible* (CEB), *Free Bible Version,* NT Psalms

*6. Family New International Version (*NIV) and NEB, 'relatives' Berwick (Ber), 'friends' KJV, Nestle's 21st Ed. Greek 'the ones with Him'

7. *Twenty-Sixth Edition of the Nestle Aland Greek New Testament* and in the *Third Edition of the United Bible Societies' Greek New Testament*

8. Complete Jewish Bible (CJB).

9. *The Merged Gospel* (MG)

10. NKJV and Darby and *Strong's Exhaustive Concordance*

11. WEB margin notes, *The Zondervan Parallel New Testament in Greek and English,* and the *Amplified Bible*

12. The Nestle-Uland (NU) text, *New English Translation*, Amplified Bible

13. Henry Alford New Testament, The Moffat translation

14. Family NIV and NEB, Berwick, KJV, Nestle's 21st Ed. Greek

15. Twenty-Sixth Edition of the Nestle Aland Greek New Testament and in the *Third Edition of the United Bible Societies' Greek New Testament*, Received Text of the Latin Vulgate

16. Complete Jewish Bible (CJB)

17. WEB margin notes, *The Zondervan Parallel New Testament in Greek and English*, and the *Amplified Bible*

18. NU text, *New English Translation, Amplified Bible*

19. The New International Version (NIV)

20. NKJV, *The Authorized Version*, Knox's translation, and E.V. Rieu's *The Four Gospels,* The Nelson Greek manuscript

21. Nestle Greek text. NKJV, *American Standard Version* (ASV), the Greek text known as the Alexandrian or Egyptian text as published in the *Nestle-Aland Greek New Testament* and in the United Bible Societies' Third Edition

22. NU, WEB, *Greek Majority Text New Testament* but also the *Textus Receptus/Received Text* (TR)

23. NKJV, KJV, NEB, *The New Holman Bible, Young's Literal Translation*

Mark 1:12–13 – Weymouth translation from Twenty-Six Translations of the Bible, Volume III

Luke 1:46-54 King James Version

Luke 5:17 – New English Bible, alternate reading, NU manuscript

Luke 8:17 – Greek has "covered," an allusion to the covering basket or bed earlier in the parable. NKJV and WEB have "made secret." I chose to use 'covered up' from CJB Complete Jewish Bible.

Mark 2:15 – From NKJV, GNT, CEB, Free Bible Version, NT Psalms

Matthew 11:2 – CEB translation used here, adding words "word by."

Mark 3:21 – Family NIV and NEB, 'relatives' Berwick, 'friends' KJV, Nestle's 21st Ed. Greek 'the ones with Him' οι παρ.

Mark 3:32 – The Alexandrian or Egyptian text, published in the Twenty-Sixth Edition of the Nestle Aland Greek New Testament and in the Third Edition of the United Bible Societies' Greek New Testament has "and your sisters" as well by the majority of ancient Greek manuscripts, known as the Received Text.

Matthew 13:1 – This seals the placement of Jesus's family's visit—

He was inside the house and then went outside. The family was outside, wanting to come inside and talk to Him. Likely, He responded to His family and went out to talk with them and then taught outside where He could reach more people.

Mark 4:22 – Greek has "covered," an allusion to the covering basket or bed earlier in the parable. NKJV and WEB have "made secret." I chose to use "covered up" from Complete Jewish Bible (CJB).

Mark 4:24 – Greek *blepeke* in both Mark 4:24 and Luke 8:18. Also translated "beware" or "be careful." "Beware" may be superior. I think Jesus is referring to His own teaching here.

Matthew 8:28 – This phrasing/interpretation came from *The Merged Gospel*, which infers one of the two men was exceptionally fierce and noteworthy. This was the man recounted by Mark and Luke.

Matthew 14:6 – NKJV and Darby have "celebrated." Greek #1096 in Strong's "*genomenois*, gerund of *ginomai*. 3. to arise, appear in history, come upon the stage of men appearing in public".[240]

John 6:27 – The WEB margin notes, The Zondervan Parallel New Testament in Greek and English, and the Amplified Bible have "I AM."

John 6:31 – Greek and Hebrew use the same word for "heaven," "the heavens," "the sky," and "the air."

Luke 9:35 – From the NU text, New English Translation, Amplified

Luke 17:21 – The Greek word vo (entos), which the WEB translates as "within," is better translated as "among." The Henry Alford New Testament renders this word as "among." The Moffat translation translates it as "in your midst." The context indicates that Jesus was referring to Himself in the midst of the Pharisees rather than the Kingdom being in the hearts or minds of the Pharisees, who actually opposed Christ, and thus the Kingdom.

Matthew 19:29 – From KJV

---

[240] Ginomai, "The KJV New Testament Greek Lexicon," *Bible Study Tools,* accessed September 19, 2019, https://www.biblestudytools.com/lexicons/greek/kjv/ginomai.html

Matthew 23:21 – Nestle Uland text reads "lives."

Matthew 23:27 – Textus Receptus (received text of Vulgate) reads "self-indulgence" instead of "unrighteousness."

John 13:2 – The Greek renders this phrase as "during supper" rather than "after supper" as the King James has it. The NIV translates the expression as "the evening meal was being served."

John 14:16 – Greek παρακλητον (*parakleton*): Counselor, Helper, Intercessor, Advocate, and Comforter.

John 15:26 – Greek *parakletos*: Counselor, Helper, Advocate, Intercessor, and Comforter.

John 17:12 – Lost (*apoleto*) GR; destruction (*apoleias*) GR same word. Goodspeed shows this.

Matthew 26:50 – Or "Jesus told him, 'Do what you have come for.'" NIV and Nestle's Greek.

Matthew 26:68 – Or forecourt or entryway

Luke 22:70 – The NKJV supplies the word "rightly" in between "You" and "say." The Authorized Version, Knox's translation, and E.V. Rieu's *The Four Gospels* do not use "rightly." Also, "rightly" is not in the Nelson Greek manuscript. Considering that Jesus knew that to say "you are right" would be condemnatory, it seems more logical He would reply evasively and ironically. Obviously, the Jews took His statement with the word "rightly" inserted.

Luke 23:15 – Nestle Greek text. This translation seems to make more sense than the NKJV. It is a reading by the ASV, also according to the Greek text known as the Alexandrian or Egyptian text as published in the Nestle-Aland Greek New Testament and in the United Bible Societies' Third Edition. The NKJV reads "for I sent you back to him."

Matthew 27:25 – TR adds "that it might be fulfilled which was spoken by the prophet:

> 'They divided my garments among them, and for My clothing they cast lots'" (see Psalm 22:18 and John 19:24).

John 19:28 – NU, TR read "knowing" instead of "seeing."

Mark 16:9–20 – NU includes the text of verses 9–20, but mentions in a footnote that a few manuscripts omitted it. The translators of the WEB regard Mark 16:9–20 as reliable based on an overwhelming majority of textual evidence, including not only the authoritative Greek Majority Text New Testament but also the TR and many of the manuscripts cited in the NU text.

Mark 16:9 – "Early on the first day of the week, after He had risen." The NKJV has "rose," but the KJV reads "was risen," which in modern English would be translated "had risen," as the NEB has it. The New Holman Bible has "after He had risen;" Young's Literal Translation has "And he, having risen in the morning of the first of the Sabbaths."

Appendix G: Gospel Sequence Decisions

Matthew 12:46 – *The Merged Gospel* puts this during or after Jesus's parables in Matthew 13 (Pericope 92). It seems to fit better, based upon Matthew and Mark in this location, probably Peter's house in Capernaum, associated with the healing of the blind and deaf demonic man. The phrase "while He was still speaking" binds this strongly to the healing, not the parables, as Luke places it.

Matthew 13:1–9 – This seals the placement of Jesus's family's visit. He was inside the house and then went outside. The family was outside, wanting to come inside and talk to Him. Likely, He responded to His family and went out to talk with them and then taught outside where He could reach more people.

Matthew 13:8; Mark 4:8 – I can't tell which order is correct, increasing or decreasing. Most likely, Jesus repeated this parable several times and varied how He told it.

Matthew 27:31 – *The Merged Gospel* puts this before the scene with Pilate, but He appears with Pilate in the robe. MG splits verse 31 at the comma. I cannot break a sentence at a comma.

Mark 4:21 – *The Merged Gospel* has Luke's comment first and then Mark's questions. I rather think Jesus would begin this parable with the startling questions and then answer them.

Mark 4:25 – *The Merged Gospel* adds Matthew 13:12 here, but that seems out of context. Matthew 13:12 focuses on those who don't understand and this parable is to the disciples who do understand.

John 5:1–47 – Timing of the Feast of the Jews: The reasons for identification of this Feast as the fall festival season are

1. Subject matter of judgment: trumpets, atonement, tabernacles, and last great day all deal with judgment.

2. Subject matter of resurrection: Feast of Trumpets and the Last Great Day both foreshadow resurrections.

3. John the Baptist is referred to as still alive.

4. Coordination with other Gospels. 4.1 harvest time; 4.2 "ordination" of the twelve; and 4.3 two years of training complete.

5. John 2:13–14 refers to the first Passover, and John 6:4 refers to the third Passover. The fall is halfway between the two.

6. John's internal structure, based on holy day seasons. John 1–Fall. John 2–4 – Spring. John 5 – Fall. John 6 – Spring. John 7–10 – Fall. John 11–21 – Spring.

Luke 8:34 – *The Merged Gospel* puts this phrase about the whole city coming out to Jesus later, where they beg him to depart from their region. It seems clear from the man getting dressed and listening to Jesus teach that some time had passed before they came to see Jesus. More time passed as they heard firsthand accounts.

Matthew 9:32–34; Luke 11:14–28 – There are two episodes of the Pharisees accusing Jesus of casting out demons by Beelzebul: Matthew 9 and Luke 11, where He healed a mute man; and Mark 3 and Matthew 12, where He heals a blind and mute man. The MG puts Matthew 9 first and then merges Matthew 12, Mark 3, and Luke 11. I put Mark 3 and Matthew 12 first because of their similarity and then Matthew 9 and Luke 11. The clincher is Luke 11:14, which clearly says Jesus healed a mute man. Thus Luke 11 and Matthew 9 must be together.

Mark 6:53–56 – This section is after John 6, which is in Capernaum. Mark and Matthew place the next event in Gennesaret, which is on the other side of the lake from Capernaum.

Mark 7:32 – This healing is only found in Mark. I have put it before the general healing section of Matthew 15:30–31, thinking one great healing would lead to multitudes coming to Jesus.

Matthew 17:4; Mark 9:4; Luke 9:33 – Which word did Peter really say? Since the Word of God cannot be broken (John 10:35) and is truth (John 17:17), he must have said all three! It looks ridiculous in print, but orally it is conceivable, especially considering that Luke says that Peter was "not knowing what he said." Consider the possibility he was stammering, trying to think of something to say. The only issue remaining is the order of his stammering. Without further insight, it seemed best to leave it in the order of the Gospels.

Matthew 17:24 – Matthew places this before the greatest teaching, yet it makes more sense following it. "When they had come" is past completed action, which means any time after they arrived. The greatest argument occurred on the road, and Jesus addressed it immediately when they were in the house in Capernaum.

Matthew 18:11 – This verse seems to introduce the next parable.

Luke 10:38–42 – Mary and Martha's house is in Bethany on the Mount of Olives. Jesus hid in their home when He was in Jerusalem. This is the logical place to put this passage, during the Feast of Tabernacles when He was hiding for the first half (four days) of the feast.

Luke 14:14; Acts 20:35 – The apostle Paul said this to the elders of Ephesus, and it is not recorded in the four Gospels. The words seem to fit best here.

Matthew 21:12; Mark 11:11 – There is a conflict between Matthew, who shows cleaning the temple on Nisan 10, and Mark, who shows it on Nisan 11. Friday Nisan 10 is more logical since buyers and sellers weren't likely to be selling on Saturday. But Mark clearly says it was evening and "He looked around," and He did it the first thing in the morning the next day. I went with Mark's account because of the clear time specification. Matthew was likely summarizing events without specifying time.

John 13:36 – Traditionally, Jesus's prediction of Peter's denial has been placed after they left the upper room despite John's inclusion of it during the Last Supper. Some harmonies have coordinated all the accounts so that they all take place during supper. Matthew and Mark's Gospels clearly indicate Jesus spoke of Peter's denial after they left the upper room while John's Gospel clearly shows He spoke of it during dinner. So there must have been two conversations (or more) on this subject. Luke is somewhat ambiguous regarding the timing of this conversation. However, Luke's phrasing seems closer to John's, and so Luke is merged with John's account.

Appendix H: Draft History

I began writing The Gospel Medley in longhand in 1981 as my daily Bible study. I had just finished it in 1988 when we bought our first computer. I transferred it to PC Write. I revised it when I changed computers in 1993 and again in 1998. In 2012, I used Dr. Crossland's Merged Gospel to further refine it. I made my final updates in 2018 when I converted to the World English Bible translation. In 2019 I submitted to my editor, Lisa Thompson who refined the form and found errors. I double-checked the whole book by reading it aloud in 2021. Then I checked all the footnotes, appendices, table of contents, and indices.

Scripture Index

Subject Index

Bolded entries are section titles, not in the gospels, not inspired

Jeffry J. Smith Biography

Born and reared in Cleveland, Ohio, Jeffry grew up with a lively interest in dinosaurs, outer space, and all things scientific. Upon learning the meaning of "agnostic" at age eight, he applied that to himself. However, at age twelve, while investigating cosmology and its related theories, he realized God had to exist in order for the universe to come from nothing. He then converted to Christianity and began a life-long study of the Bible.

During his career in information technology and process improvement, Jeffry began harmonizing the four Gospels into a single narrative. After releasing seven books under the pseudonym Andy Zach, he is finally publishing The Gospel Medley under his own name.

Jeffry is now retired and writes full-time. He lives with his wife and children in Peoria, Illinois.

www.ingramcontent.com/pod-product-compliance
Lightning Source LLC
LaVergne TN
LVHW010641110826
845149LV00014B/2914